Mastering PyCharm

Use PyCharm with fluid efficiency

Quazi Nafiul Islam

[PACKT]

PUBLISHING

BIRMINGHAM - MUMBAI

Mastering PyCharm

First published: October 2015

Production reference: 1201015

Published by Packt Publishing Ltd.
Livery Place
35 Livery Street
Birmingham B3 2PB, UK.

ISBN 978-1-78355-131-6

www.packtpub.com

Credits

Author

Quazi Nafiul Islam

Reviewers

Frederic De Groef

Ivan Kleshnin

Acquisition Editor

Richard Brookes-Bland

Content Development Editor

Anand Singh

Technical Editor

Ankita Thakur

Copy Editor

Swati Priya

Project Coordinator

Paushali Desai

Proofreader

Safis Editing

Indexer

Monica Ajmera Mehta

Graphics

Disha Haria

Production Coordinator

Arvindkumar Gupta

Cover Work

Arvindkumar Gupta

About the Author

Quazi Nafiul Islam is a consultant and an occasional speaker, and has worked professionally with Python for 3 years while completing his bachelor's degree in computer science. He blogs regularly on his website, `nafiulis.me`.

He struggled to find the right tools that could aid his workflow when working on large Python projects until he was introduced to PyCharm. He loved it so much that he wrote a book on it, his very first one.

About the Reviewers

Frederic De Groef has an MSc in computer science from the Brussels University, Belgium. He previously worked as a researcher in an applied sciences laboratory at the same university. There, he worked on immersive 3D visualization systems and successfully campaigned for the use of Python as the favored tool by students, both as the research and introductory programming language.

He is currently working as a software engineer at SoftKinetic Systems, a subsidiary of Sony that develops time-of-flight sensors and cameras as well as computer vision libraries for gesture recognition, body tracking, and 3D scanning. For 2 years, his focus shifted towards engineering productivity, automation, quality assurance and validation, and API design. Nowadays, his daily work includes extensive use of Python for supporting research and development of machine learning methods, computer vision algorithms, and ToF cameras.

He can be reached at `f.degroef@gmail.com`.

Ivan Kleshnin is a self-employed web developer and consultant. He uses JetBrain's IDEs extensively for his everyday tasks. Ivan likes functional programming, LISP, math, interfaces, and everything in between. Nowadays, he develops rich web applications in JavaScript and Clojure for his commercial and personal projects. Besides programming and reading tech books, he enjoys traveling. He can be reached at `ivan@paqmind.com`.

www.PacktPub.com

Support files, eBooks, discount offers, and more

For support files and downloads related to your book, please visit www.PacktPub.com.

Did you know that Packt offers eBook versions of every book published, with PDF and ePub files available? You can upgrade to the eBook version at www.PacktPub.com and as a print book customer, you are entitled to a discount on the eBook copy. Get in touch with us at service@packtpub.com for more details.

At www.PacktPub.com, you can also read a collection of free technical articles, sign up for a range of free newsletters and receive exclusive discounts and offers on Packt books and eBooks.

PACKTLIB

https://www2.packtpub.com/books/subscription/packtlib

Do you need instant solutions to your IT questions? PacktLib is Packt's online digital book library. Here, you can search, access, and read Packt's entire library of books.

Why subscribe?

- Fully searchable across every book published by Packt
- Copy and paste, print, and bookmark content
- On demand and accessible via a web browser

Free access for Packt account holders

If you have an account with Packt at www.PacktPub.com, you can use this to access PacktLib today and view 9 entirely free books. Simply use your login credentials for immediate access.

To Mr. Jon Storer for teaching me the importance of context and being the best teacher I've ever had.

Table of Contents

Preface

TLDR: So you want more PyCharm productivity, but don't want to read a book. I get that! So, just head over to the main menu, go over to Help and then Productivity Guide. If you want to get down to the best tools, read *Chapter 4*, *Editing*, *Chapter 5*, *Interpreters and Consoles*, and *Chapter 6*, *Debugging*. However, if you read this book, you'll get a lot more.

Welcome to *Mastering PyCharm*. If you've bought this book, then you probably want to become more effective with PyCharm in your day-to-day work. However, whether you can truly master a tool as multifaceted as PyCharm is completely up for debate since PyCharm changes so fast and so quickly. However, what I can promise you is that you will learn a great deal not only about how to use PyCharm, but how PyCharm works as part of the IntelliJ ecosystem of IDEs and what that means in terms of tooling and extensibility.

What this book covers

Chapter 1, *Getting the Right Look*, will help you make PyCharm look the exact way you want it to. So, whether you want too many buttons or too few or you want to change the theme or modify it more effectively, PyCharm will help you do all these.

Chapter 2, *Understanding the Keymap*, will help you map all the actions to their shortcuts and search for the actions using the action name or by invoking the shortcut. If that doesn't make sense, it means you've been missing out on something. This chapter also covers how to overcome known problems with keyboard shortcuts.

Chapter 3, *Getting Places*, covers a host of tools that PyCharm has. These tools will help you navigate everything from a really large file to huge codebases with loads of packages.

Chapter 4, *Editing*, will explain all the tools and help you learn more about writing error-free code quickly.

Chapter 5, Interpreters and Consoles, covers a lot of interpreters that Python has. PyCharm can support a whole host of them and provide code completion inside the console and much more. If you don't read this chapter, you're really going to miss out on some of the most powerful tools PyCharm has to offer.

Chapter 6, Debugging, being an iterative chapter, covers how to incorporate PyCharm's powerful debugger in to your debugging workflow. Buckle up; this one's going to get greasy.

Chapter 7, The PyCharm Ecosystem, answers PyCharm's existential questions. Who makes it? How does it work? How do you extend it? Where do plugins come from? Oh, and a lot more.

Chapter 8, File Templates and Snippets, covers the powerful set of snippets and file templates that PyCharm has. This will help you pump out code as fast as you can hit Tab. This chapter also talks about how to make your own file templates and snippets and extend the ones that already exist, using the velocity templating language. After all, don't you hate writing the same stuff all over again, such as getters and setters or function declarations?

Chapter 9, Version Control Integration, is a short chapter on some of the good parts of PyCharm's version control features that support multiple version control systems.

Chapter 10, HTML and JavaScript Tools, covers a set of tools that PyCharm comes with, which will help you work with JavaScript efficiently. JavaScript is (unfortunately) everywhere!

Chapter 11, Web Development with PyCharm, talks about picking a web framework, any framework. Chances are that PyCharm supports it as well as the tools that support those frameworks such as SQLAlchemy and templating languages such as Jinja2 and Mako.

What you need for this book

Basic Python knowledge, such as what functions are, what docstrings are, and so on, is needed. For *Chapter 9, Version Control Integration,* you'll need a basic understanding of at least one version control system and for *Chapter 10, HTML and JavaScript Tools* and *Chapter 11, Web Development with PyCharm,* you'll need to know quite a bit of Python as well as how the different Python frameworks operate.

Who this book is for

This book is for those who want to learn how to use PyCharm more effectively.

Conventions

In this book, you will find a number of text styles that distinguish between different kinds of information. Here are some examples of these styles and an explanation of their meaning.

Code words in text, database table names, folder names, filenames, file extensions, pathnames, dummy URLs, user input, and Twitter handles are shown as follows: "You should be then presented with a `.jar` file, which you can save."

A block of code is set as follows:

```
def add_one(n):
    return n + 1


def foo(func, n):
    return func(n)



foo(add_one, 2)
```

Any command-line input or output is written as follows:

```
pip install ipython[all]
```

New terms and **important words** are shown in bold. Words that you see on the screen, for example, in menus or dialog boxes, appear in the text like this: "What I've tried to do is put in the name of the action being done so that you can take a look in your **Keymap** (by navigating to **File | Settings...**)."

> Warnings or important notes appear in a box like this.

> Tips and tricks appear like this.

Reader feedback

Feedback from our readers is always welcome. Let us know what you think about this book—what you liked or disliked. Reader feedback is important for us as it helps us develop titles that you will really get the most out of.

To send us general feedback, simply e-mail `feedback@packtpub.com`, and mention the book's title in the subject of your message.

If there is a topic that you have expertise in and you are interested in either writing or contributing to a book, see our author guide at `www.packtpub.com/authors`.

Customer support

Now that you are the proud owner of a Packt book, we have a number of things to help you to get the most from your purchase.

Downloading the example code

You can download the example code files from your account at `http://www.packtpub.com` for all the Packt Publishing books you have purchased. If you purchased this book elsewhere, you can visit `http://www.packtpub.com/support` and register to have the files e-mailed directly to you.

Downloading the color images of this book

We also provide you with a PDF file that has color images of the screenshots/diagrams used in this book. The color images will help you better understand the changes in the output. You can download this file from: `https://www.packtpub.com/sites/default/files/downloads/1316OT_ColorImages.pdf`.

Errata

Although we have taken every care to ensure the accuracy of our content, mistakes do happen. If you find a mistake in one of our books—maybe a mistake in the text or the code—we would be grateful if you could report this to us. By doing so, you can save other readers from frustration and help us improve subsequent versions of this book. If you find any errata, please report them by visiting `http://www.packtpub.com/submit-errata`, selecting your book, clicking on the **Errata Submission Form** link, and entering the details of your errata. Once your errata are verified, your submission will be accepted and the errata will be uploaded to our website or added to any list of existing errata under the Errata section of that title.

To view the previously submitted errata, go to `https://www.packtpub.com/books/content/support` and enter the name of the book in the search field. The required information will appear under the **Errata** section.

Piracy

Piracy of copyrighted material on the Internet is an ongoing problem across all media. At Packt, we take the protection of our copyright and licenses very seriously. If you come across any illegal copies of our works in any form on the Internet, please provide us with the location address or website name immediately so that we can pursue a remedy.

Please contact us at `copyright@packtpub.com` with a link to the suspected pirated material.

We appreciate your help in protecting our authors and our ability to bring you valuable content.

Questions

If you have a problem with any aspect of this book, you can contact us at `questions@packtpub.com`, and we will do our best to address the problem.

1
Getting the Right Look

"Simplicity is the ultimate sophistication."

– Leonardo da Vinci

I fell in love with Python for its elegance. I love how there are no semicolons, how you can make a block through a simple indentation, how you can make multiline strings without having to concatenate them, and how you can make lambdas in a single line. I love how readable it all is, and how the documentation (docstrings) is built right into the language.

I think we all appreciate beauty. Think about it; you have a favorite font, a favorite color-scheme, and the list can go on. In essence, the code you write needs to be beautiful in your perspective, not just the syntax, but how it looks—the colors, the font, the highlighting—everything must be just right.

In this chapter, we are going to work toward making PyCharm beautiful. We'll progress from changing the overall appearance to some of the predefined appearances available us on PyCharm. After that, we'll get into fonts and how the highlighting/coloring works in PyCharm. With the most difficult part of this chapter under our belt, we'll dive into exporting and importing styles and themes.

If you appreciate how your code looks and how you can make it as beautiful as possible, then this chapter will equip you with all the things necessary to make PyCharm as vibrant as you want it to be. I've tried to make this chapter light so that you can experiment yourself with it, and most things are pretty self-explanatory.

A short note on keyboard shortcuts

The keyboard shortcuts used in this chapter are the defaults for when you install PyCharm on Windows. PyCharm supports a wide range of shortcut schemes, and hence, it is impossible to include them all here (also, you might have made your own customizations). What I've tried to do is put in the name of the action being done so that you can take a look in your **Keymap** (by navigating to **File | Settings...**).

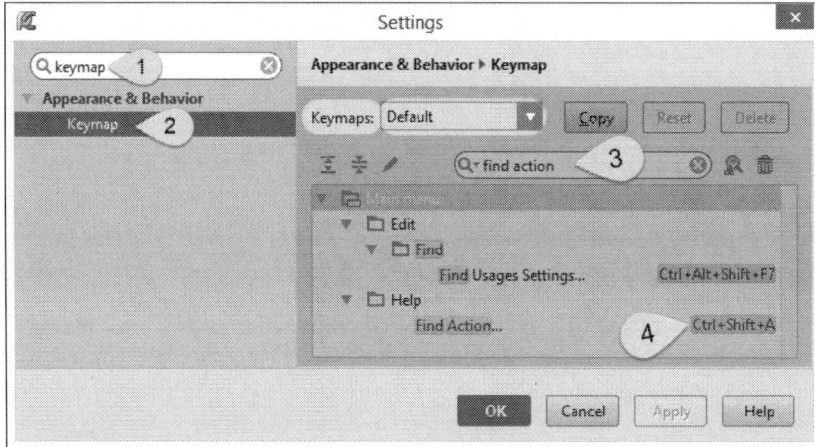

The basics

The first time you install PyCharm, the theme will default to *IntelliJ*. But, if you prefer something darker, I suggest you use Darcula. I personally prefer a darker IDE, so I go with a custom version of Darcula that's tailored to my tastes.

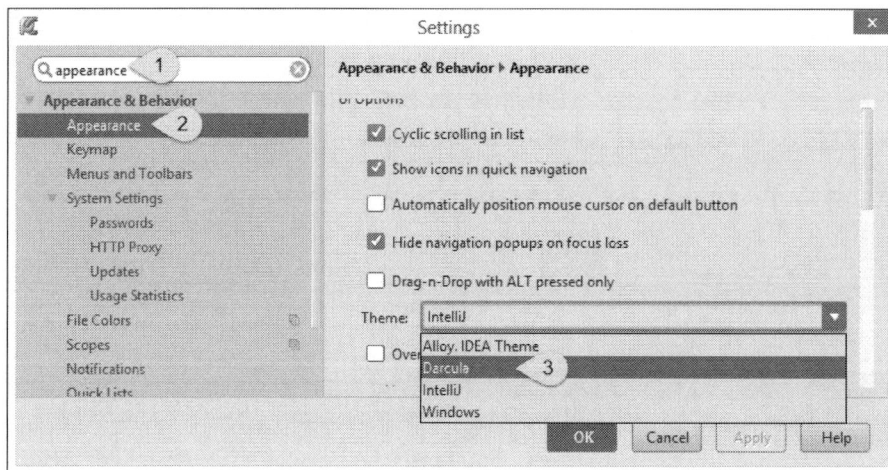

However, let's start with the default UI and see how we can make PyCharm look a little better.

The first change – fonts

The first thing that hit me when I opened up PyCharm was the hideous font set by default to be *Courier New*. Let's change this:

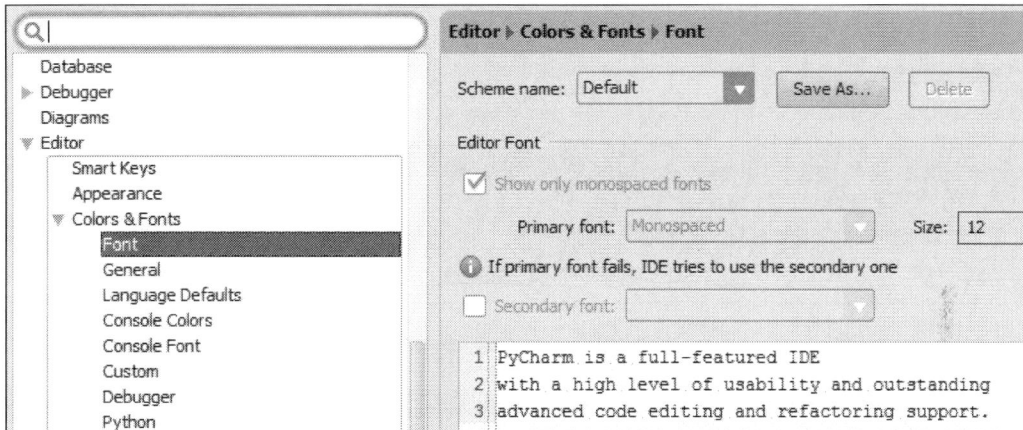

With the color scheme set to **Default**, you will need to save your new color scheme with a different name before you can go about making any changes to the scheme. You can just click on **Save As...** and then simply enter the name of your scheme in the popup. After doing so, you are free to make any changes you wish.

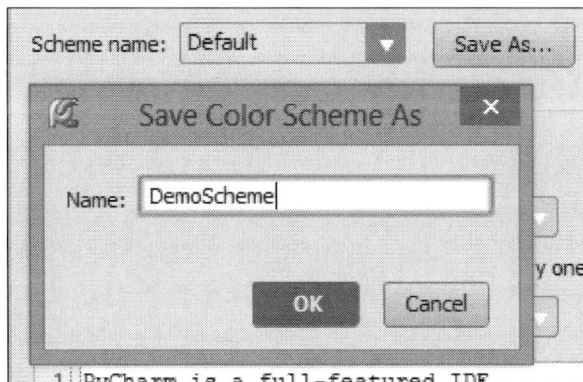

The **Show only monospaced fonts** option is enabled by default, but you can change it to include other fonts such as Arial or Times New Roman as well. Also the choice of a secondary font is important when you're trying to import your settings to another computer that does not have your desired font.

A typical example would be Consolas; it's only available on Windows machines, so when you try to import your font settings to Ubuntu or Mac, you likely get the default monospaced font. I usually set my default font to Consolas and my secondary font to Ubuntu Mono since it's free and can be made available on all the machines.

Now that the font business is taken care of, let's get down to a couple of other features. We will revisit this part of PyCharm pretty soon.

The layout

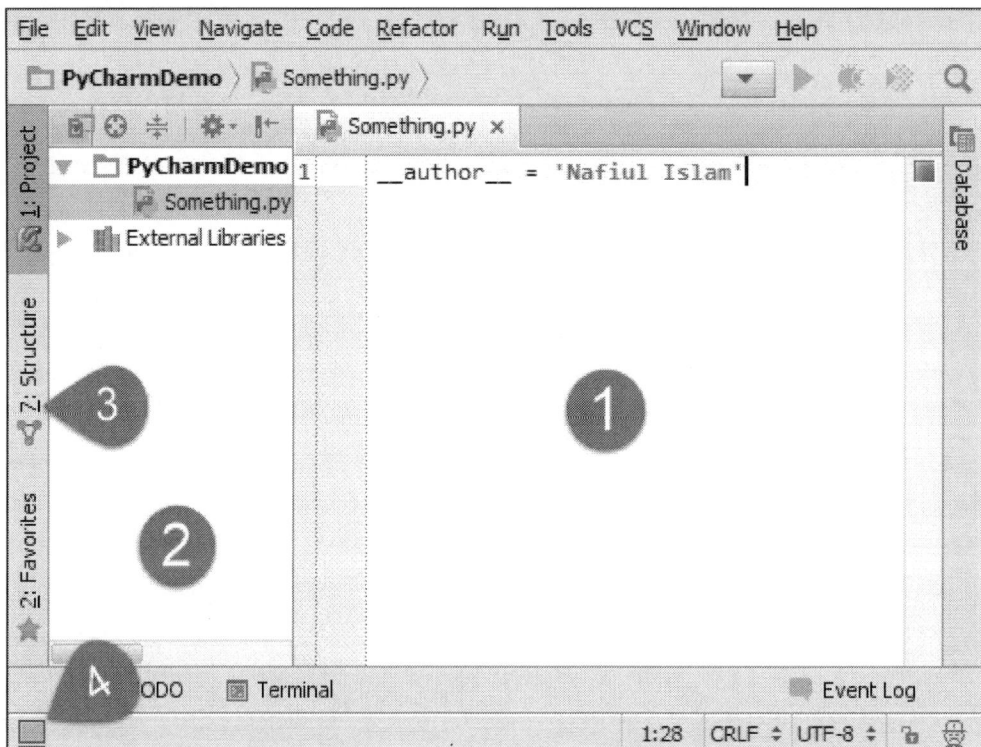

The default PyCharm layout is quite minimal. With reference to the preceding screenshot, you get an editor in [1], and the list of your directories and files in [2]. Actually, [2] is a sidebar, so if you click on [3], you get a totally different sidebar popping up.

You can show/hide it using *Alt* + number indicated by the underline. So, in this case, if you were to press *Alt* + 7, the panel indicated by [3] (**Structure**) would show up. Once you're familiar with the layout, you can hide all the panel buttons by clicking on [4].

The minimalist

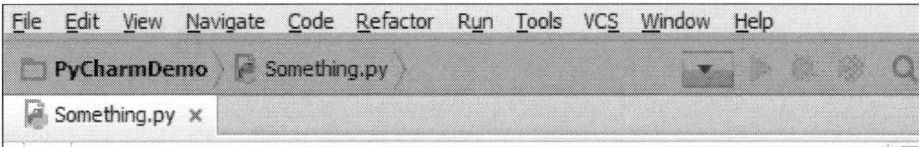

If you'd like to focus completely on the code, you ideally want a minimalistic layout without all the extra tools taking up your screen. Let's see how PyCharm can help us with this.

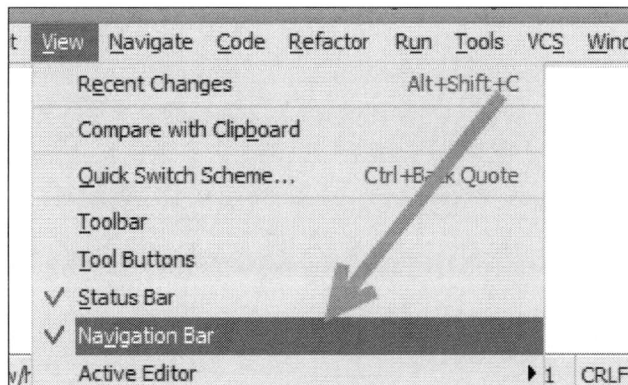

So far, we can hide panels; now let's get rid of all the other distractions as well. The area highlighted with the arrow in the preceding screenshot is called the navigation bar; if you'd like to get rid of it, you can deselect the **Navigation Bar** option in the **View** option menu.

Note that with the **Navigation Bar** option, you also lose the **Run, Debug, Coverage,** and **Search Anywhere** buttons; but don't worry, there are plenty of shortcuts available so that you can do everything you want from your keyboard.

You can make the navigation bar appear as a popup instead of being a permanent bar by pressing *Alt + Home* (if this is not your shortcut, search for navigation bar in the **Keymap**):

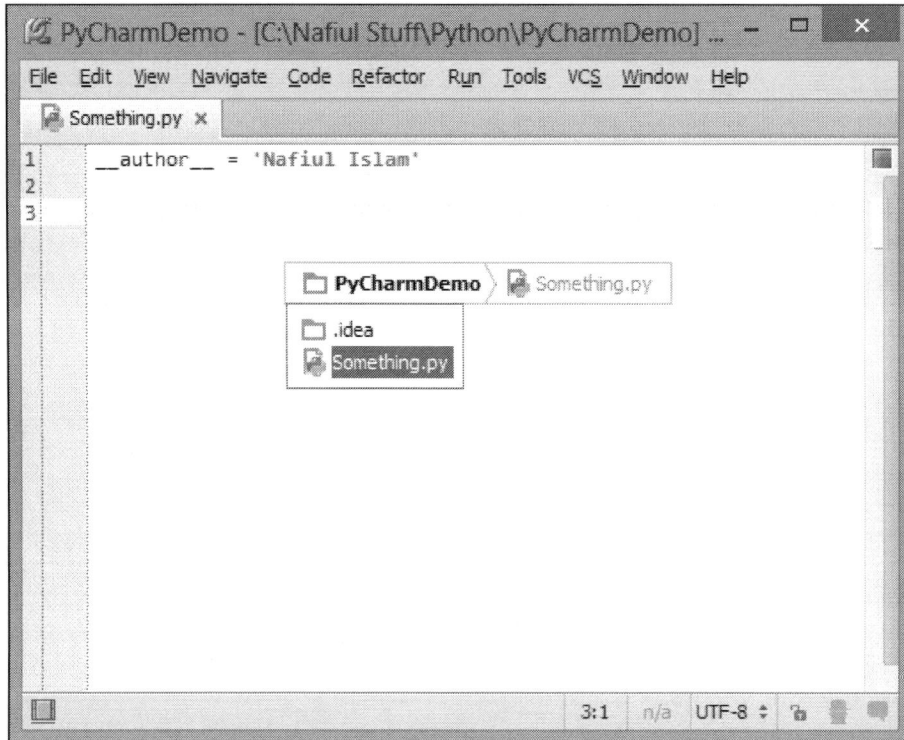

As for the **Debug** and other buttons that we got rid of, you can always get them through **Find Action**, *Ctrl + Shift + A*.

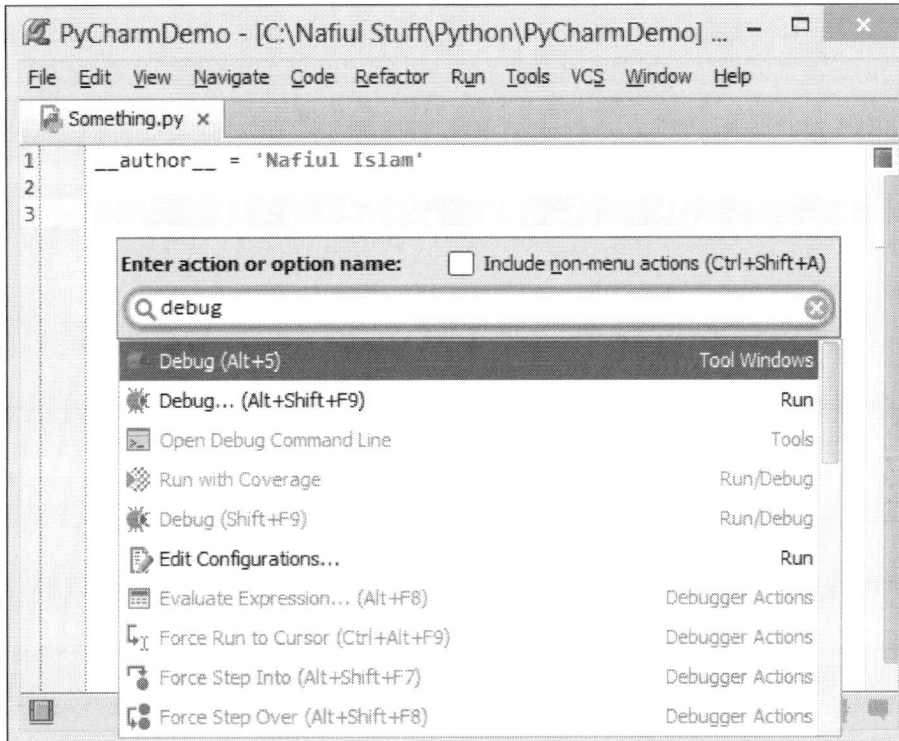

Search Everywhere searches files, actions, classes, objects, and pretty much everything using double *Shift* (pressing *Shift* twice in quick succession):

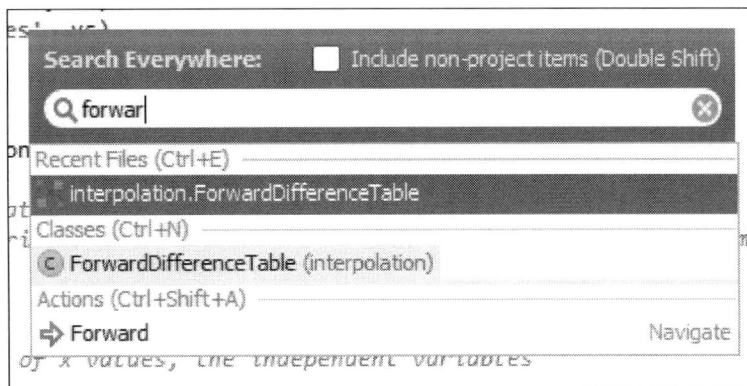

PyCharm can also go to full screen mode (it even gives you a nice helpful clock in the top right):

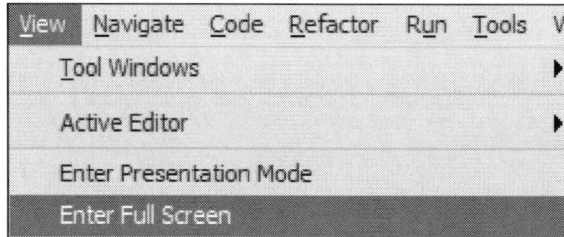

I never use this mode because with my start menu minimized, with no navigation bar, and a collapsible **Project** sidebar, I have plenty of screen space to get the job done.

Another tool that I really appreciate is **Switcher**, which can be invoked with *Ctrl + Tab*. It appears as a floating window:

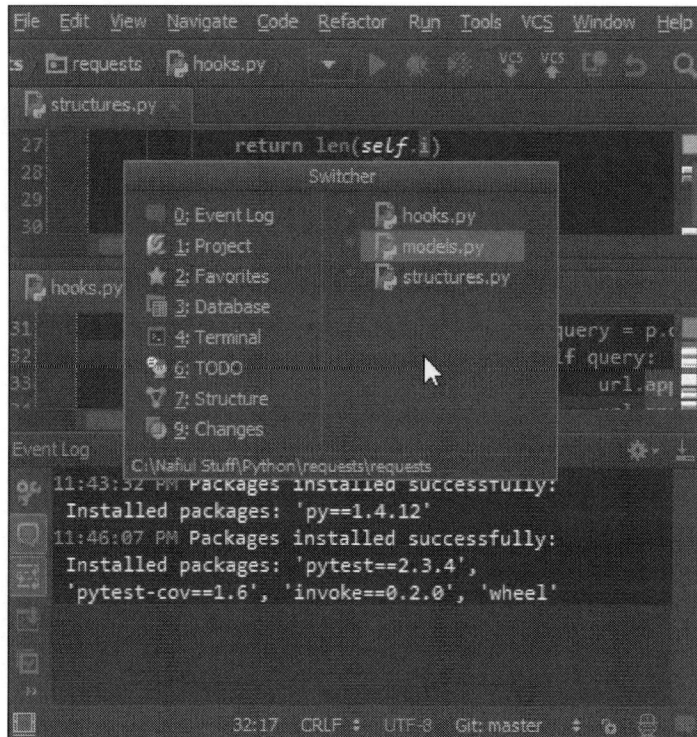

You can quickly navigate through your open files on the right-hand side of the window, and on the left-hand side you have some commonly used tools. You can navigate by pressing *Tab* again, and this will proceed through the list. You can also use the arrow keys. However, note that you will need to keep the *Ctrl* key pressed down as long as you're using **Switcher**.

You can quickly get to them by pressing the key underlined. In this case, you can quickly get to **Terminal** through first pressing *Ctrl + Tab* to bring up **Switcher**; if, while holding down the *Ctrl* key, you press 4, (in the preceding screenshot, **Terminal** is 4, but you might get a different number), you can open up **Terminal**.

You can close anything, that is, a tool panel or an editor tab using *Ctrl + F4*.

Beautiful code

We looked at themes briefly in the *The basics* section, and frankly there isn't much else left to themes in PyCharm. Right now you have your choices limited to a couple of themes if you're using IntelliJ IDEA Platform 130.* and above. In older versions of IntelliJ, there used to be a lot more.

Editor

This is where you are going to be spending most of your time in PyCharm, so it makes sense to make it look as good as possible.

Getting the right colors

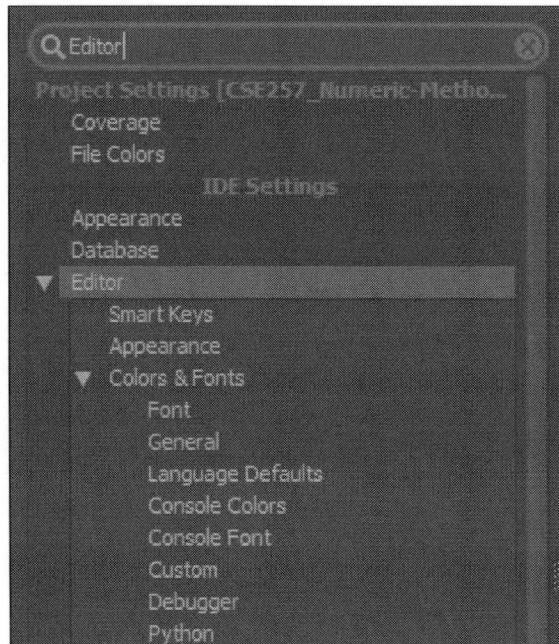

Each language has its own color scheme under **Editor**; if you can't find it, just look it up in the search bar, and underneath **Editor**, you should be able to find **Python**. Most of the options here are the same for all the IDEs built using the IntelliJ Platform, so this is nothing native to PyCharm.

Underneath **Colors & Fonts**, you should be able to see a whole bunch of choices. We have already changed the font, and the other options will become more relevant as we progress through this chapter, but first let's make a couple of changes to the scheme for Python.

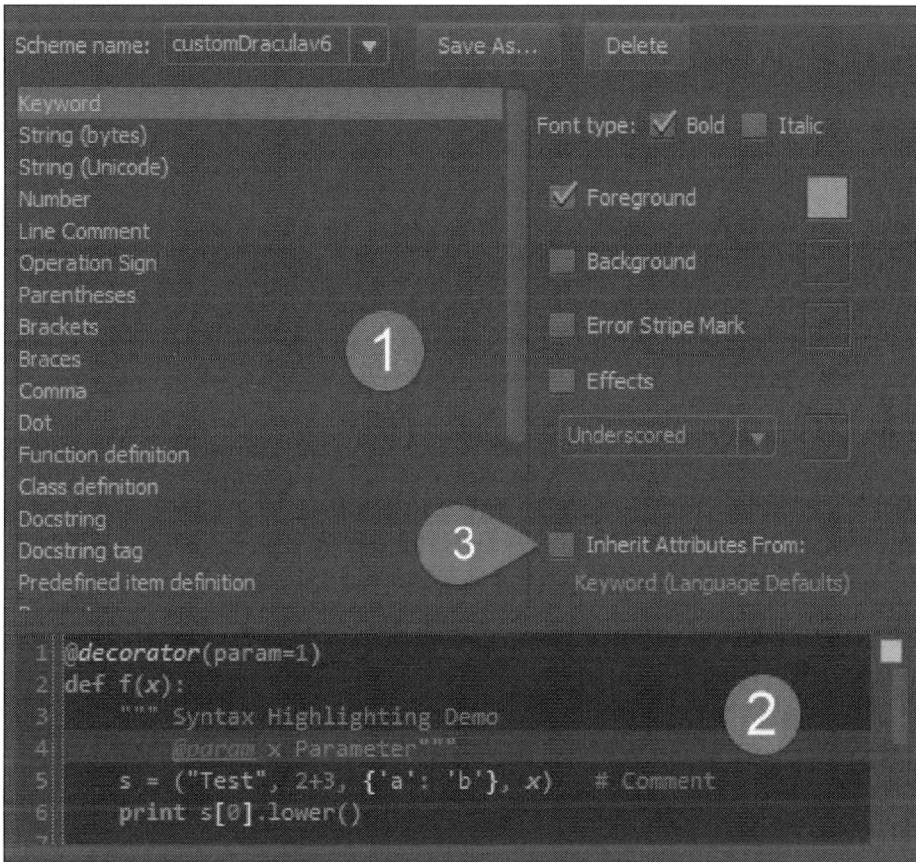

The list in [1] is merely the different elements in a file that can be styled. The best way to go about changing the style is not using [1]; however, it's clicking on the elements in [2], which directly takes you to the element in question. Note that you cannot change the text in [2].

> Whenever we change any of the default schemes, we need to save it as a new scheme all together, which we can later make changes to. PyCharm will prompt you for a new theme name.

So, in this example, if you want to know the category for a decorator in Python, all you have to do is click on the decorator in [2], and that will lead you to the corresponding name of the said element. An interesting option is [3], which we will touch upon soon.

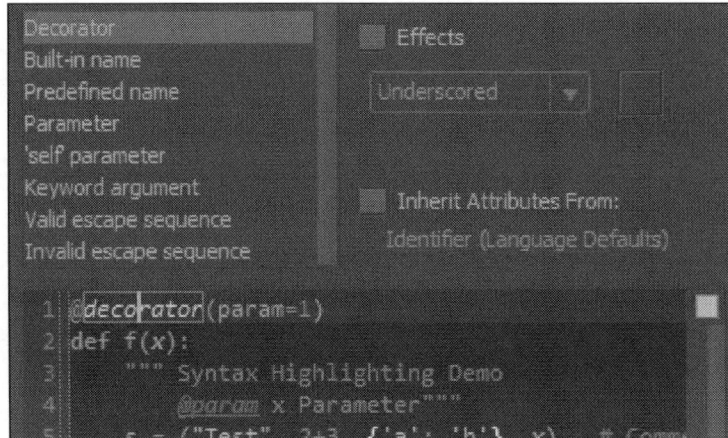

As you can see, when we clicked on decorator, it auto-scrolled straight to **Decorator** in the list. However, it's not always obvious what something is called, so clicking on it again will help us identify what element it is:

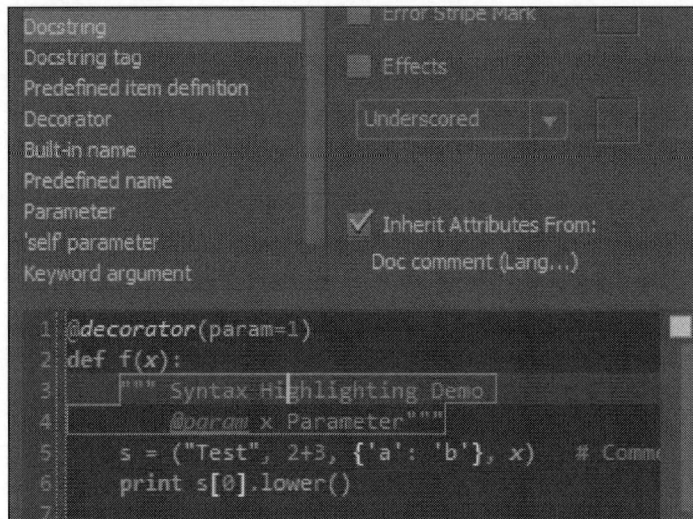

PyCharm has two different styles for docstrings and string; in this case, what we clicked on was a docstring and not a normal string, which is a lighter blue color in this case.

Style hierarchies

PyCharm's style system can work on hierarchies; what this simply means is that a lot of the common elements in different languages are handled by central rules. This is useful since in this way, you have a common set of colors for all your languages.

For example, documentation comments are common in most languages, so PyCharm allows you to control how documentation looks in all the languages, so the colors stay consistent. Let's take a look at this:

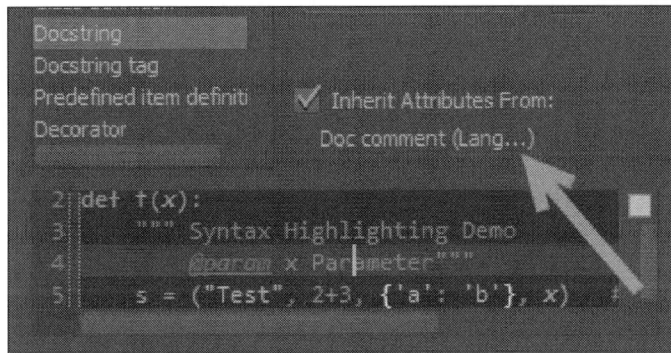

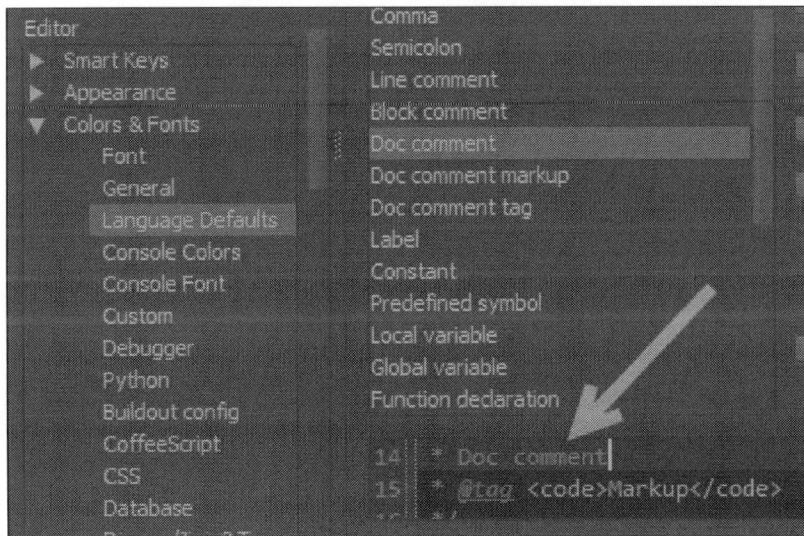

Here it says that it does inherit from another set of styles; in this case, it is **Language Defaults**, which has been abbreviated by PyCharm, so let's head over there, and we can see that, yes indeed, there is a **Doc comment** element and its styled the same way docstring is.

Styling on steroids

Note that the editor isn't the *only* region that you can style; you can style just about anything. For example, if you wanted to change the colors for the in-built terminal, you'd have to change the console colors; both the terminal and console share a common style setting.

A common problem that I faced when I initially installed PyCharm was that, even though my terminal was *actually* styled, I did not get the styling when I opened up the **Terminal** in PyCharm, and this is because I did not set up my console colors correctly:

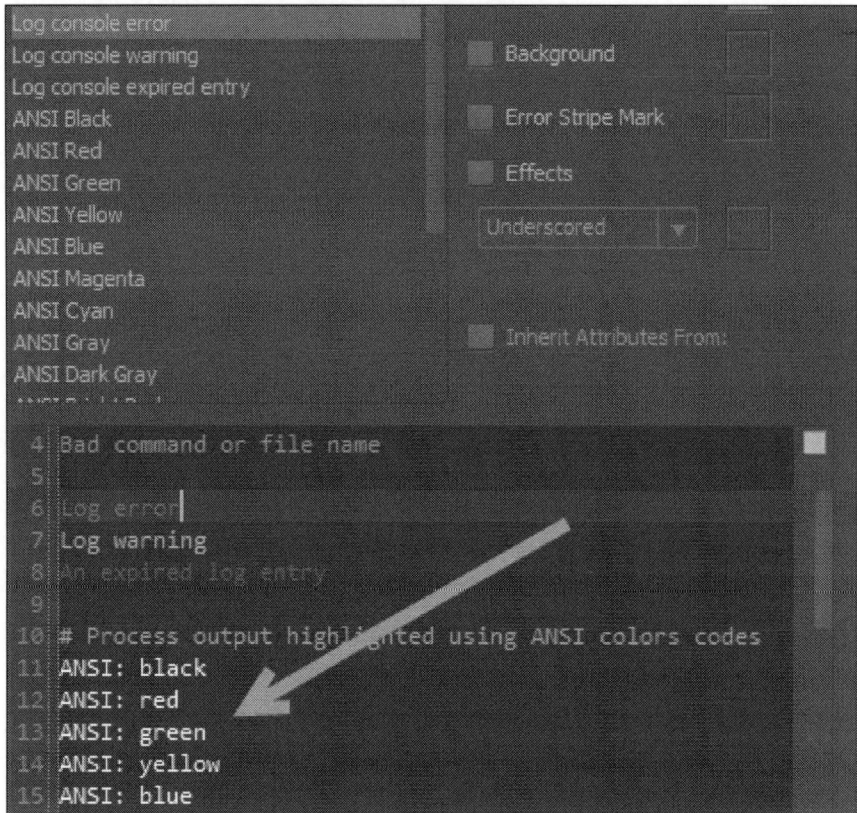

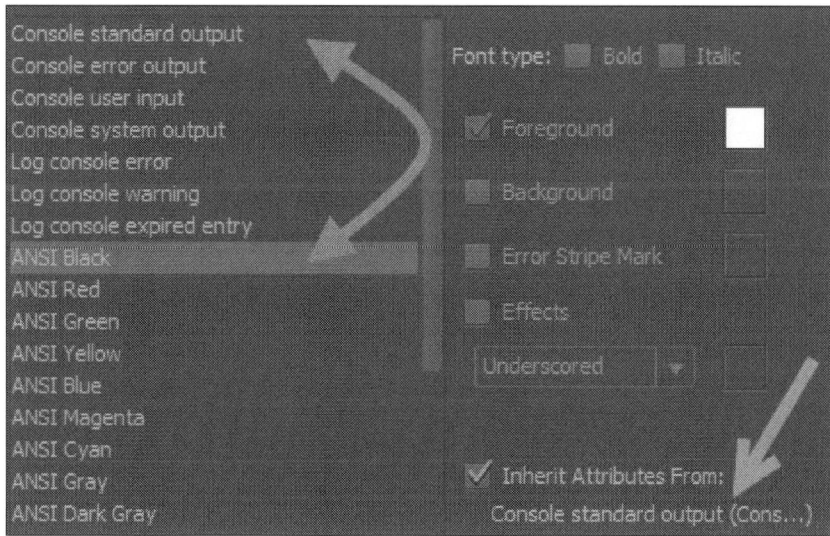

As you can see in the preceding screenshot, my ANSI colors have not been set right, and hence, all my output just comes out in blue and red; thus, I had to manually change the colors. Note that some elements can also inherit their color from within the same category.

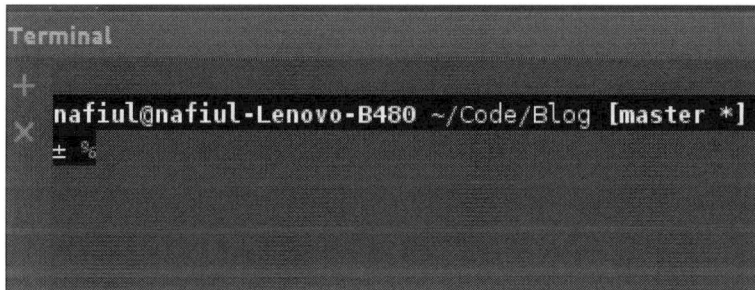

So my terminal used to look similar to this:

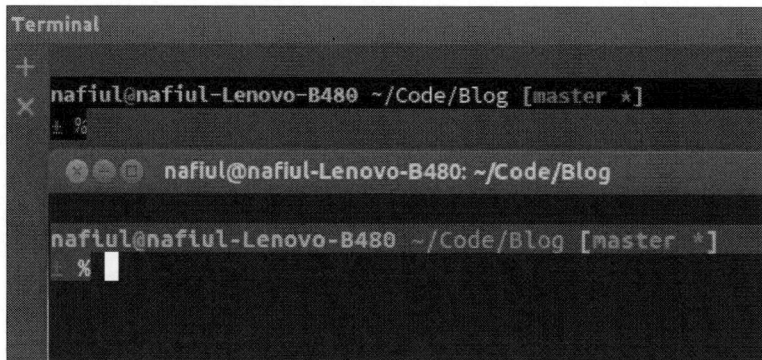

However, after the change, I was able to make it look more like my real terminal, although you cannot replicate it exactly.

You can of course go ahead and choose the appropriate colors, but it's best to let the color picker (shown on the right-hand side in the following screenshot) do it for you:

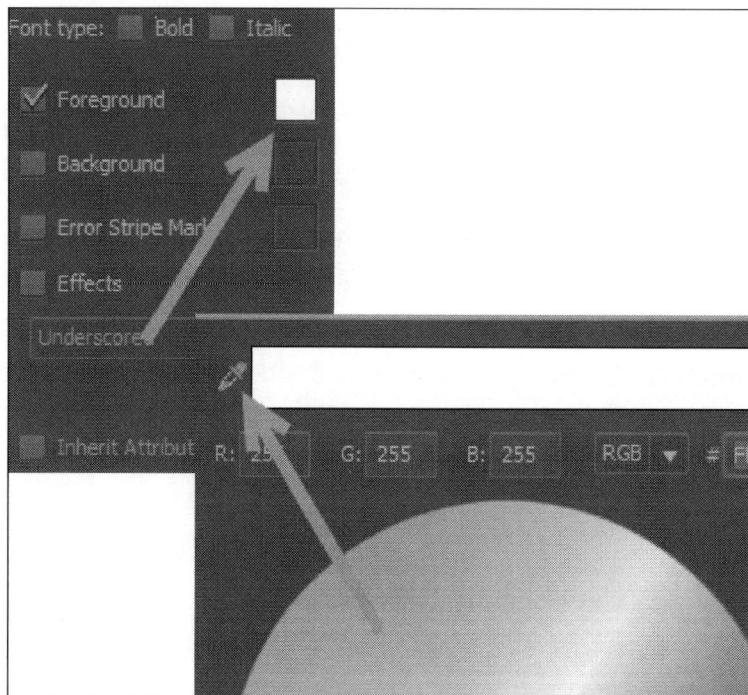

> If you hover over your chosen color for just a second using the color picker, PyCharm will show the color you've chosen in the color circle.

Here are a few pointers on where things are located:

- **General** is for the different parts of the IDE that you see. For example, when you try to find something in your editor, and your editor highlights the search item in question, you determine that via **Text search result** in this tab. This is really handy when you want to change things such as the color of your line numbers, for example.

- **CSS**, **Python**, **HTML**, **CoffeeScript**, and so on are all language-specific element stylings.

- **Language Defaults** provides the styling for generic language elements, such as doc comments, variables, keywords, and so on.

- **Console Colors** is for styling the terminal and console (when you run something, it opens up the **Console** window).

- **Console Font** is the font used in the terminal and console.

- **Debugger** is for debugger-specific styling (I would not change this if I were you; the defaults are pretty intuitive).

Imports and exports

The best way to import a theme is to simply import it as a setting file; these are typically `.jar` files. Remember, we mentioned that PyCharm is a derivative of the IntelliJ Platform? Well, you can use all the themes that are available to the Platform in PyCharm as well. One of the first places to look for themes is `http://ideacolorthemes.org/themes/`.

This gives you a good set of themes, and also shows you the languages that a theme will work with. So, we can just quickly download a theme; in this case, we will be downloading **Solarized Dark** (one of my all-time favorites).

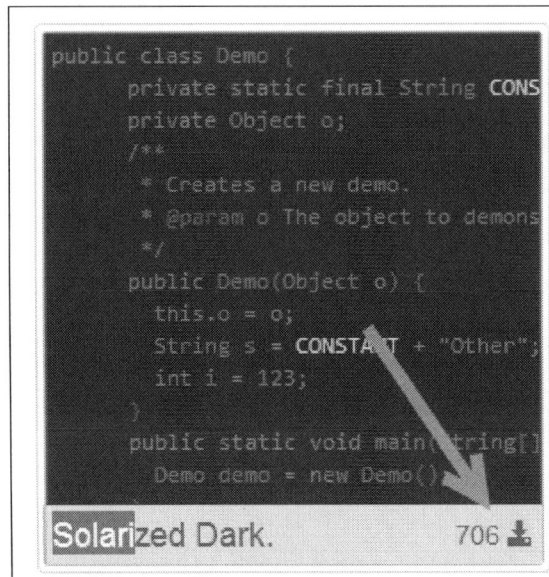

To download and install Solarized Dark, perform the following steps:

1. Head over and just click on **Download Theme**:

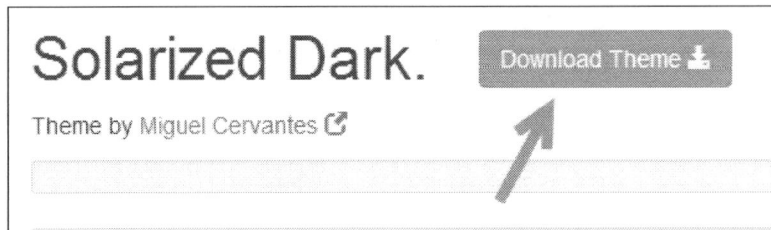

2. You should be then presented with a `.jar` file, which you can save:

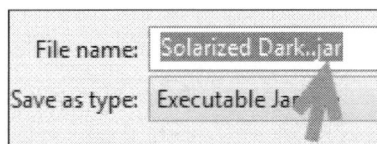

3. Click on **Import Settings…** to open up a dialog box for importing the JAR file:

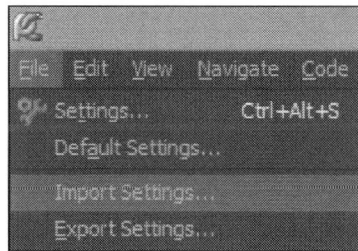

4. Just choose the file that you want and click on **OK**:

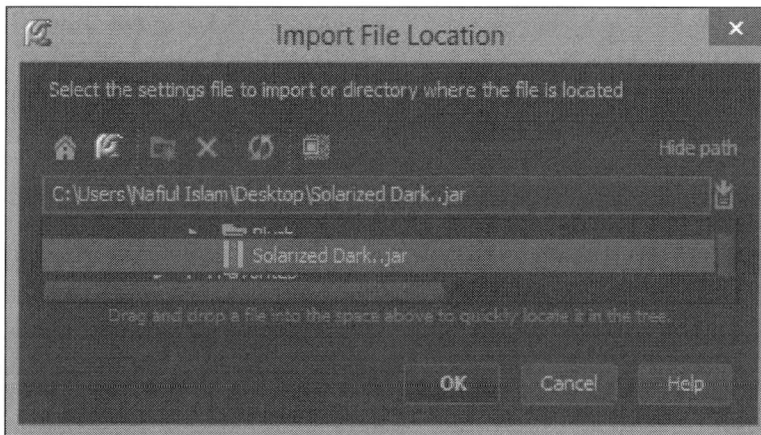

5. Make sure that **Editor Colors** is selected and then simply press **OK**:

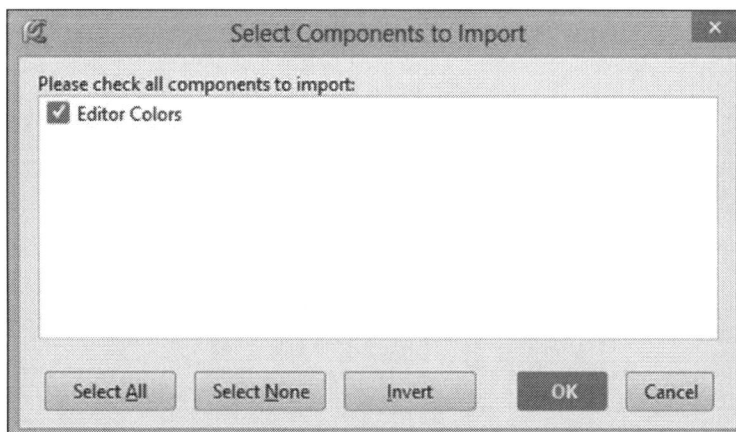

You should now be able to see a new option in your **Scheme** menu:

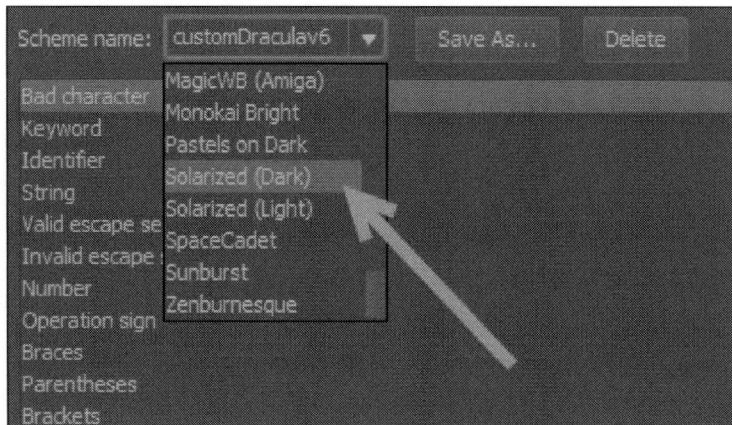

That's all there is to it. You can export quite simply as well:

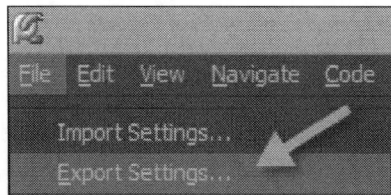

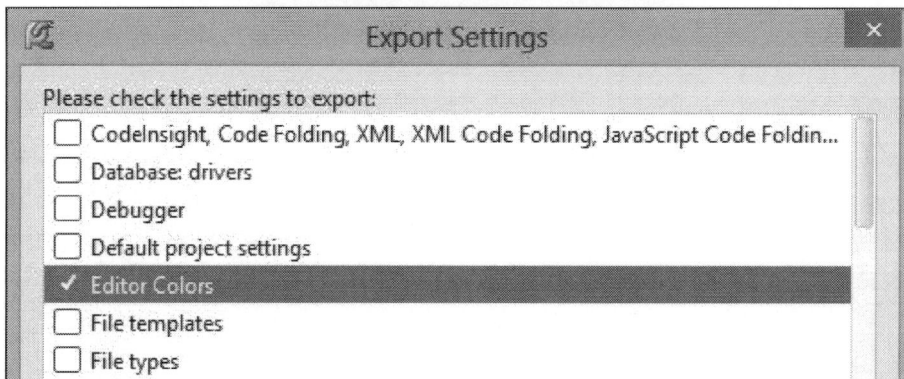

The **Color schemes** option must be selected, and at the end of it, you will get a
settings.jar file that you can import into another PyCharm installation.

TextMate bundles

You can also import your TextMate bundles in PyCharm:

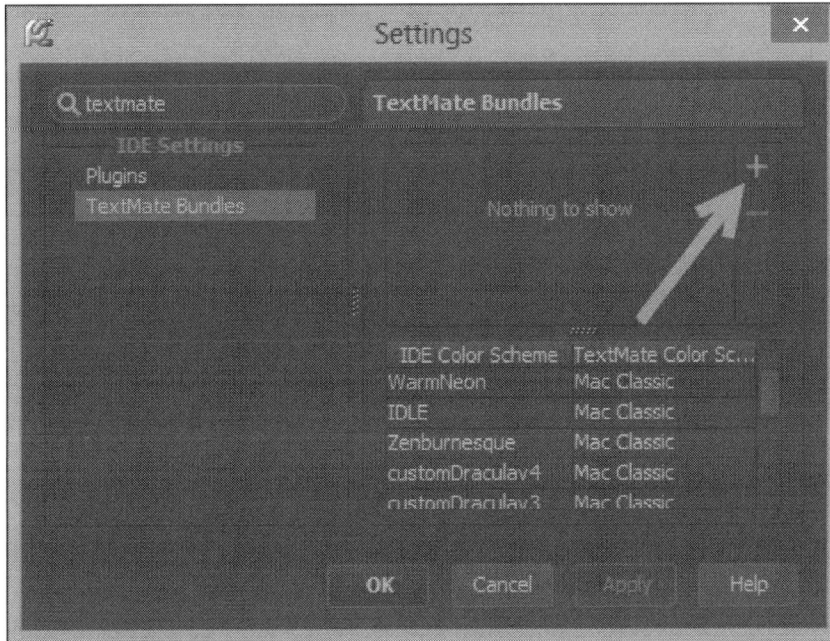

Summary

We covered a lot in this chapter. From fonts to styles to hierarchies, we saw a lot of what we could do with the styling system in PyCharm. We took a look at a minimalistic layout without compromising on what tools were quickly available to us, using **Find Action** and **Search Everywhere**. In the end, we showed how we can import themes and export them as well.

2
Understanding the Keymap

The keymap is one of the most powerful features that PyCharm has to offer. It allows you to set your keyboard shortcuts and find the keyboard shortcuts you've seen other people use. It also allows you to use a familiar set of keyboard shortcuts that you're used to such as Eclipse and Emacs. This chapter is very much a standalone chapter, and if you understand how keymaps work, you're well on your way to using the most powerful features that PyCharm has to offer with ease.

In this chapter, we are going to go over the following topics:

- **Different keymaps**: PyCharm assumes that you might have had prior experience with a separate IDE or editor, so you can quickly adapt PyCharm to predetermined keyboard shortcuts.

- **Finding shortcuts**: A lot of times, you will see other people using keyboard shortcuts, but you won't know what they're called. This section will remedy that.

- **Setting shortcuts**: We will customize our own keyboard and mouse shortcuts as we see fit. We will also make our own abbreviations.

- **Troubleshooting on Mac**: Unlike Windows and Linux, Mac comes with support for a lot of special characters that can get in the way of using keyboard shortcuts. This section will remedy that problem.

Different keymaps

PyCharm has a default keymap and even a nice PDF to show you all the most used commands when you navigate to **Help | Default Keymap Reference** (the same on Mac, Windows, and Linux).

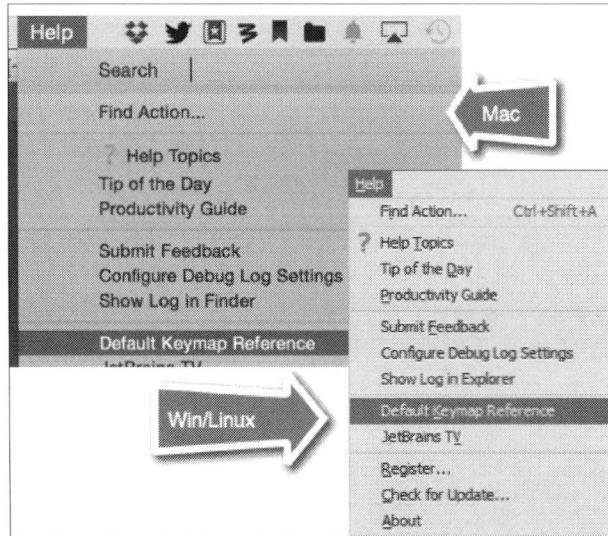

On Mac, the default keymap is **OSX 10.5+**, and on both Windows and Linux, the default keymap is called **Default**. This can easily be changed by changing the keymap by going to **Preferences** (Mac) or **Settings…** (Windows/Linux).

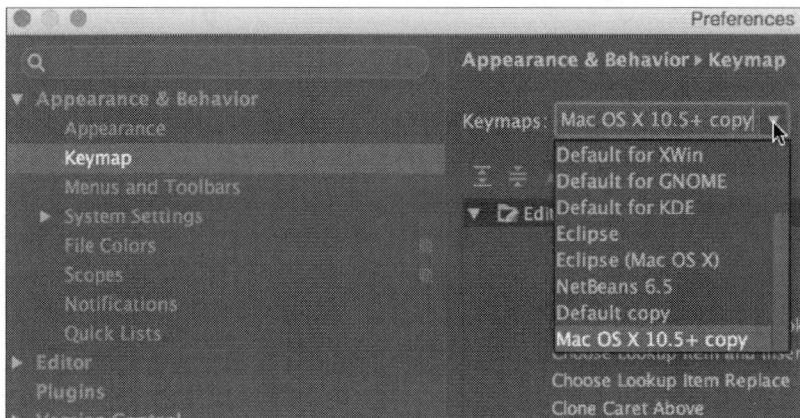

Notice how my keymap is **Mac OS X 10.5+ copy**. This is because you cannot override a predefined configuration; you can only make your own copy of it. If my list is different from yours, it's because I imported some of my keymaps; in this case, **Default copy** from my Windows installation. Just like themes, you can import and export keymaps.

Finding shortcuts

Now you can easily search for the keyboard shortcut that you're looking for in the find bar, for example, if we want **Find Action...**, we can search for it like this:

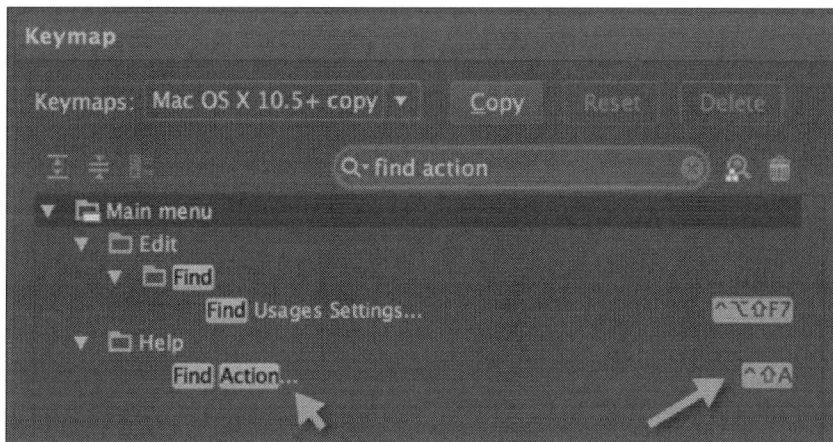

However, you can also do just the reverse by inputting the shortcut to find out what it's called (this is incredibly useful when you're trying to explain what you're doing to someone else on another platform with a different set of default keyboard shortcuts).

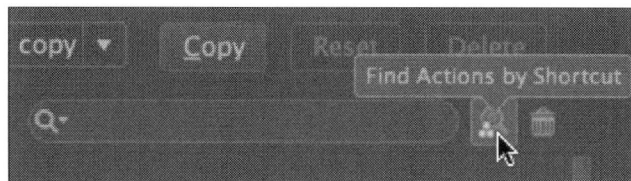

So, if we wanted to find what *Alt + Q* does, we would have done this:

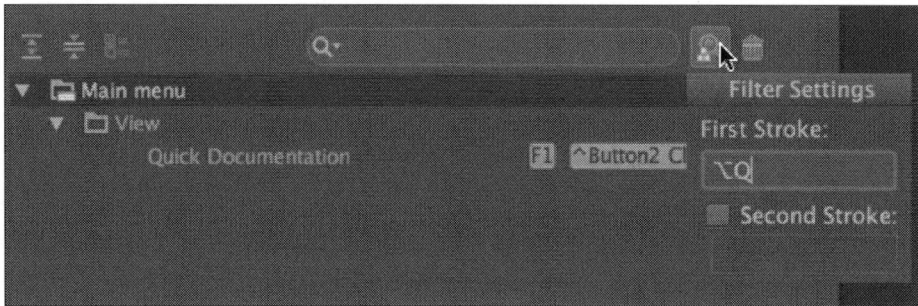

At this point, I feel that it would be prudent to note that Mac shortcuts have special symbols in them, while Windows/Linux don't (you can skip the next page). When I was first using Mac with PyCharm, I found this quite perplexing because other than the command key (⌘), there were no other symbols on my Mac's keyboard. These characters are explained in the bottom-right corner of the **Default Keymap Reference** for Mac (which is a PDF).

However, if you cannot, for some reason or another, gain access to the PDF, here is a reference, just in case (although mine contains a few more useful symbols):

⌘	command
⌥	option
^	control
⇧	shift
⇪	caps lock
⌫	delete
⌦	del
↩	return
⎋	escape
⏏	eject
⇥	tab
←↑→↓	arrow keys
↖	home
↘	end
⇞	page up
⇟	page down

Setting shortcuts

Now that we've got all the basics down, it's (finally) time to make a keyboard shortcut of our own, and we are going to start by making a keyboard shortcut for the terminal. I have my terminal set to open up at [*command + Shift + ;*]. So, let's see how we can get around to doing that.

First, we are going to look up for terminal and see what we get:

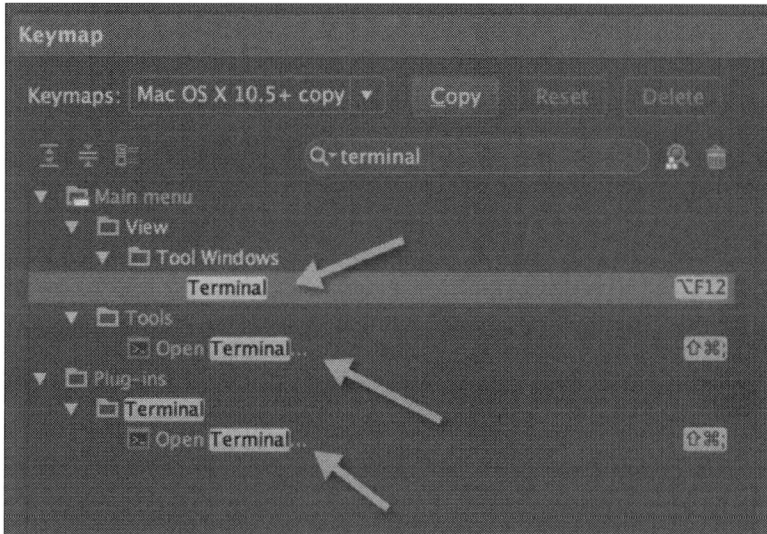

If you take a look, you will see that we have three options, and it turns out that they all do the same thing. Now, notice how **Terminal** pops up in three separate places. This is because the terminal inside PyCharm is in fact two things: one being a bundled plugin and another being a tool. This is why you see **Terminal** appearing in several places. This **Terminal** tool can be invoked by both [*command + Shift + ;*] and [*Alt + F12*]. Now, I don't really like [*Alt + F12*], so I am going to get rid of it, by right-clicking (or double-clicking) on the highlighted row:

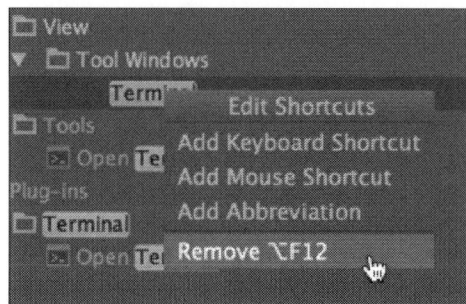

Now I am assigning a new shortcut by clicking on **Add Keyboard Shortcut**:

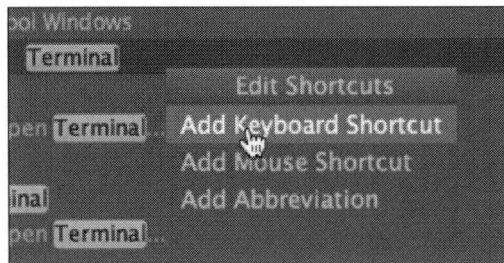

Press [*command + Shift + ;*] in one go:

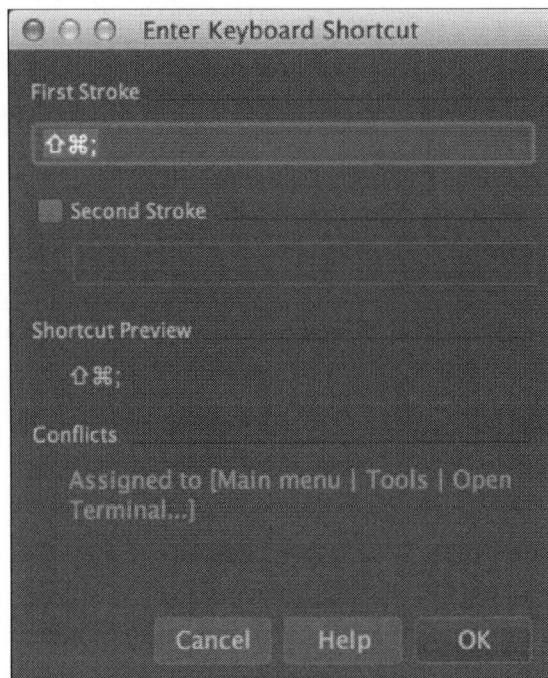

If you had another action with the same shortcut, PyCharm will show you conflicts. Now, in my own settings, the conflict lies with the **Open Terminal** action, which does the same thing, so when the following screenshot pops up, I will choose **Leave**:

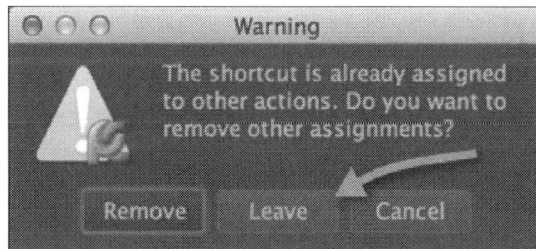

With that, you can now open up your terminal with [*command + Shift + ;*].

You might have also noticed something else; there was a way to add **Second Stroke**. This is, in essence, just doing what we did previously, but adding a second stroke. So, say, if we wanted to open up the terminal by pressing [*command + Alt + ,*] for the first and the second key stroke, this is how we would do it:

1. First, just enter the first keystroke and then enable the second keystroke by clicking on the **Second Stroke** checkbox:

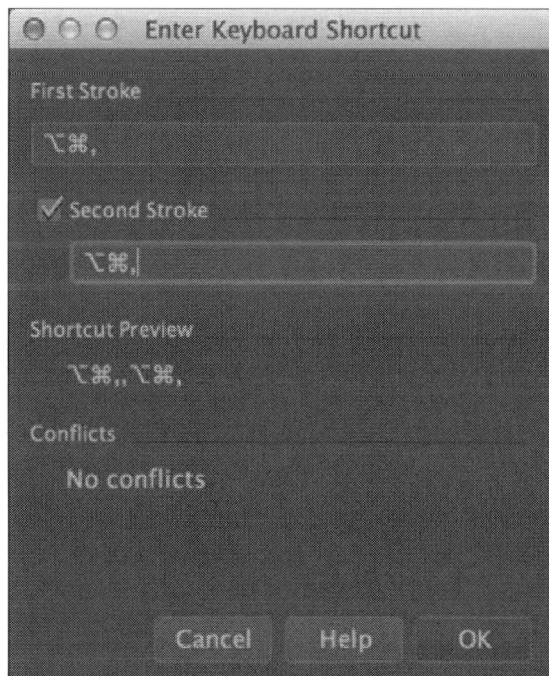

2. When invoking this, after we've entered the first keystroke, PyCharm will tell us that a prefix key has been pressed:

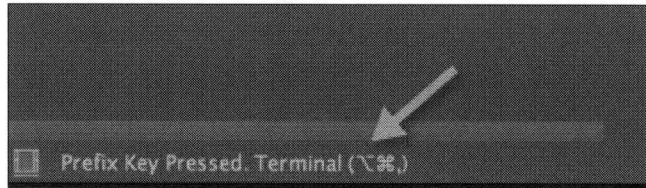

So by pressing [*command* + *Alt* + ,] twice, you can get the terminal. PyCharm will show up all the possible actions. In this case, the only thing with a second stroke and with this particular first stroke (also known as the **Prefix Key**) is Terminal.

Making a mouse shortcut is just as easy; you simply click on **Add Mouse Shortcut**:

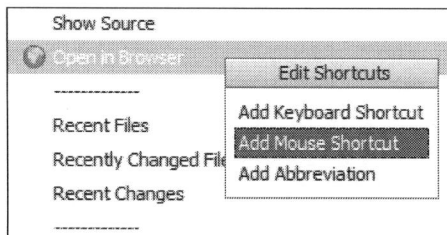

Like before, you simply enter the combination of keys that you would like:

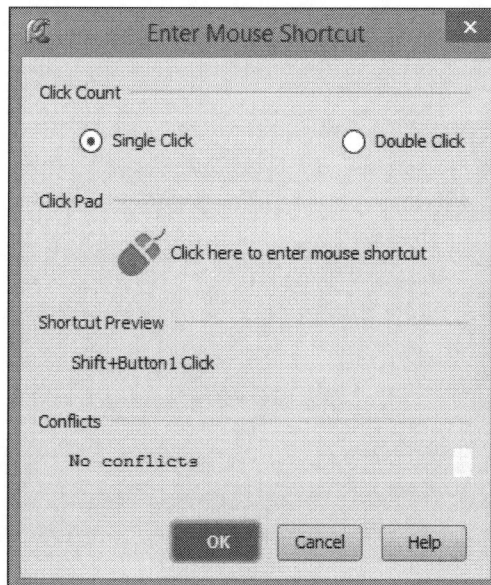

You might have also noticed that we have the ability to add an abbreviation; this is a way to quickly find the action in the **Search Everywhere** action, which is invoked by a double *Shift* (pressing *Shift* twice in quick succession). So, say we wanted to add an abbreviation for the **Open in Browser** action, all we need to do is head over to the **Keymap** again, right-click on the **Open in Browser** action, and choose **Add Abbreviation**:

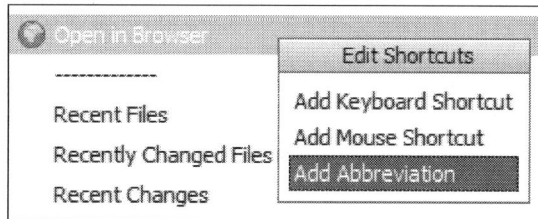

We would then get a dialog box for the abbreviation:

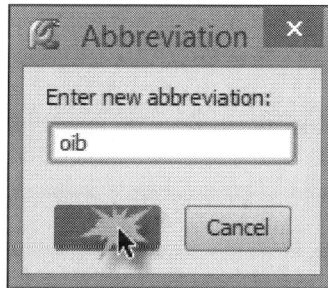

Once that is done, we should be able to see **oib**, but in a green tag:

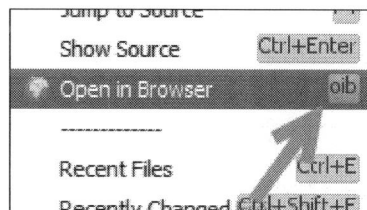

And with that, if we type `oib` into our **Search Everywhere** bar, we get this:

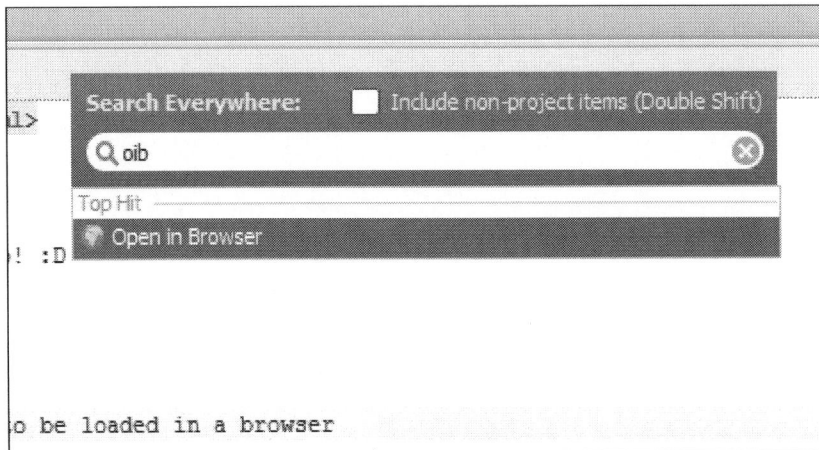

This can be a far better way to do things rather than using a second stroke in a keyboard shortcut. But, abbreviations can be even more powerful than this. We can group a couple of items with the same abbreviation so that we can make our own list of favorite actions that will come up in the **Top Hits** section of **Search Everywhere**. Let's have a look.

What we're going to do is assign two abbreviations to each of these two actions:

* **Open in Browser**
* **Reload in Browser**

So, we are going to assign the abbreviation **b** to both of them, as well as assigning their own unique abbreviations:

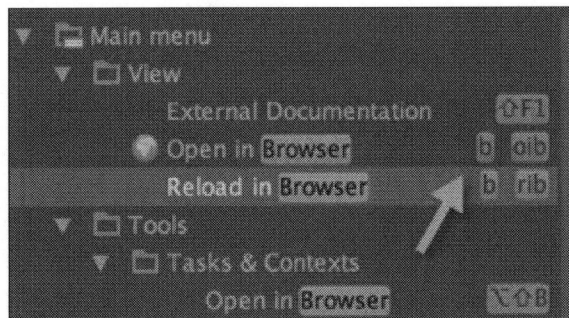

As you can see, the two browser actions have one common abbreviation, so we try to look it up in **Search Everywhere**:

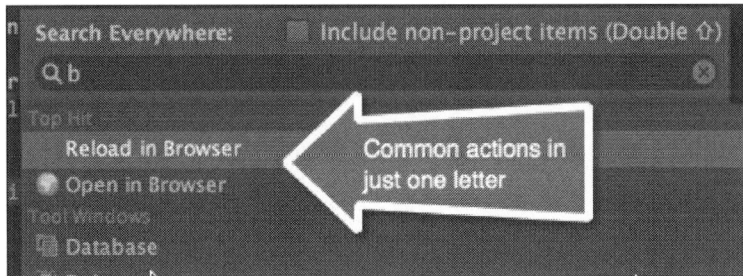

But we can still look them up individually:

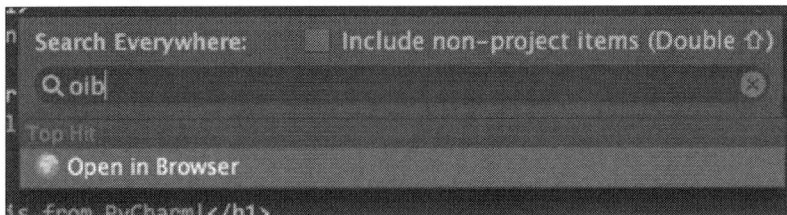

This means you can get access to all your favorite actions with just a few keystrokes. This functionality has made me much more productive.

Troubleshooting on Mac

One problem I faced when I first set up my Mac was that the keyboard shortcuts did not work; instead of getting the desired action, I got weird Greek letters appearing here and there. At first, I thought this was PyCharm's fault, but it wasn't.

The main problem was that the keyboard layout I was using, U.S., had special characters appearing when the *Alt/Option* key was pressed. In order to actually use my keyboard shortcuts, I had to change my layout to something that did not have these special characters appearing. Here is the solution to this problem.

1. Download the key mapping file from Packt's website.

2. After you've downloaded it, move it to `~/Library/Keyboard Layouts`.

3. Once you've saved the file there, all you need to do is make it your main keyboard layout. To do this, you need to head over to **System Preferences**:

    1. Go to **Keyboard**:

    2. And then, choose to add a new one by clicking on the **+** button:

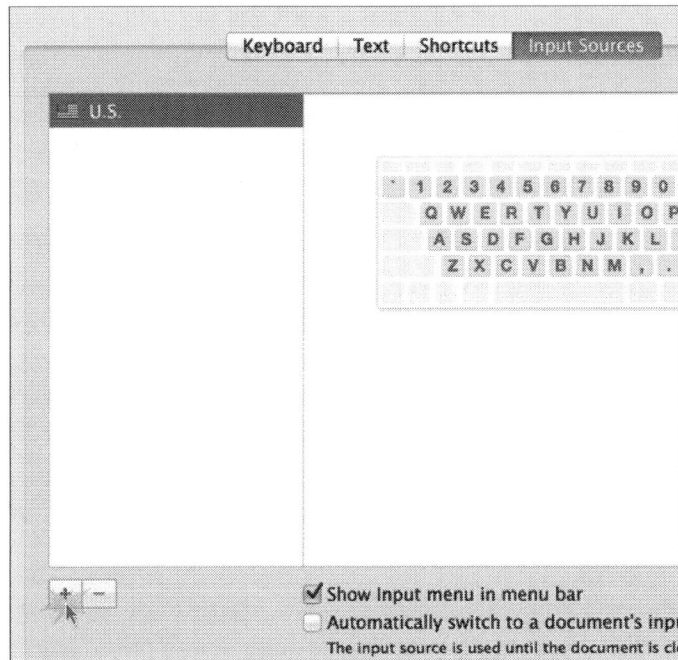

3. Choose **Others**, as shown in the following screenshot:

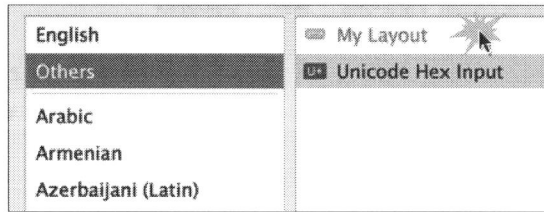

4. Once you've added it, you can now use **My Layout**:

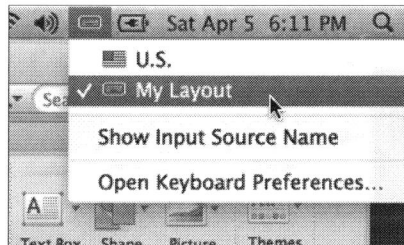

Your keyboard shortcuts should now function as expected.

Summary

In this chapter, we covered what is perhaps the most important part of using any IDE. We also looked at the common problems that one might have with setting up keyboard shortcuts on Mac.

The contents of this chapter will serve us well in the future as it will allow us to talk about keyboard shortcuts by reference to what they are called instead of having to provide a long list of possible shortcuts depending on our mapping.

3
Getting Places

This chapter is all about navigation. It is divided into three parts. The first part is called *Omni*, which deals with getting to anywhere from any place. The second is called *Macro*, which deals with navigating to places of significance. The third and final part is about moving within a file and it is called *Micro*.

By the end of this chapter, you should be able to navigate freely and quickly within PyCharm, and use the right tool for the job to do so.

Veteran PyCharm users may not find their favorite navigation tool mentioned or explained. This is because the methods of navigation described throughout this chapter will lead readers to discover their own tools that they prefer over others.

Omni

In this section, we will discuss the tools that PyCharm provides for a user to go from anywhere to any place. You could be in your project directory one second; the next, you could be inside the Python standard library or a class in your file. These tools are generally slow or at least slower than more precise tools of navigation provided.

Back and Forward

The **Back** and **Forward** actions allow you to move your cursor back to the place where it was previously for more than a few seconds or where you've made edits. This information persists throughout sessions, so even if you exit the IDE, you can still get back to the positions that you were in before you quit.

This falls into the Omni category because these two actions could potentially get you from any place within a file to any place within a file in your directory (that you have been to) to even parts of the standard library that you've looked into as well as your third-party Python packages. The **Back** and **Forward** actions are perhaps two of my most used navigation actions, and you can use **Keymap** (see *Chapter 2, Understanding the Keymap*). Or, one can simply click on the **Navigate** menu to see the keyboard shortcuts:

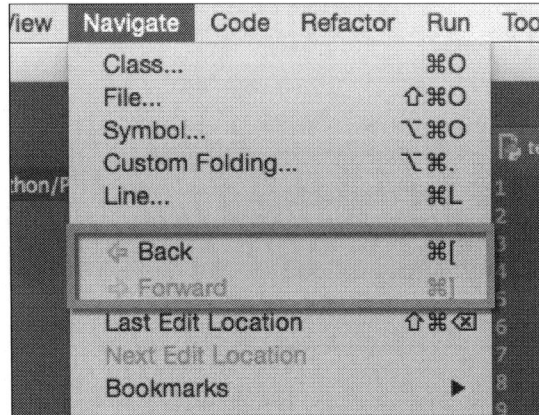

Macro

The difference between Macro and Omni is subtle. Omni allows you to go to the exact location of a place, even a place of no particular significance (say, the third line of a documentation string) in any file. Macro, on the other hand, allows you to navigate anywhere of significance, such as a function definition, class declaration, or particular class method.

Go to definition or navigate to declaration

Go to definition is the old name for *navigate to declaration* in PyCharm. This action, like the one previously discussed, could lead you anywhere—a class inside your project or a third-party library function. What this action does is allow you to go to the source file declaration of a module, package, class, function, and so on. Keymap is once again useful in finding the shortcut for this particular action.

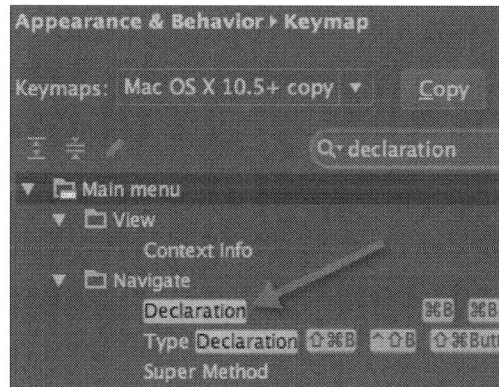

Using this action will move your cursor to the file where the class or function is declared, may it be in your project or elsewhere. Just place your cursor on the function or class and invoke the action. Your cursor will now be directly where the function or class was declared.

There is, however, a slight problem with this. If one tries to go to the declaration of a .so object, such as the datetime module or the select module, what one will encounter is a stub file (discussed in detail later). These are helper files that allow PyCharm to give you the code completion that it does. Modules that are .so files are indicated by a terminal icon, as shown here:

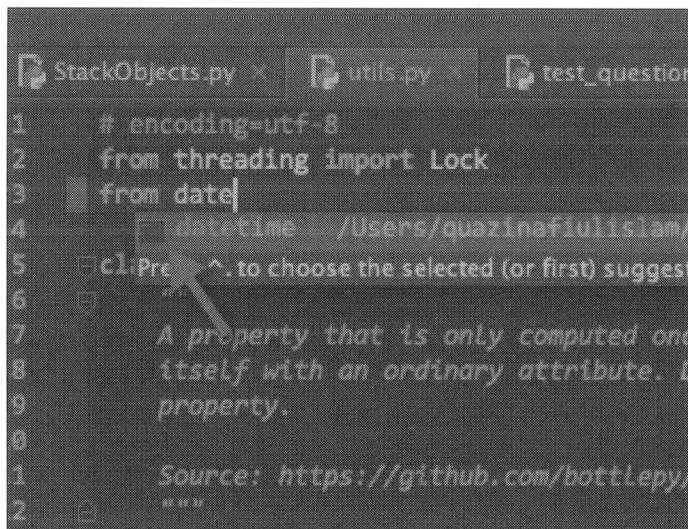

Search Everywhere

The action speaks for itself. You search for classes, files, methods, and even actions. Universally invoked using double *Shift* (pressing *Shift* twice in quick succession), this nifty action looks similar to any other search bar. **Search Everywhere** searches only inside your project, by default; however, one can also use it to search non-project items as well. Not using this option leads to faster searches and a lower memory footprint.

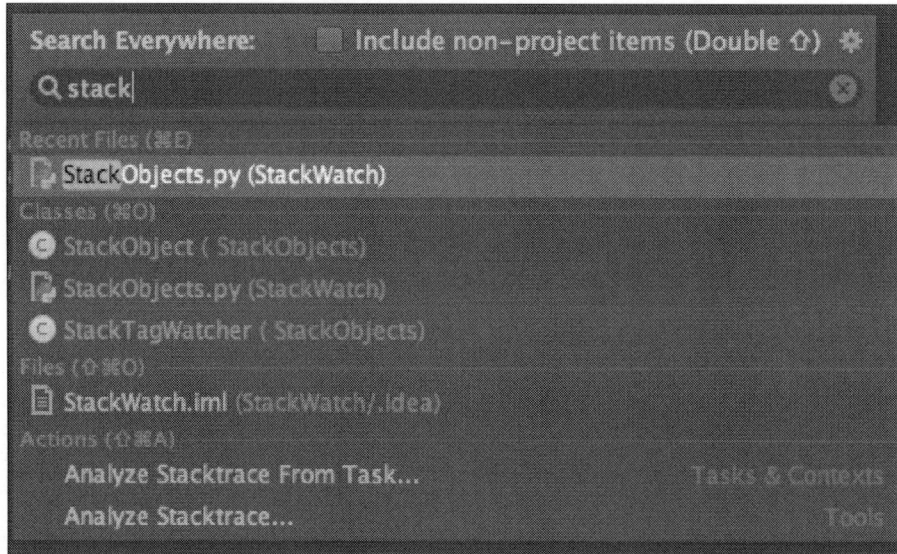

Search Everywhere is a gateway to other search actions available in PyCharm. In the preceding screenshot, one can see that **Search Everywhere** has separate parts, such as **Recent Files** and **Classes**. Each of these parts has a shortcut next to its section name. If you find yourself using **Search Everywhere** for **Classes** all the time, you might start using the **Navigate Class** action instead, which is much faster.

The Switcher tool

The **Switcher** tool allows you to quickly navigate through your currently open tabs, recently opened files as well as all of your panels.

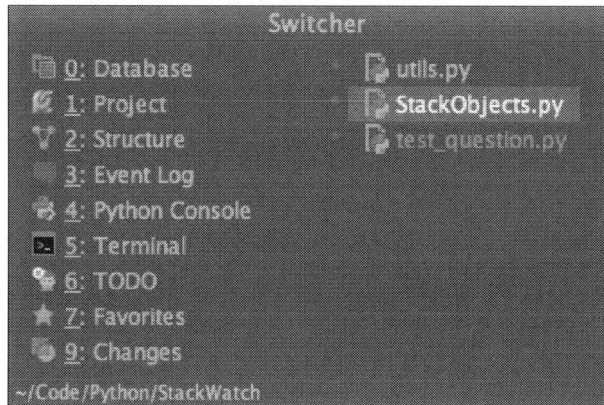

This tool is essential since you always navigate between tabs. A star to the left indicates open tabs; everything else is a recently opened or edited file. If you just have one file open, **Switcher** will show more of your recently opened files. It's really handy this way since almost always the files that you want to go to are options in **Switcher**.

The Project panel

The **Project** panel is what I use to see the structure of my project as well as search for files that I can't find with **Switcher**. This panel is by far the most used panel of all, and for good reason. The **Project** panel also supports search; just open it up and start typing to find your file.

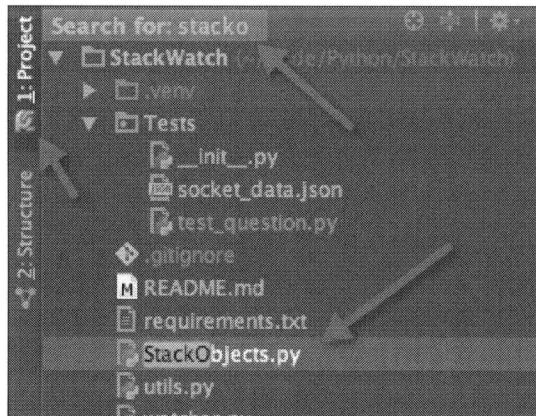

However, the **Project** panel can give you even more of an understanding of what your code looks similar to if you have **Show Members** enabled.

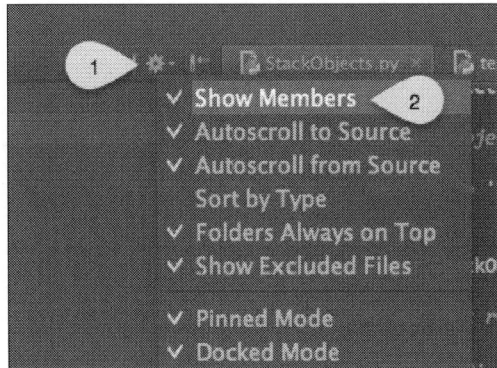

Once this is enabled, you can see the classes as well as the declared methods inside your files.

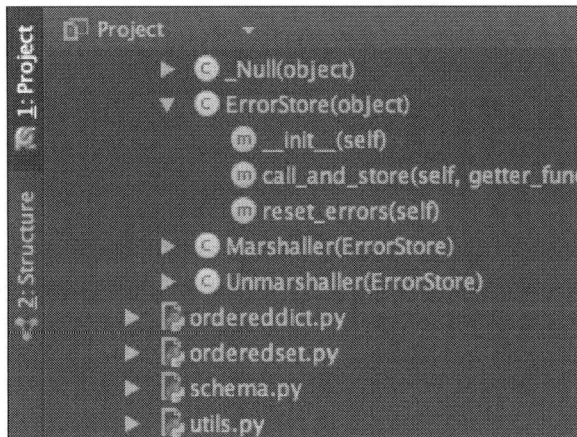

Note that a search works just like before, meaning that your search is limited to only the files/objects that you can see; if you collapse everything, you won't be able to search either your files or the classes and methods in them.

Micro

Micro deals with getting places within a file. These tools are perhaps what I end up using the most in my development.

The Structure panel

The **Structure** panel gives you a bird's eye view of the file that you are currently have your cursor on. This panel is indispensable when trying to understand a project that one is not familiar with.

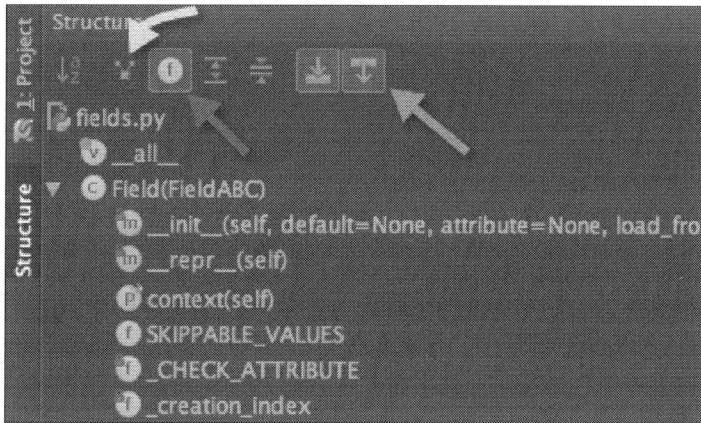

The yellow arrow indicates the option to show inherited fields and methods. The red arrow indicates the option to show field names, meaning that, if it is turned off, you will only see properties and methods. The orange arrow indicates the option to scroll to and from the source. If both are turned on (scroll to and scroll from), where your cursor is will be synchronized with whatever method, field, or property is highlighted in the structure panel. Inherited fields are grayed out in the display.

Ace Jump

This is my favorite navigation plugin, and was made by John Lindquist who is a developer at JetBrains (creators of PyCharm). Ace Jump is inspired by the Emacs mode with the same name. It allows you to *jump* from one place to another within the same file. Before one can use Ace Jump, one has to install the plugin for it (see *Chapter 7, The PyCharm Ecosystem*). Ace Jump is usually invoked using *Ctrl* or *command + ;* (semicolon). You can search for Ace Jump in **Keymap** as well, and it is called **Ace Jump**. Once invoked, you get a small box in which you can input a letter. Choose a letter from the word that you want to navigate to, and you will see letters on that letter pop up immediately.

If we were to hit *D*, the cursor would move to the position indicated by D. This might seem long winded, but it actually leads to really fast navigation.

If we wanted to select the word indicated by the letter, then we'd invoke Ace Jump twice before entering a letter.

This turns the Ace Jump box red. Upon hitting *B*, the named parameter rounding will be selected.

Often, we don't want to go to a word, but rather the beginning or the end of a line. In order to do this, just hit **Invoke Ace Jump** and then the left arrow for line beginnings or the right arrow for line endings.

In this case, we'd just hit *V* to jump to the beginning of the line that starts with `num_type`.

This is an example where we hit left arrow instead of the right one, and we get line-ending options.

Summary

In this chapter, I discussed some of the best tools for navigation. This is by no means an exhaustive list. However, these tools will serve as a gateway to more precise tools available for navigation in PyCharm. I generally use **Ace Jump**, **Back**, **Forward**, and **Switcher** the most when I write code. The **Project** panel is always open for me, with the most used files having their classes and methods expanded for quick search.

4
Editing

Editing is what we are going to be doing the most in PyCharm, and hence, this is one of the most important chapters. This chapter does not try to cover a wide range of feature sets; it instead tries to provide a comprehensive look at some of the best tools available for editing. The most important part of this chapter is enhancing code completion in PyCharm. This IDE has a remarkably powerful engine that can understand your code, and it allows for things such as better code completion (even when we haven't specified the types), method hierarchies, and a lot more.

This chapter has several parts:

- **Improving code completion**: This section will take a comprehensive look at the tools at our disposal that enhance PyCharm's code completion, giving us more completion options and smarter completions.

- **Writing code**: This section will cover some of the best tools that PyCharm offers to write code quickly and effectively.

- **Setting up IPython Notebook**: IPython Notebook has become the de facto document format for Python's scientific community, and for good reason. This section will take a look at how to set up IPython Notebook in PyCharm so that we can get the benefits of code completion inside the notebook.

- **Editor plugins**: This section will cover a few select plugins to help you get used to PyCharm if you come from other editors such as Emacs and Vim. This section will also showcase support markdown.

- **Reading code**: This section looks at the different tools at your disposal to better read code such as diagrams and method hierarchies.

Improving code completion

Code completion in PyCharm is really quite something, and there are many things that you can do to enhance it even further. PyCharm normally gives you code completion options as you type:

```
class Meta:

    def __init__(self):
        se
        P  self
        c  set
        m  setattr(p_object, name, value)
        m  license(args, kwargs)
        raise
```

However, if you press *Ctrl* + spacebar while this popup is on the screen, you will get even more code completion options:

```
class Meta:

    def __init__(self):
        is
        is
        c  islice (itertools)
        iso2022_jp
        iso2022_jp_1
```

Note that `islice` is not even imported, yet PyCharm can smartly tell you that you can use it, and if you chose to do so, it will be automatically imported. PyCharm also supports **Cyclic Word Completion** also known as **Hippe Complete** (*Alt* + /), which can prove to be very useful when you want completion in strings:

```
def __init__(self):
    """

    super sammy susie sarah stephan shape source
    """

    some_long_variable_name_here_muhahahahahaha = ''
    bad_variable_name = 's'
```

```
    super sammy susie sarah stephan shape source
    """
    some_long_variable_name_here_muhahahahahaha = ''
    bad_variable_name = 'some_long_variable_name_here_muhahahahahaha'
```

```
__init__(self):
    """

    super sammy susie sarah stephan shape source
    """

    some_long_variable_name_here_muhahahahahaha = ''
    bad_variable_name = 'source'
```

Furthermore, you can fine-tune your completion options:

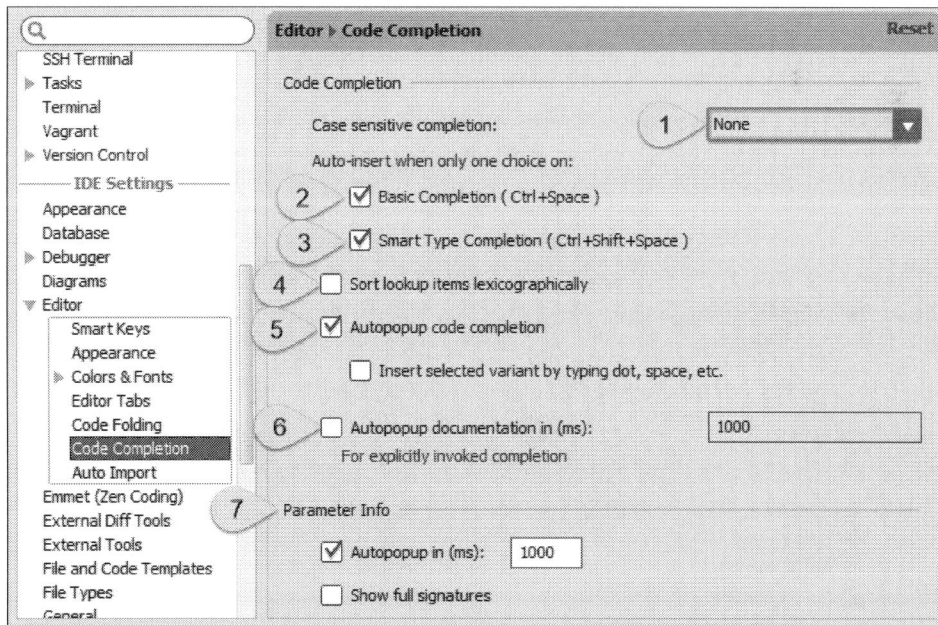

Here, [1] is, by default, set to *first letter*, and I feel it's best to demonstrate this with an example.

With first letter, you will need to type in a capital к in order to get **KeyboardInterrrupt**; otherwise, it will never show up in your completion options:

```
if __name__ == '__main__':
    while True:
        try:
            time.sleep(2)
            print("zzzz")
    except K
            KeyboardInterrupt
        C KeyError
        C LookupError
        Press Ctrl+Period to choose the selected (or first) suggestion
```

But, with the setting set to **None**, you don't need to type in a capital к:

```
        print("zzzz")
    except k
        C KeyboardInterrupt
        C KeyError
        C LookupError
        Press Ctrl+Period to choose the select
```

I set my case sensitivity to **None** because I'm too lazy to press *Shift*.

What [2] and [3] do is pretty self-explanatory, however, you might be confused at what **Smart Type Completion** does, and you're right to be. It has nothing to do with Python, but it's a JavaScript feature in PyCharm that gives you better code completion options when you're writing JavaScript.

This would be a good time to tell you that PyCharm has what I like to call *Fuzzy Completion*, which means that in the preceding example, if you were to type in `ki`, it would take you to **KeboardInterrupt**, but this is not limited to camel case alone, it also extends to underscores:

```
def some_normal_func():
    pass


def some_happy_func():
    pass


def some_super_awesome_func():
    pass



if __name__ == '__main__':
    print(ssa)
        m some_super_awesome_func ()
        Ctrl+Down and Ctrl+Up will move caret down and up in
```

Again, [4] is self-explanatory. It will simply arrange your options in a certain way (basically, alphabetical, but numbers appear before letters). Toggling [5] will allow completion options to display commas, semicolons, and a whole host of other characters. This can slow down PyCharm quite a lot on slow systems. Option [6] will automatically open documentation when you press *Ctrl* + spacebar on a completion option:

```
inspect.cl
    m classify_class_attrs (cls)      inspect          Documentation for classify_class_attrs
    m cleandoc (doc)                  inspect      ⇐ ⇒ ⬆      < Python 2.7.6 (C:/Python27/python.exe) >  ⚙
    m getclasstree (classes, unique) inspect
    m isclass (object)                inspect  π   def classify_class_attrs(cls)
                                                   Inferred type: (cls: unknown) -> list

                                                   Return list of attribute-descriptor tuples.

                                                   For each name in dir(cls), the return list contains
                                                   with these elements:
```

The **Parameter Info** popup, [7], shows you the parameter information that looks similar to a little callout:

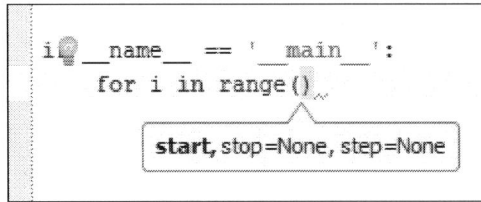

```
i  __name__ == '__main__':
    for i in range ()
              /\
        start, stop=None, step=None
```

This will automatically pop up, and if it goes away for some reason, you can always bring it back with *Ctrl + P* (**Parameter Info**).

Understanding what intentions can do for you

If you've ever wondered about what that yellow light bulb means, it's simply an indication that there are possible intention actions at your disposal. Intentions in PyCharm are context-specific actions that you can invoke with *Alt + Enter* (**Show Intention Actions**). One very useful example of intentions at work is when using language injection in strings.

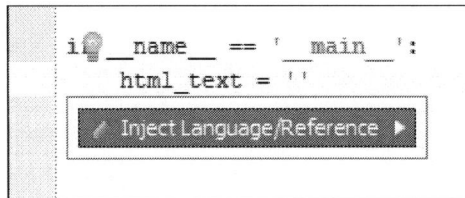

```
i  __name__ == '__main__':
    html_text = ''
    /  Inject Language/Reference  ▶
```

And with that, we can insert the many different languages that PyCharm supports:

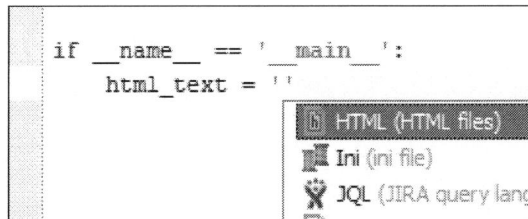

```
if __name__ == '__main__':
    html_text = ''
                  HTML (HTML files)
                  Ini (ini file)
                  JQL (JIRA query lang
```

The best part is that you get syntax highlighting and snippet completion within the string as well:

```python
if __name__ == '__main__':
    html_text = '<html>' \
                '<body>' \
                '    <div class="container">' \
                '        Hello World!' \
                '</div>' \
                '</body>' \
                '</html>'
```

But, injections are not limited to languages alone, for example, you can have things such as file paths:

```
                '</body>' \
                '</htm
                          Q file
    demo_html_path = '
                          File Reference
                          Localization file (Localiz
```

You can have a look at all the intentions at your disposal here:

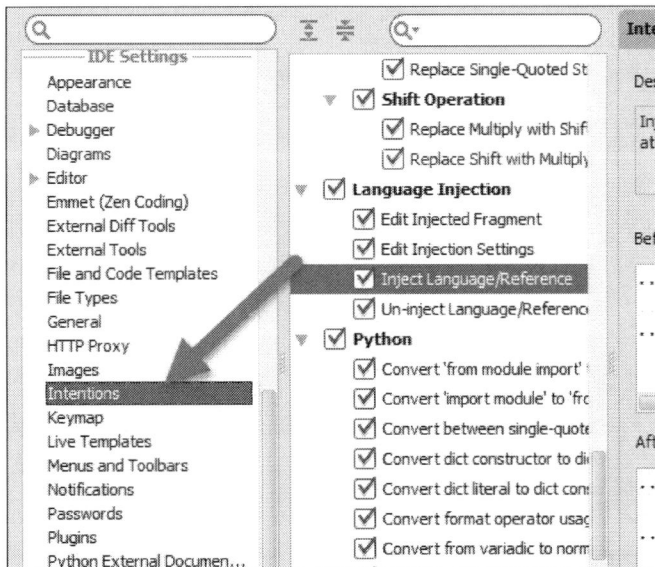

All the intentions are context-specific; sometimes, they're tuned specifically for languages and others are often more general purpose. For example, in Python, you have the intention to convert from a single-quoted string into a double-quoted string, however, language injections work across different languages. You can get a good idea of what these intentions do just by looking at its individual page:

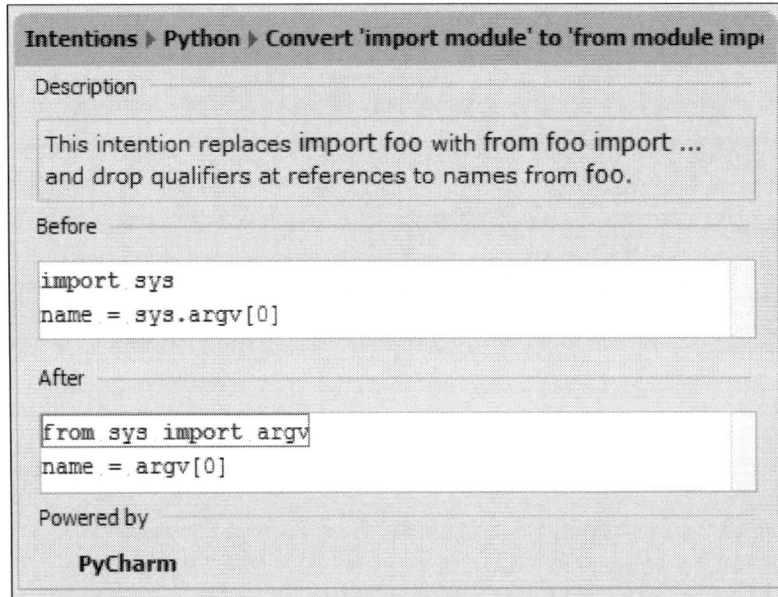

Intentions ▸ Python ▸ Convert 'import module' to 'from module impı

Description

This intention replaces import foo with from foo import ... and drop qualifiers at references to names from foo.

Before

```
import sys
name = sys.argv[0]
```

After

```
from sys import argv
name = argv[0]
```

Powered by

PyCharm

It gives you everything that you wanted to know about intentions, but notice what it is powered by. In this case, this is one of PyCharm's core functionalities, but some intentions are powered by plugins, so if one does not work, you can figure out what is causing the problem.

Collecting runtime types

Code completion is probably the reason why most of us use PyCharm. The PyCharm team spends a lot of their time improving and refining completion options not only in PyCharm but also in other IDEs. One of the easiest ways to improve code completion is to gather runtime data.

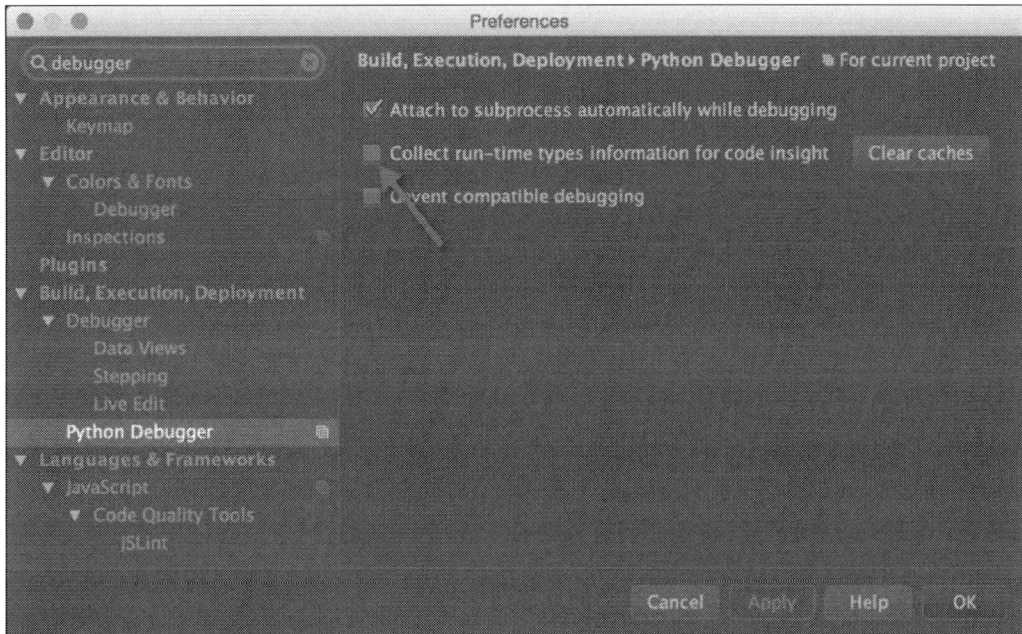

Collecting runtime types allows PyCharm to provide better code completion. This runtime data is collected every time one *debugs* a program, not when one simply runs it. If by any chance, PyCharm shows you the wrong types, then clearing the caches is the best way to solve the problem.

Adding docstrings and type information

Docstrings are parsed and used by PyCharm to give you better code completion as well as better quick documentation information. Here is an example, using **Intentions**.

```
class Person:

    def __init__(self, name, age, gender, country_of_origin):
        self.age = age
        self.name = name
                                    Add field 'gender' to class Person    ▶

                                    Insert documentation string stub       ▶
                                    Specify type for reference in docstring ▶
```

Say we wanted to make a `Person` class so that we can declare the class and add a few parameters to its `__init__` function:

```
class Person:

    def __init__(self, name, age, gender, country_of_origin):
        self.age = age
        self.name = name
                                    Add field 'gender' to class Person    ▶

                                    Insert documentation string stub       ▶
                                    Specify type for reference in docstring ▶
```

We can also add parameter info through docstrings or annotations (in Python 3) and since docstrings work for both Python 2 and 3, we're going to stick with them.

```
class Person:

    def __init__(self, name, age, gender, country_of_origin):
        self.country_of_o    Insert documentation string stub       ▶
        self.gender = gen    Specify type for reference in docstring ▶
        self.age = age
        self.name = name
```

This causes PyCharm to generate a lot of documentation for me (for free!):

```
def __init__(self, name, age, gender,
    """

    :param name:
    :param age:
    :param gender:
    :param country_of_origin:
    """
```

Let me take a step back to say that this docstring is in a particular format, that is, it's in rst or **reStructuredText**. This means that PyCharm can parse the string and get information regarding the parameters to the init function and class it is initializing. Note that you have the choice between **Epytext** and **reStructuredText**. I suggest using **reStructuredText** because that is what PyCharm uses to generate documentation skeletons for a variety of stdlib classes. Here is where all of these options are set:

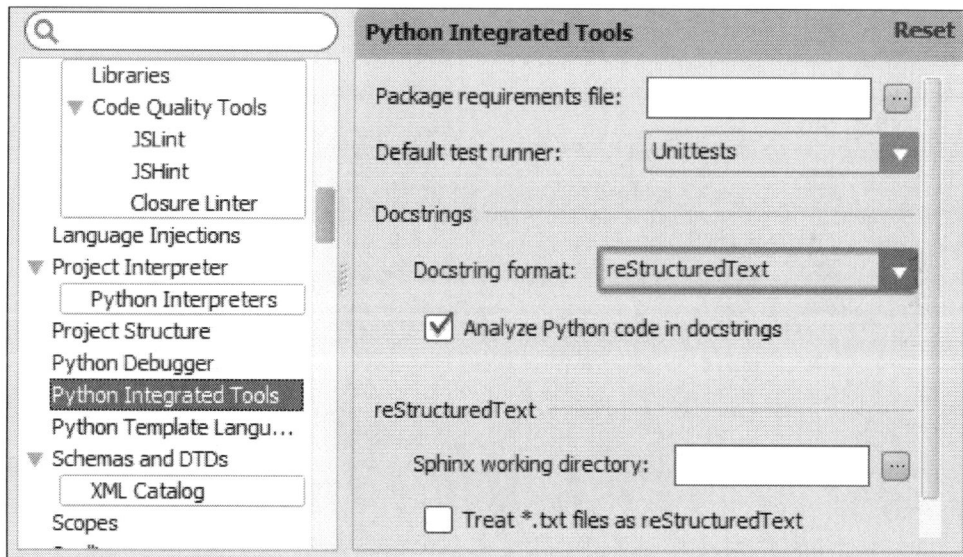

Now that we've put in some information regarding our `Person` object, let's see what the **Quick Documentation** (*Ctrl + Q*) brings up:

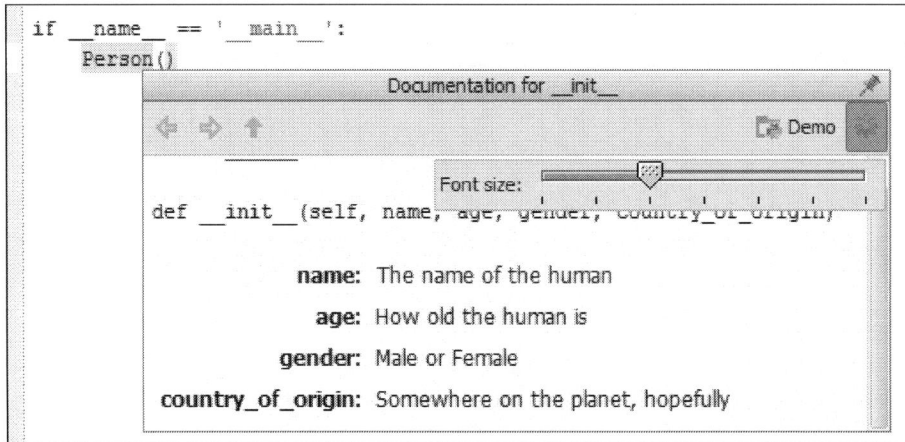

```
if __name__ == '__main__':
    Person()
```

Documentation for __init__

Demo

Font size:

```
def __init__(self, name, age, gender, country_or_origin)
```

name:	The name of the human
age:	How old the human is
gender:	Male or Female
country_of_origin:	Somewhere on the planet, hopefully

This is great, but we can get even more information out of docstrings. So now using another intention option, we can generate the parameter types for each of the arguments for `Person`:

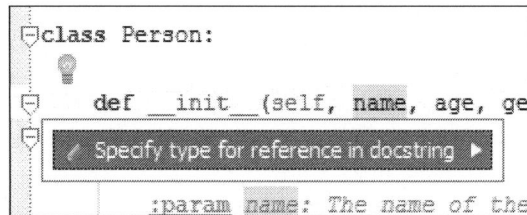

```
class Person:

    def __init__(self, name, age, ge
```
Specify type for reference in docstring ▶
```
        :param name: The name of the
```

And with this, we can say that the name will be of type `str`:

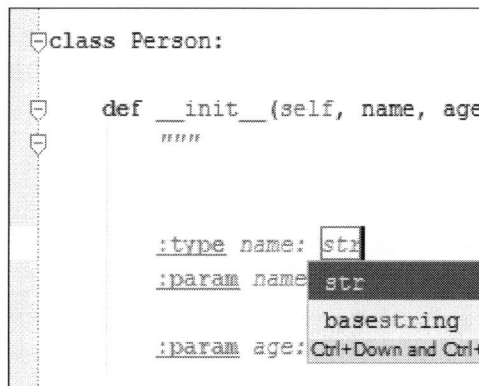

```
class Person:

    def __init__(self, name, age
        """

        :type name: str
        :param name  str
                     basestring
        :param age: Ctrl+Down and Ctrl+
```

With this, you get even more information from **Quick Documentation**:

Please note that you need to be careful when adding docstrings because they require special formatting. So, in this case, we have the following:

```
i  __name__ == '__main__':
    Person()
```

Documentation for __init__	

⇐ ⇒ ⬆   Demo ⚙

```
def __init__(self, name, age, gender, country_of_origin)
```

name:	(str)	The name of the human
age:	(int)	How old the human is
gender:	(str)	Male or Female
country_of_origin:	(str)	Somewhere on the planet, hopefully

```
    """
    :type name: str
    :param name: The name of the human

    :type age: int
    :param age: How old the human is


    :type gender: str
    :param gender: Male or Female

    :type country_of_origin: str
    :param country_of_origin: Somewhere on the planet, hopefully
```

See how we have the type of the parameter first, then its description, and finally a blank line between parameters. This is best practice, so even without PyCharm someone can quickly read about and understand the different parameters. This is how you need to arrange the information in your docstring in order for PyCharm to give you useful quick documentation. Docstrings can also be used by PyCharm to help you write more accurate code:

```
i  __name__ == '__main__':
      Person('hello', 'hello', 'cheese', 1)

      Expected type 'int', got 'str' instead more... (Ctrl+F1)
```

PyCharm correctly points out that you've put in the wrong parameters, and this kind of static analysis can be very helpful. Also, note that you can choose to tell PyCharm to ignore the problem (by pressing the right arrow after we've selected **Inspect 'Type checker' options**):

```
i  __name__ == '__main__':
      Person('hello', 'hello', 'cheese', 1)

   Inspection 'Type checker' options          ▶      Type checker

   Convert single-quoted string to double-quoted string  ▶     Edit inspection profile setting
   Inject Language/Reference                   ▶      Run inspection on ...
   Specify return type in docstring            ▶   X  Disable inspection
                                                      Suppress for statement
```

This will add a new command above the line, telling PyCharm to ignore the type checking for this statement:

```
if __name__ == '__main__':
    # noinspection PyTypeChecker
       Person('hello', 'hello', 'cheese', 1)
```

Docstrings can provide a lot of code completion options for functions, however, they often fall short when it comes to providing code completion options for metaclasses. This is to be expected since docstrings provide static analysis.

The skeletons in PyCharm's closet

No, it's not that PyCharm has something to hide; it's just that it has a lot of skeletons generated for different modules, and you can take a look at them too:

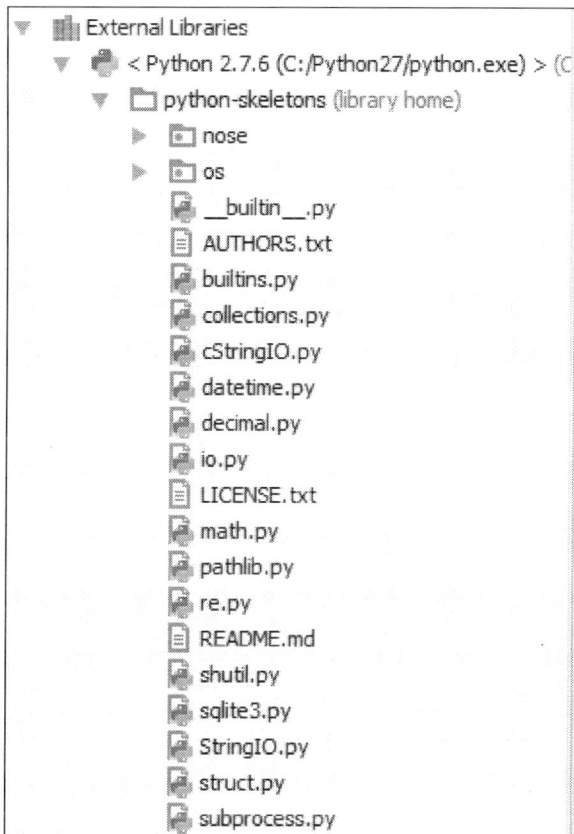

```
▼  📚 External Libraries
    ▼  🐍 < Python 2.7.6 (C:/Python27/python.exe) > (C
        ▼  📁 python-skeletons (library home)
            ▶  📦 nose
            ▶  📦 os
                📄 __builtin__.py
                📄 AUTHORS.txt
                📄 builtins.py
                📄 collections.py
                📄 cStringIO.py
                📄 datetime.py
                📄 decimal.py
                📄 io.py
                📄 LICENSE.txt
                📄 math.py
                📄 pathlib.py
                📄 re.py
                📄 README.md
                📄 shutil.py
                📄 sqlite3.py
                📄 StringIO.py
                📄 struct.py
                📄 subprocess.py
```

Python skeletons provide a lot of the code completion that you see in PyCharm, and all are hosted on an open source GitHub repository at `https://github.com/JetBrains/python-skeletons`.

And when I said skeletons, I meant skeletons! These are not implementations; they are merely something that PyCharm can statically analyze. Let's look at the decimal.py file:

```python
class Decimal(object):
    """Floating point class for decimal arithmetic."""

    def __add__(self, other, context=None):
        """Returns self + other.

        :type other: numbers.Number
        :type context: decimal.Context | None
        :rtype: decimal.Decimal
        """
        return decimal.Decimal()
```

There's no implementation here, just the bare information that PyCharm needs to give you the code completion options you need. The skeletons are still a work in progress but are getting better every day.

Setting up IPython Notebook

Support for the IPython Notebook is one of PyCharm's newer additions. Before we can do anything, we need to make sure that IPython is installed as one of our packages in the interpreter. Unfortunately, if we install IPython through PyCharm's package installer, all the requirements will not be installed. So, the best way to install IPython is through the following command line:

```
pip install ipython[all]
```

This will install IPython and all its requirements. Now, we can create a new notebook with the extension of `.ipynb`, and PyCharm will recognize this. If all the requirements are not installed, PyCharm will complain that the connection to the server is being refused. Once we make a `.ipynb` file, we will see a different interface from other Python files.

This is just like the IPython Notebook interface that we're used to. The only difference is that we can now get code completion too.

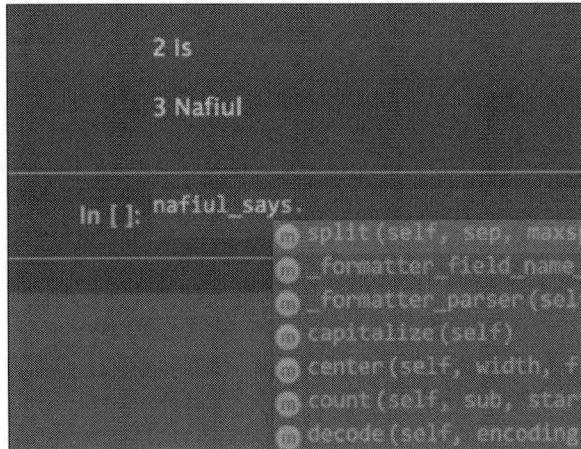

Editor plugins

PyCharm is extended through plugins, and one can install them by simply browsing the **Plugins** catalog in PyCharm:

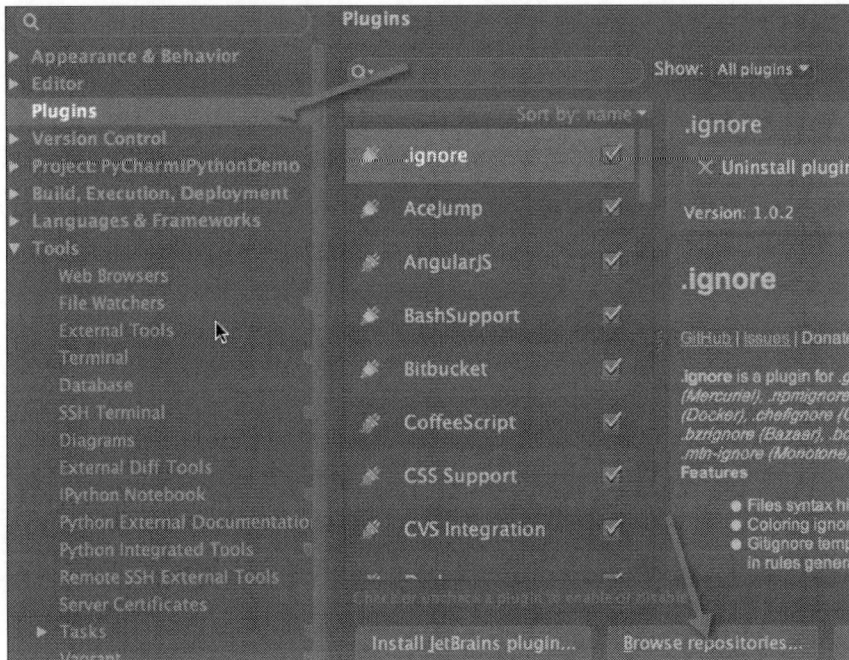

The PyCharm plugin ecosystem is so large and so important that there is an entire chapter dedicated to it in this book. However, in this section, we will look at two plugins in particular: **IdeaVim** and **emacsIDEAs**.

IdeaVim was created by JetBrains. It offers full emulation of Vim and is freely available on the repositories.

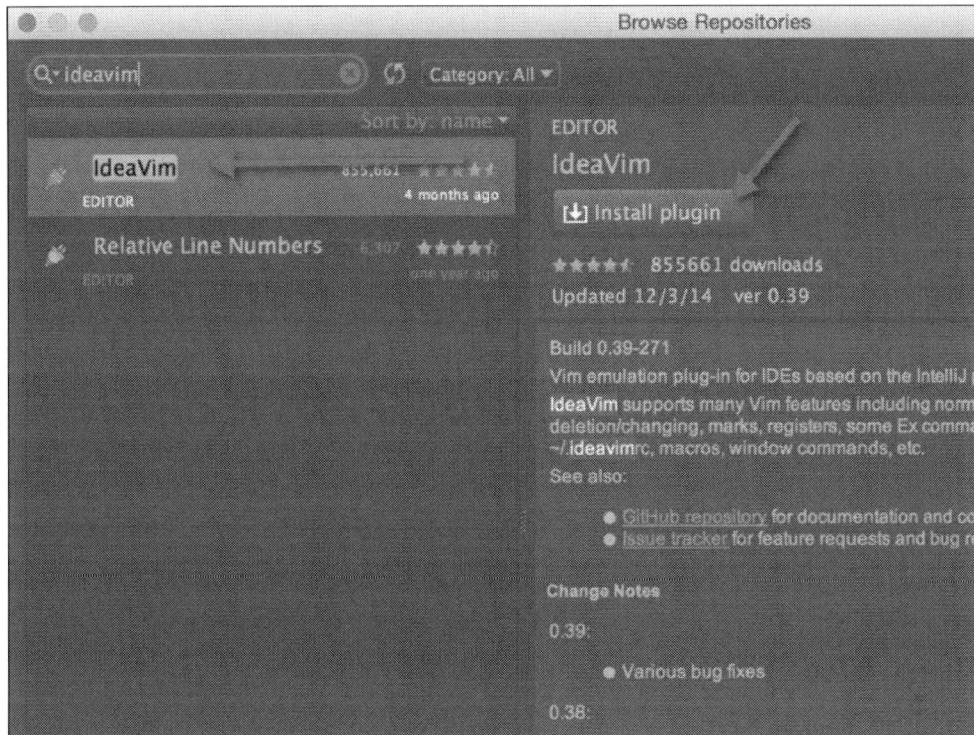

However, the other plugin, emacsIDEAs, is not supported by JetBrains. This is a third-party plugin, but has a high rating and is regularly updated.

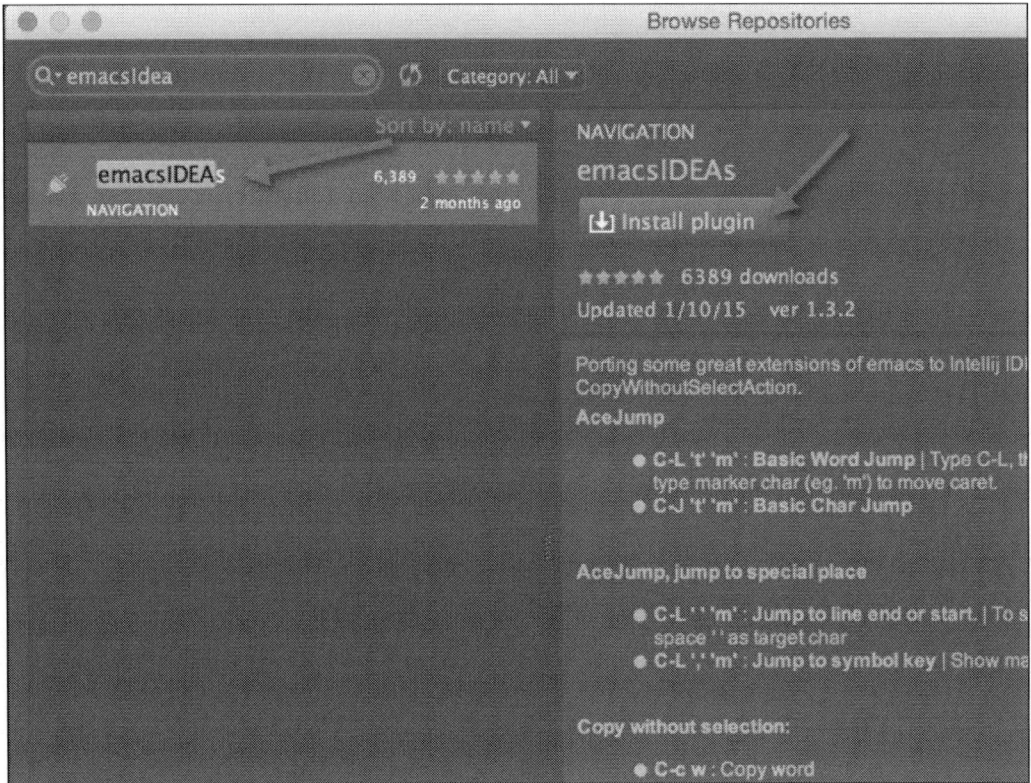

Writing code

This section has been purposely kept short and only showcases three powerful features that many PyCharm users are not completely aware of. The first two features are very simple and require us to simply use a keyboard shortcut, while the other feature requires a little more work.

Refactoring

Refactoring is one of PyCharm's most powerful features and its capabilities go beyond a single file. One of the simplest ways to see this feature at work is renaming a variable or a function:

```
def add_one(n):
    return n + 1


def foo(func, n):
    return func(n)


foo(add_one, 2)
```

In the preceding example, we want to change the function name `foo` to `apply` (because it makes more sense). This is of course a simple example, but helps prove a point.

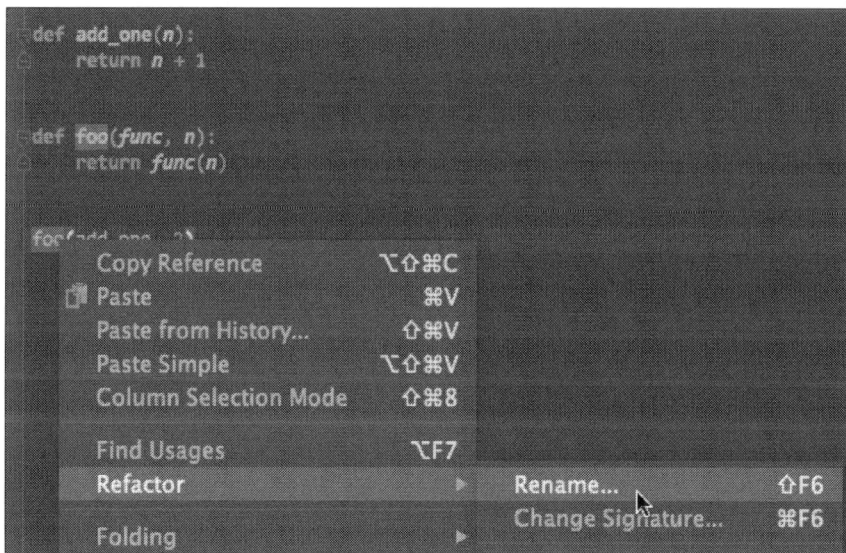

This brings up another window that gives us a few options:

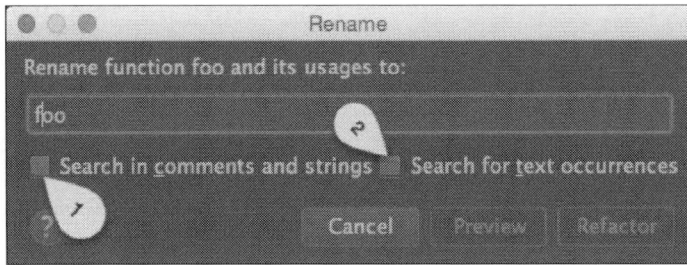

Here, [1] is very useful if we have put docstrings into the functions that describe variables. [2] will search for text documents such as `.rst` and `.md`. This already shows you how far PyCharm can go in its analysis. In this simple example, we don't need to turn on [1] or [2], so let's see what happens when we just go ahead with what we have.

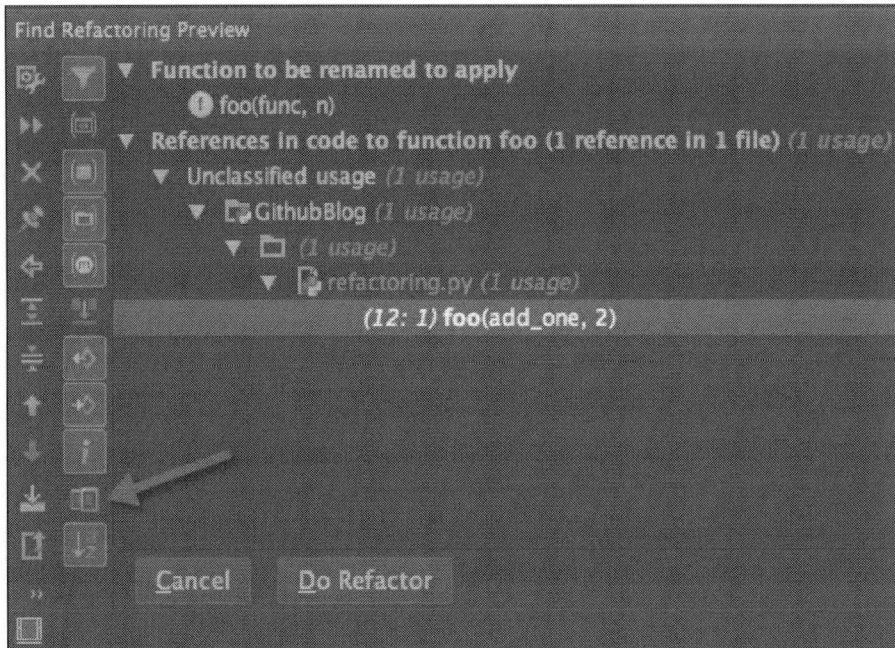

This panel might seem complicated, and we don't have to understand what all the buttons do to take advantage of what this panel has to offer. We can see the function that we are going to name, in this case foo, and the places where it is referenced. By default, things are grouped by directories and then by files, and it's best to keep it this way (although we can change this as well). In this case, we have only one use case of foo, and that is being shown under the aptly named file, refactoring.py. However, one of the buttons that I do find very useful is the one indicated by the arrow that will show the exact code in a side panel (although we cannot edit in the panel).

Once we hit the **Do Refactor** button, we can see that foo is now renamed apply. As I've mentioned before, this is a simple example because this can be used to refactor everything from module names to setting variables in totally different packages with usages all over the place. As long as PyCharm knows that a file exists, that is, it is in the PYTHONPATH, it will search the file for relevant usages.

Multiple cursors

Multiple cursors has been a long-awaited feature in PyCharm and its addition has everything to do with sublime text championing this much-loved feature. Placing cursors is easy; all we need to do is add or remove a caret (*Shift* + *Alt* + click). Clicking on the same place a second time after a cursor has been placed will remove the cursor. This is rather difficult to show in a book, but it looks similar to this:

We can also get multiple cursors by invoking **Add Selection for Next Occurrence**. This allows us to place a cursor on the same occurrence of a symbol.

We can also use *Alt* + drag to get a straight perpendicular line of cursors.

This can be really useful when trying to add trailing commas at the end of each item in a list or dictionary, for example.

doc_mode

This is something I coined myself. It is not an official feature, but rather something that you can set up in PyCharm. This mode is terribly useful when you want to explore a new library. Here we have a **Quick Documentation** popup, but what if we wanted to see the documentation in a panel and that panel updated as we invoked methods or functions?

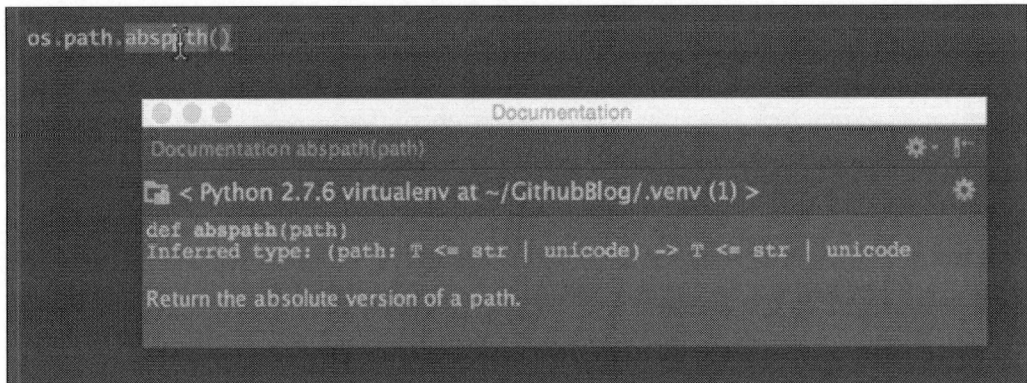

What we first need to do is change **Quick Documentation** from **Floating Mode** to **Pinned Mode**:

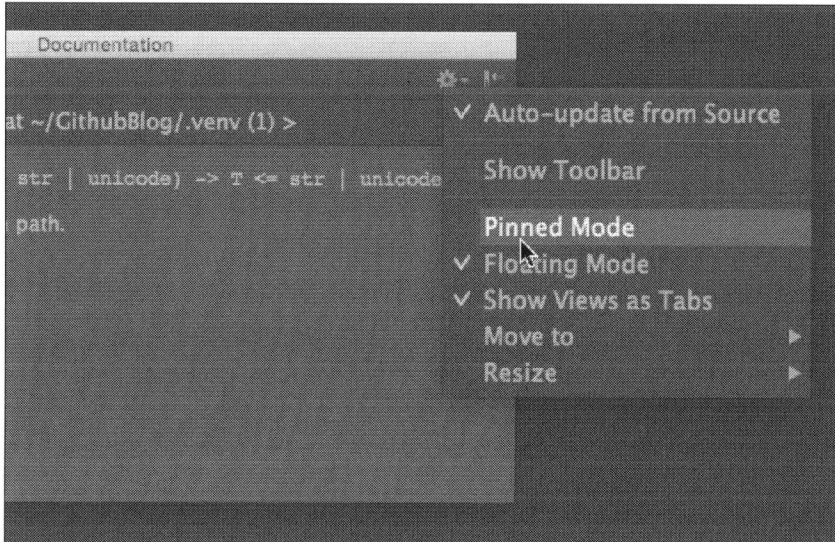

We also need to disable **Floating Mode**. This part is confusing since we need to click on the gear icon again and then disable **Floating Mode**, just like we enabled **Pinned Mode**. After it is pinned, we need to invoke **Quick Documentation** again. Click on the gear icon once more and select **Docked Mode**. Make sure that **Auto-update from Source** is also selected.

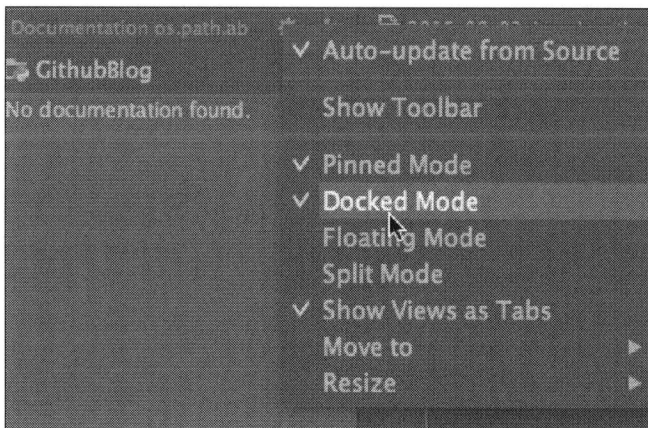

Once this is done, we can now get documentation as we type.

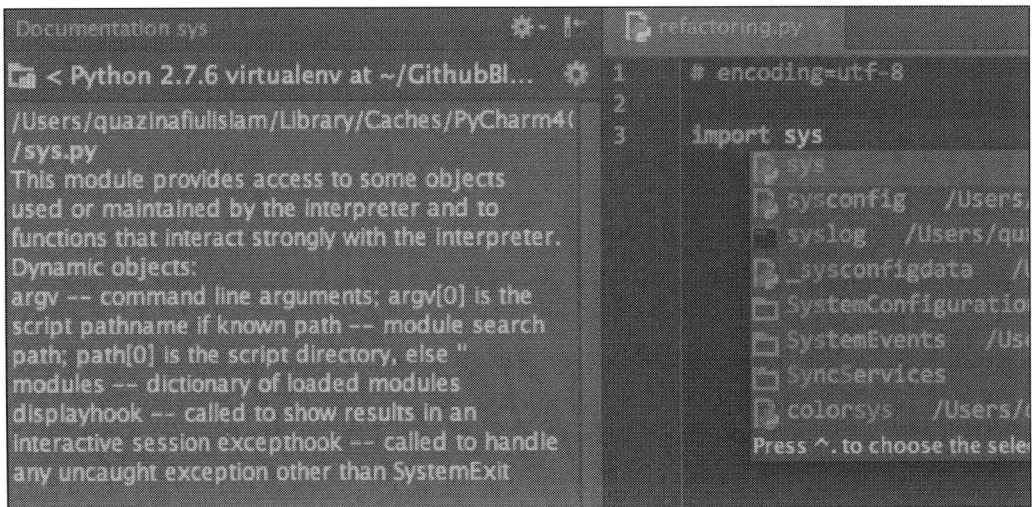

Reading code

This section covers the different tools available in PyCharm to help you read code better. This is not an exhaustive list, however, as there are so many features out there.

The lens mode

When editing, you might notice that there are different colored bars on the right-hand side. If you hover over these small bars, you will be able to see the warning, error, or information in question. This is what PyCharm calls lens mode.

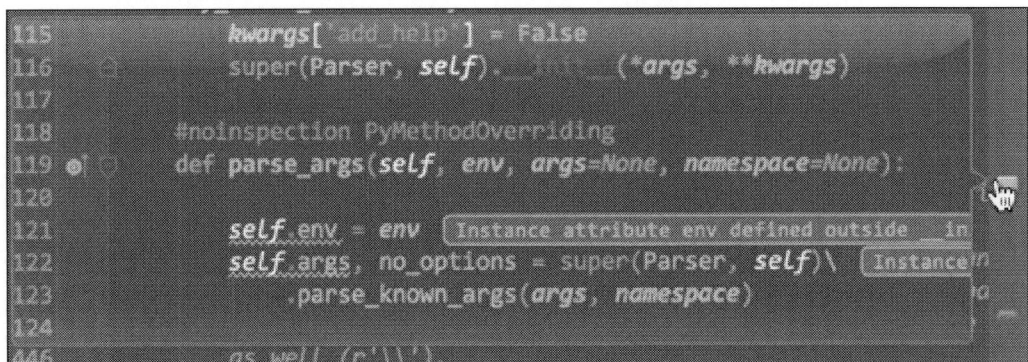

This is really quite useful when you want to take a quick look at the code. You can also see that lens mode will show you all the messages that the colored horizontal bars mean. In this case, you can see that by placing the mouse on the dark yellow bar, we can see the message that it is trying to convey. This can give you a quick bird's-eye view of your code. But, usually, when I want to see what a particular function does, I use **Quick Documentation** or **Quick Definition**.

Diagrams

The **Diagrams** option can also give you a great view of your code; you can simply go to any class and choose to see its inheritance diagram:

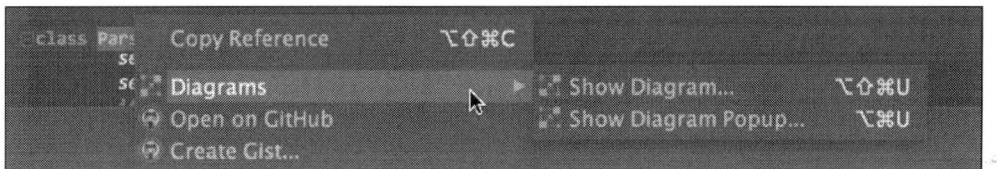

This popup will show you a quick representation:

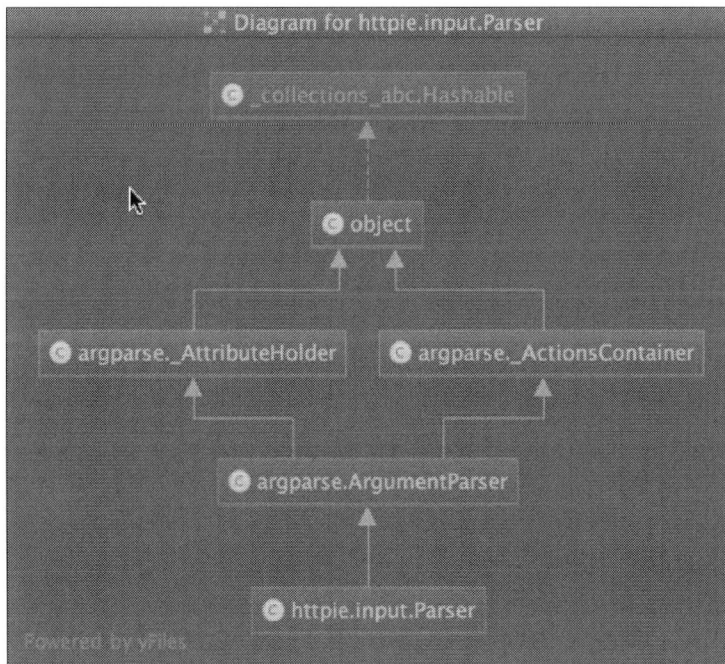

This is great if you want a quick look, and you can also choose to take a look at the variables and methods of the classes:

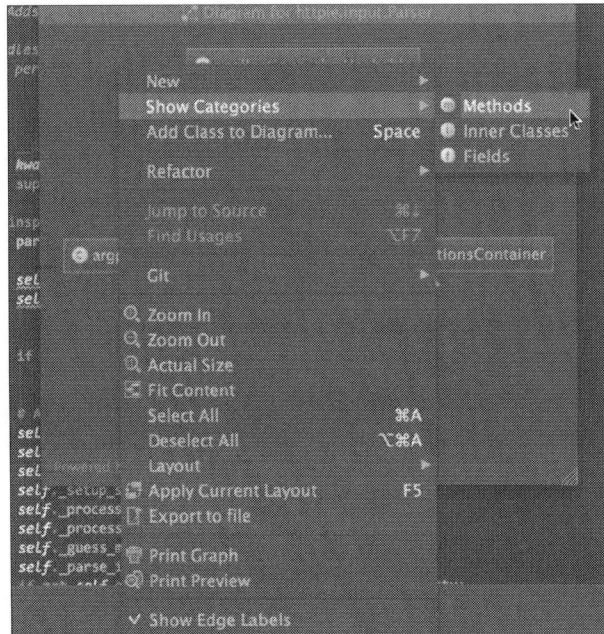

However, this can get a bit too much to see in the popup comfortably, so it's better to just look at it in a tab of its own. So, using **Show Diagram...** can instead provide a much better way of navigating large class structures easily:

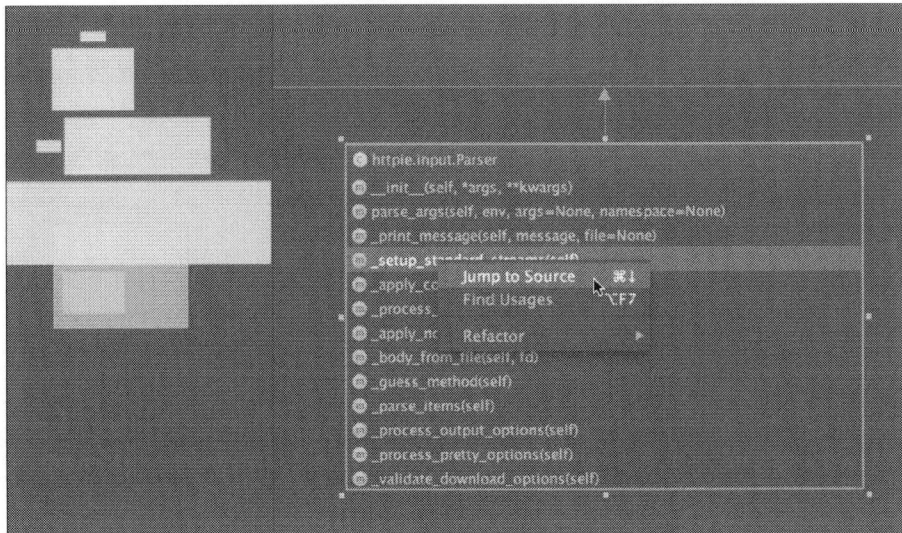

The best thing is that you can easily navigate to the source as well. These tools have helped me immensely when trying to understand open source libraries such as `requests` and `httpie`.

Method hierarchies

Method hierarchies can be very useful in trying to determine what other methods are being called to be a method as well as what methods call a particular method. If that's a mouthful, let me demonstrate with an example:

```python
# encoding=utf8
import time


def say_doing_something():
    time.sleep(1)
    print("We are doing something")


def say_we_did_something():
    print("We did something")


def do_something(a):
    say_doing_something()
    _ret = a + 1
    say_we_did_something()
    return _ret


if __name__ == '__main__':
    print(do_something(10))
```

In the preceding example, there are three simple methods. When we call do_
something, we call say_doing_something, which calls time.sleep. After say_
doing_something is called, add 1 to the initial argument, a. Then, we call say_we_
did_something. We finally return _ret. This is an improvised decorator; there are of
course far more elegant ways of writing the preceding code, but bear with me. If we
now jump into PyCharm, and ask to get all the called methods in do_something, we
not only get that, but also the methods that say_doing_something calls, by looking at
the **Callee Methods Hierarchy**. First, we must move our cursor over do_something
and then invoke **Call Hierarchy**. Once this is done, we should see a new panel with the
call hierarchy of do_something.

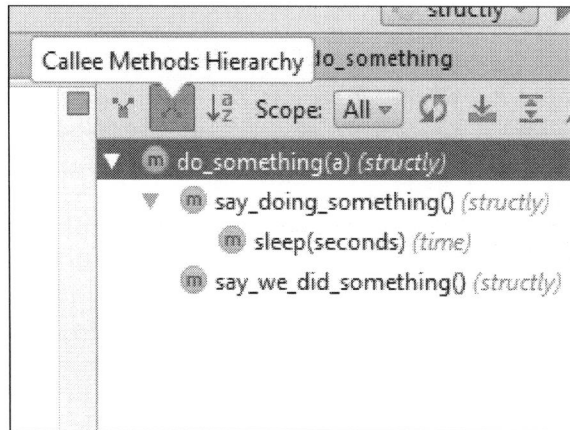

If we now place the cursor on say_doing_something and invoke **Call Hierarchy**,
we again get the same panel; this time we can take a look at the **Caller Methods
Hierarchy**.

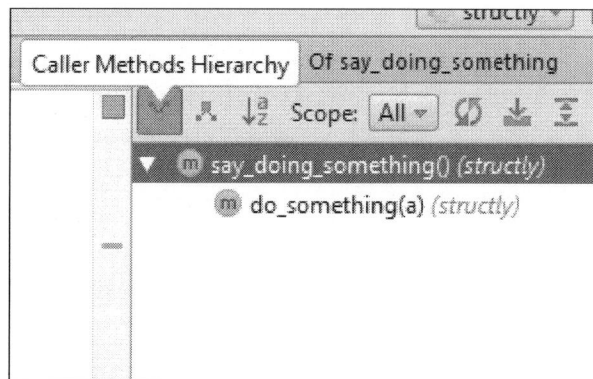

We can see that `do_something` calls `say_doing_something`. Unfortunately, however, this static analysis does not extend to real decorators. For example, take a look at the following code:

```
# encoding=utf-8
from functools import wraps

import time


def sleep_for_a_second():
    time.sleep(1)


def tell_all(func):
    @wraps(func)
    def wrapper(*args, **kwargs):
        print("we are doing something")
        sleep_for_a_second()
        out = func(*args, **kwargs)
        print("We did something")
        return out

    return wrapper


@tell_all
def do_something(a):
    return a + 1


if __name__ == '__main__':
    print(do_something(10))
```

If we place the cursor on `do_something`, we will not see `test_all` as the caller or the callee. However, if we place the cursor on `tell_all`, we can see that `do_something` is listed as a caller.

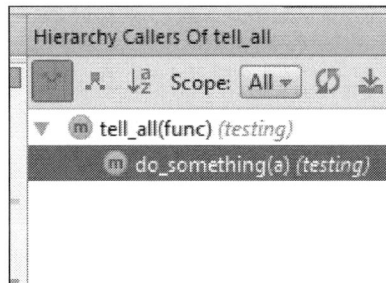

Summary

We learned a lot in this chapter—from how code completion works to how PyCharm's powerful static analysis can help you read code better. I use **reStructuredText** docstrings all the time for my own code so that it serves as documentation as well as a way for PyCharm to help me write error-free code. There are of course limitations to all these tools, most notably **reStructuredText** still does not support all kinds of types, for example, more complex types that aren't built in.

We also looked at some of the powerful tools at our disposal to write and read code. Some of these features might change over time, but I'm sure that the basic functionalities will remain the same.

5
Interpreters and Consoles

In this chapter, we are going to be diving deep into interpreter support in PyCharm. PyCharm's interpreter support is very powerful, with the ability to support almost any interpreter—from the most commonly used interpreter, CPython, to less widely used interpreters such as PyPy and Jython. PyCharm also has powerful console support. It can emulate both IPython and the normal Python interpreter, providing the syntax highlighting and code completion that we take for granted from the editor. What's even better is that code completion in the console is more powerful in PyCharm than in the editor. By reading this chapter, you'll be able to quickly install packages, make virtualenvs, and get the most out of code completion in the PyCharm console. This chapter is broken down into a few parts:

- **All about interpreters**: This section covers interpreter configuration, virtualenv creation, package management, and remote interpreters
- **The PyCharm console**: This section teaches you how to take advantage of the PyCharm console—from code completion to debugging

All about interpreters

Interpreter features in PyCharm are quite numerous. PyCharm allows you to create a new project with any interpreter that is installed on your system. It also allows you to derive a virtualenv from any interpreter installed on your system. And, it even allows you to inherit global site packages in the dialog box when creating the virtualenv. However, if you don't like this, you can always launch a project from the command line with the interpreter of your choice.

Before we start, however, I feel it is necessary to discuss virtualenv. It is a Python package for managing Python environments. It is freely available on **Python Package Index** (**PyPI**) and can be easily accessed with a pip install. If you aren't familiar with how virtualenv works, I suggest reading the documentation at `https://virtualenv.pypa.io/en/latest/`.

Adding interpreters

When starting off a **Pure Python** project in the wizard, PyCharm gives us the ability to choose any interpreter installed on our system, and it refers to such interpreters as local interpreters.

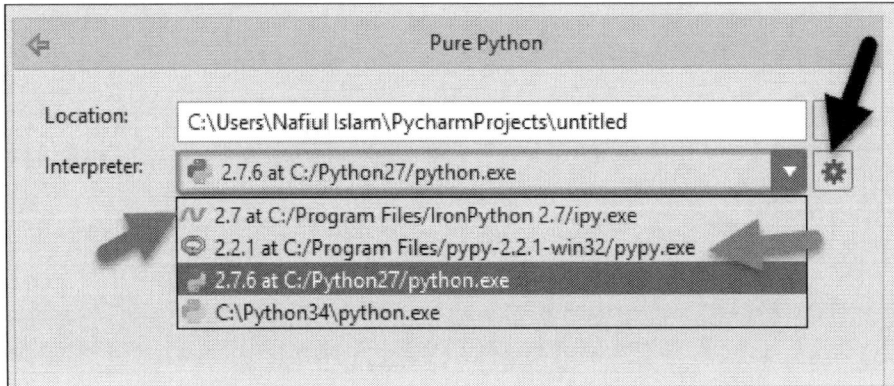

In the preceding screenshot, you can see that I've got quite a few interpreters installed. The interpreter indicated by the red arrow is IronPython, a Python implementation for the .NET platform. The green arrow indicates my PyPy interpreter. The one highlighted in blue is my default CPython interpreter. PyCharm automatically detects your interpreters for you, but in case it does not, you can always manually add a new interpreter.

The gear icon indicated by the black arrow allows us to add another interpreter manually. In this case, we're going to add a Jython interpreter (a Python interpreter that runs on the JVM). We are first going to choose to add a local interpreter since it's an interpreter installed on our machine.

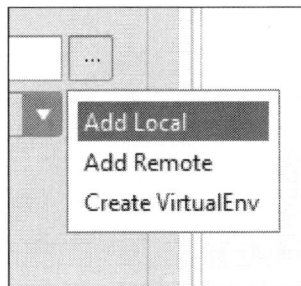

Once we chose to add a new local interpreter, PyCharm will ask us for the binary of that interpreter. In most cases, it is a .exe file, but in the case of Jython, it's a .bat file. In a *nix machine, it will just appear as an executable.

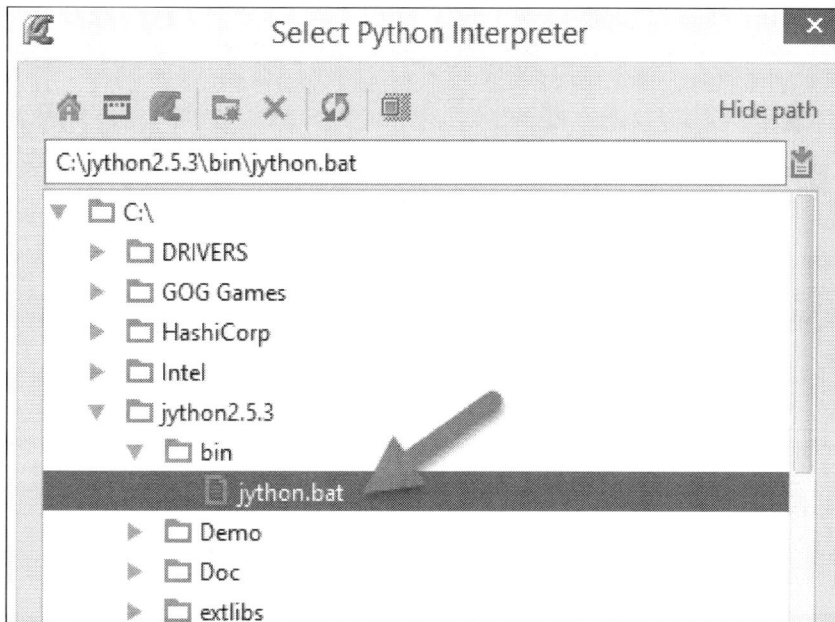

Once added, we should see a new interpreter ready and waiting to be used as one of our interpreter options.

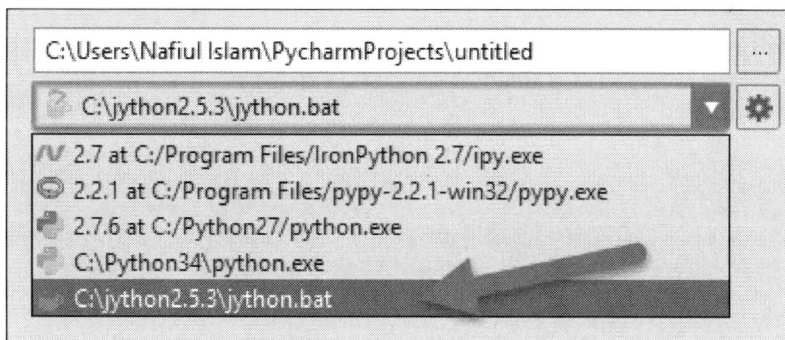

Creating virtualenvs

PyCharm also allows you to drive a virtualenv from an existing Python interpreter. Just like before, after clicking on the gear icon, we can add a new virtualenv.

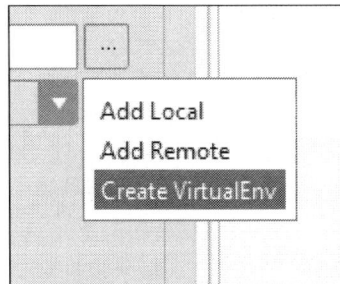

All we need to do in order to create a virtualenv is tell PyCharm what base interpreter we want to use [1], the name of the virtualenv, and finally whether we want to inherit global site packages or not (if we want to install all the third-party packages in the base Python interpreter as well) [3]. The option marked with [2] allows us to manually add a new interpreter on the fly.

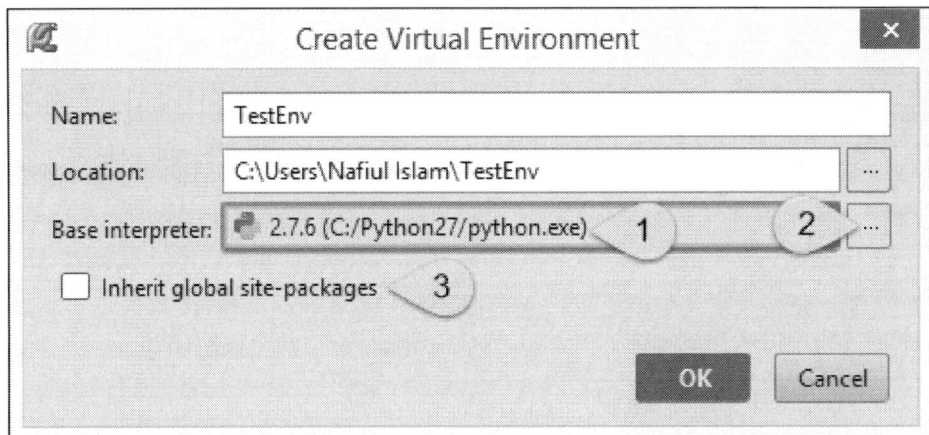

However, I dislike this way of creating a virtualenv because in this manner, virtualenvs get installed all over the place. I much prefer project creation through the command line.

Through the terminal

The project creation wizard is an absolute godsend for Windows users since they don't have to manage virtualenvs through the cmd. However, for *nix users, a far better option is using the command-line launcher. Creating a launcher is simple; all you need to do is tell PyCharm that you want one created.

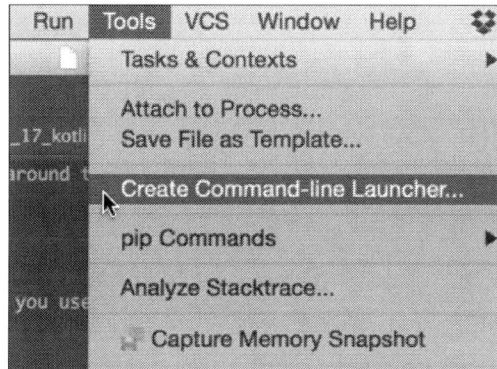

After this, we can open up PyCharm by simply using the newly created `charm` command. This is how I create my projects:

```
mkdir <Project Name>
cd <Project Name>
virtualenv .venv
source .venv/bin/activate
charm .
```

By invoking PyCharm at the end, PyCharm will use the virtualenv Python interpreter as the project's Python interpreter. In the command line, whichever interpreter is directed to by the Python command, is the interpreter that PyCharm uses.

Installing packages

PyCharm allows you to install packages for an interpreter without ever having to open up the command line. We can see a list of packages installed by going to **File | Settings... | Project | Project Interpreter**.

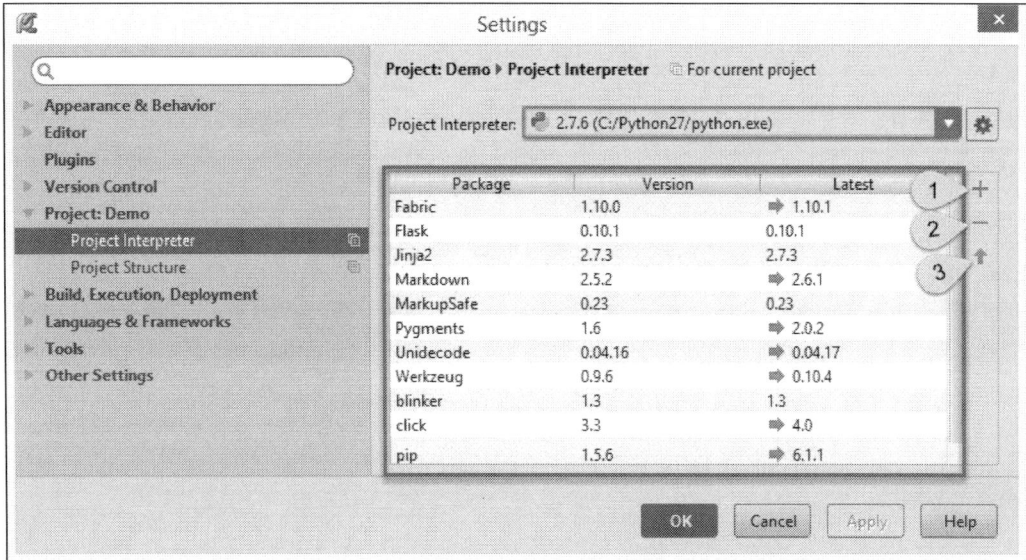

In the preceding screenshot, the area enclosed by the blue box shows a list of all the packages installed for this particular interpreter. Using [1], we can add a new packager from PyPI. Using [2], we can remove a selected package and with [3], we can upgrade a selected package.

Adding a new package is very simple; all we need to do is search for it.

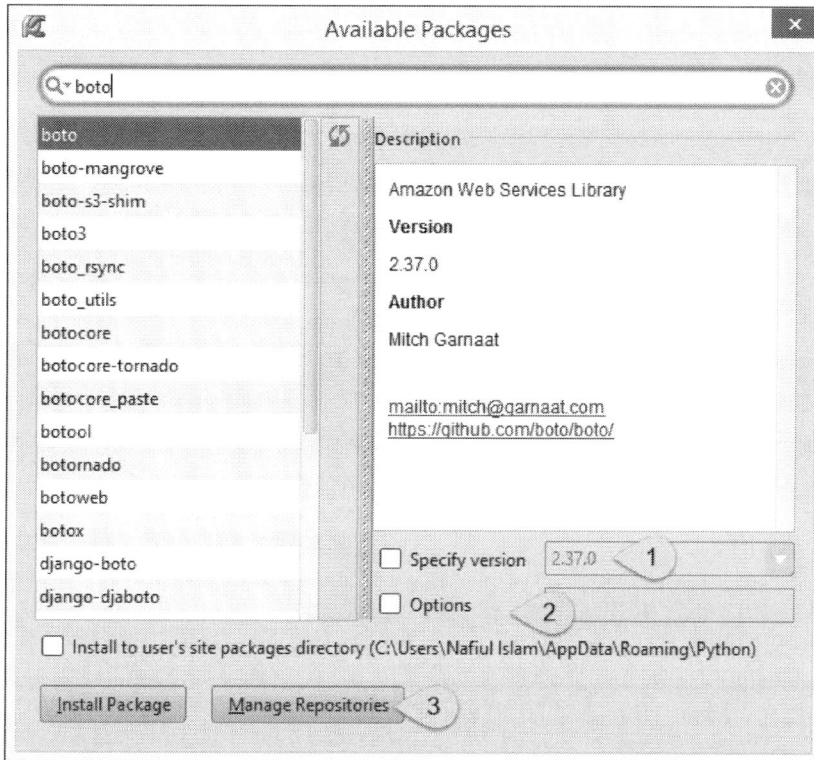

In this example, we're trying to install the `boto` package. Option [1] will allow us to install a specific version, and [2] will let us add options to the installation just as we do in pip (such as `allow-insecure`). Option [3] allows us to add other repositories (such as a Git repository) to PyCharm in case you are using a private package not available on PyPI.

Setting paths

The PYTHONPATH determines where your interpreter looks when searching for packages or modules to import. We can take a look at the list of paths included in our PYTHONPATH. We first need to select **Show All** to view all the interpreters in the project interpreter dropdown.

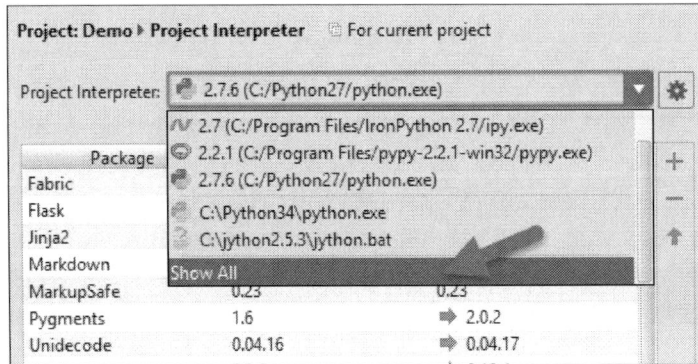

Then we select the interpreter of our choice [1]. After that, we ask to see its paths by using [2]. Finally, [3] shows us the list of all the paths available to us. Adding an extra path is often useful when working with **Google App Engine (GAE)** since you need to manually upload some of the libraries you're going to be using. By adding a path in PyCharm, we can emulate GAE circumstances.

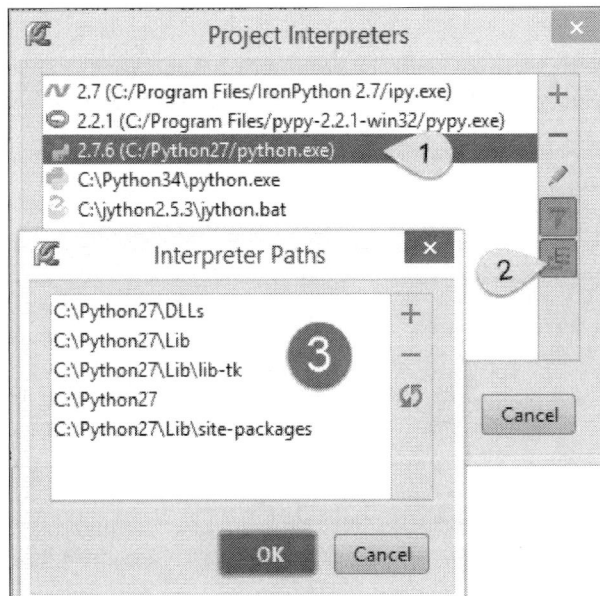

Remote interpreters

PyCharm can connect directly to your server's interpreter and use it to debug your script. All you need to do is set up your server and then configure your interpreter. Adding a server is easy enough; PyCharm uses the SFTP protocol to do so.

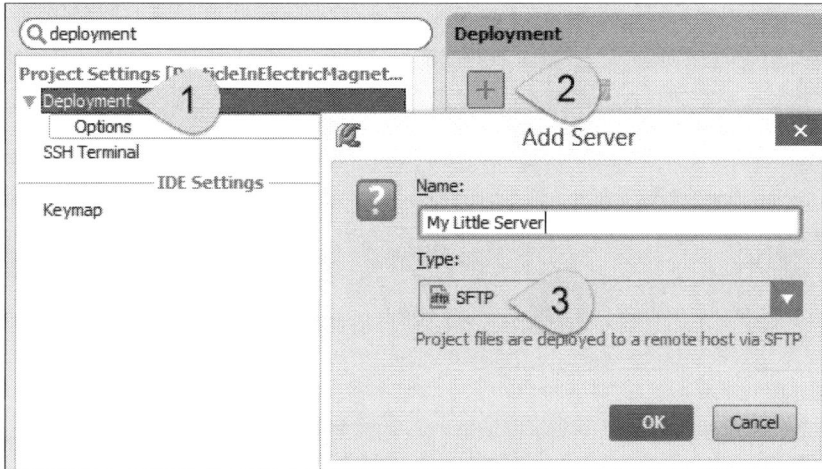

We now need to configure the server.

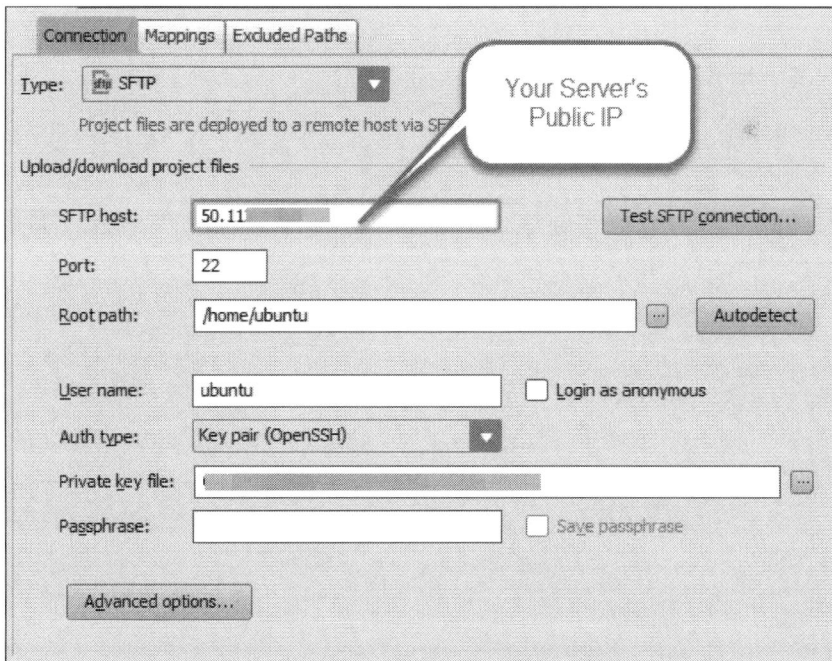

You can use your public IP or address. As for authentication, I use Amazon's EC2, so I get a .pem file, and that's why **Key pair** is selected. If you have a username and password, change **Auth type**. In **Advanced options...**, you have the ability to change the text encoding and the number of concurrent connections; alter them if you know what you're doing. Some parts are blurred out because this is a server that I actually use, and it's not that I don't trust you (the very thought of it!). It's just that I don't trust all the other people reading this book.

With this done, we're on our way to adding our remote interpreter, but with this, you also get filesystem access to your server. You can edit any file that you have rights to, you can also SSH into it any time you want with the terminal available in PyCharm.

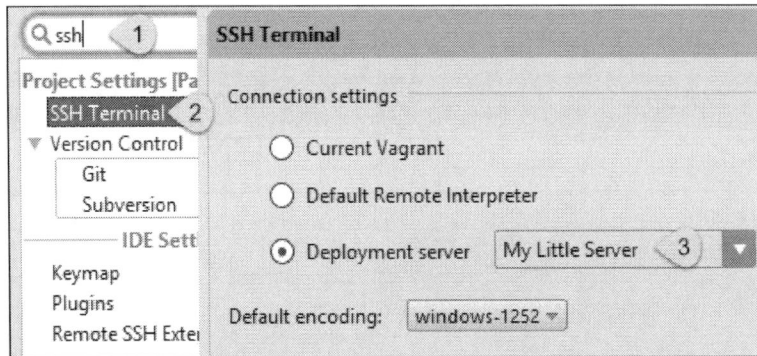

Now, you have SSH access to your server:

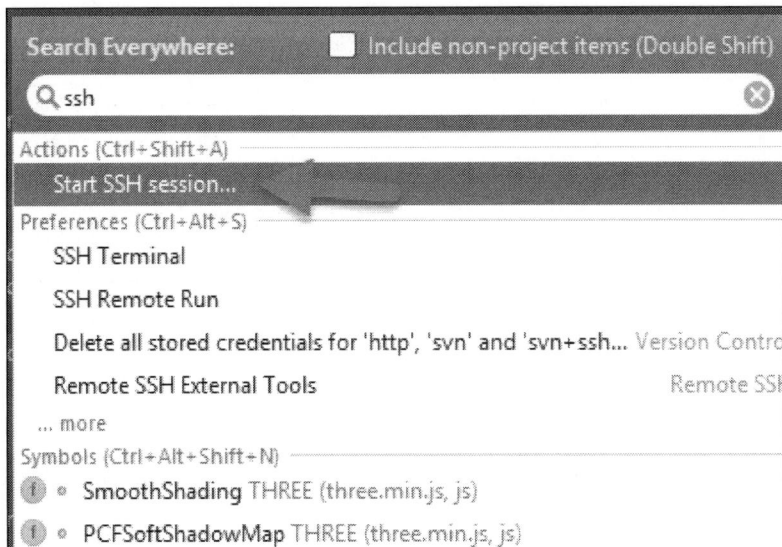

I found these tools very handy when working on a Windows machine.

Now that all of the server configuration is done, and we know how to SSH into our server, we can get started on configuring the interpreter. You will find it rather anti-climactic now that we've configured the server:

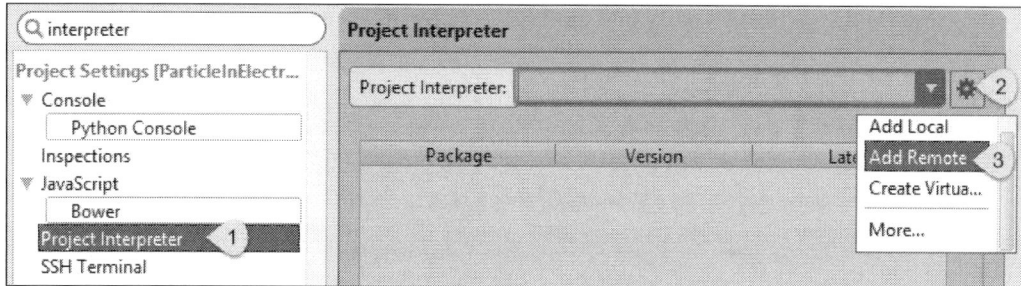

After choosing to add a remote interpreter, we will get this popup:

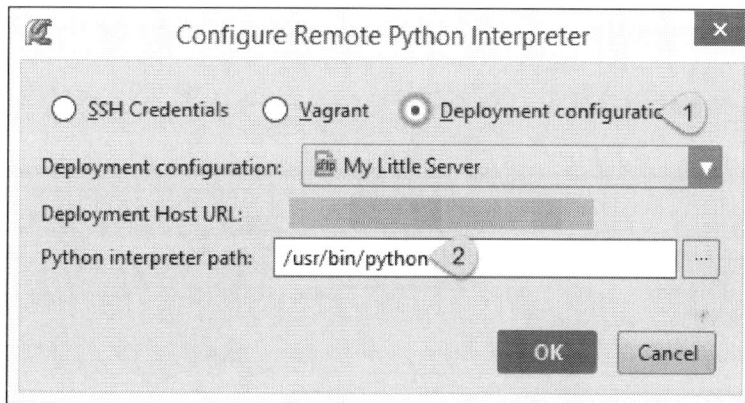

Now that all of this is done, PyCharm will upload a couple of important files to your remote interpreter that will allow you to use the interpreter as if it were right here on your local machine (this might take some time depending on your connection):

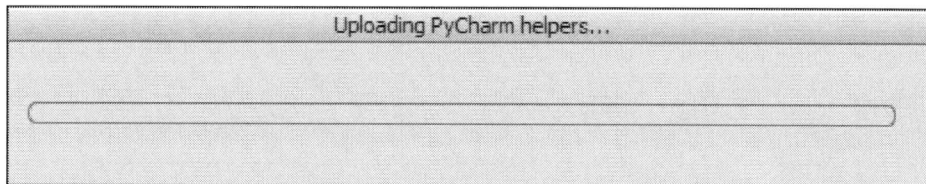

Now every time you run a script, it will be run through the remote interpreter on your server. You can always change back to the local interpreter of your choice.

Using Vagrant in PyCharm

Setting up Vagrant with a headless Linux box is so automated in PyCharm that it's almost no fun. The only prerequisite is that we have Vagrant installed on our machines and you don't even need to have a box installed. PyCharm will automatically download the default Vagrant box in case you don't have any installed on your system. We can initialize Vagrant like this:

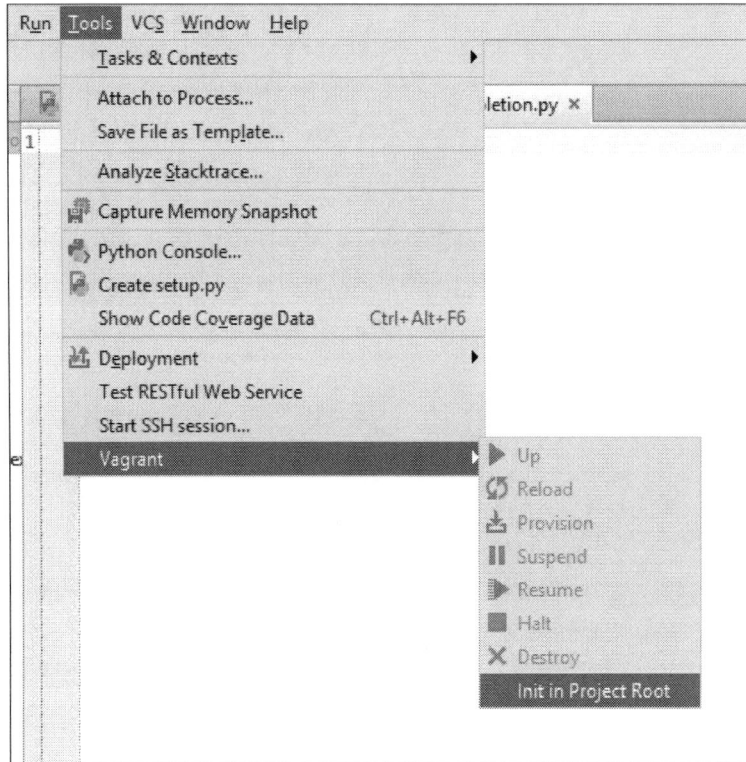

If we don't have a box handy, PyCharm will offer us the option to download a box of our choice, with lucid32's URI already in the dialog box.

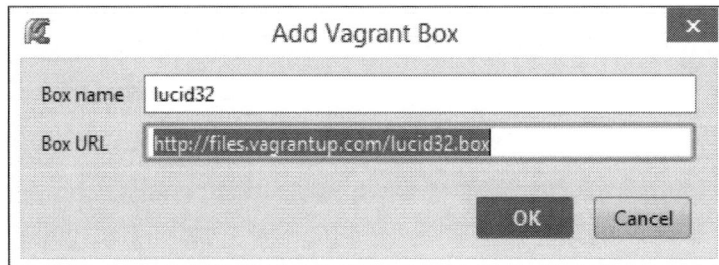

In case we already have a box installed, PyCharm will just go ahead and initialize it for us.

```
Run    vagrant init lucid32
    vagrant init lucid32
    A `Vagrantfile` has been placed in this directory. You are now
    ready to `vagrant up` your first virtual environment! Please read
    the comments in the Vagrantfile as well as documentation on
    `vagrantup.com` for more information on using Vagrant.

    Process finished with exit code 0
```

Now we can Vagrant up by navigating to **Tools** | **Vagrant** | **Up**.

```
File  Edit  View  Navigate  Code  Refactor  Run  Tools  VCS  Window  Help
 Demo   code_completion.py                    Tasks & Contexts              ▶
 Project              ⊗  ⊹  ⚙ ▾  ⊩            Attach to Process...              letion.py ×
 Demo (C:\Users\Nafiul Islam\PycharmP  1      Analyze Stacktrace...
   ▶  .vagrant                                 Capture Memory Snapshot
   ▼  src                                      Python Console...
       hello.py                                Show Code Coverage Data   Ctrl+Alt+F6
   code_completion.py                          Deployment                   ▶
   demo.html                                   Test RESTful Web Service
   demo.py                                     Start SSH session...
   init.py                                     Vagrant                      ▶   ▶ Up
Run    vagrant up                                                              Reload
    vagrant up                                                                 Provision
    Bringing machine 'default' up with 'virtualbox' provider...               Suspend
    ==> default: Clearing any previously set forwarded ports...               Resume
    ==> default: Clearing any previously set network interfaces...            Halt
    ==> default: Preparing network interfaces based on configuration...       Destroy
        default: Adapter 1: nat                                               Init in Project Root
    ==> default: Forwarding ports...
        default: 22 => 2222 (adapter 1)
    ==> default: Booting VM...
    ==> default: Waiting for machine to boot. This may take a few minutes...
        default: SSH address: 127.0.0.1:2222
        default: SSH username: vagrant
        default: SSH auth method: private key
        default: Warning: Connection timeout. Retrying...
        default: Warning: Connection timeout. Retrying...
```

Vagrant acts like a remote interpreter on your local machine, so you can actually SSH into your Vagrant machine any time you want after it has been turned on.

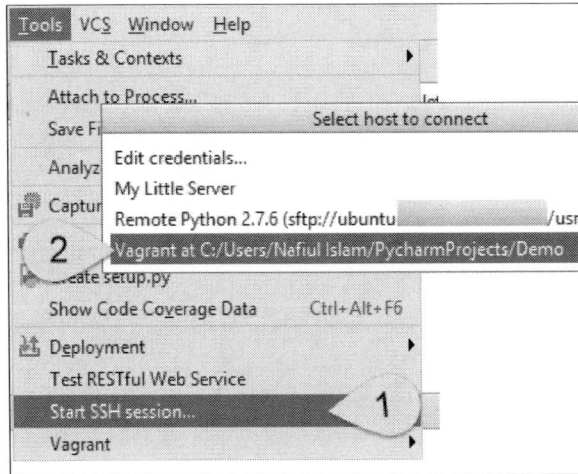

We can now add yet another remote interpreter, and load this directly from the Vagrant file, so PyCharm automatically adds it for us.

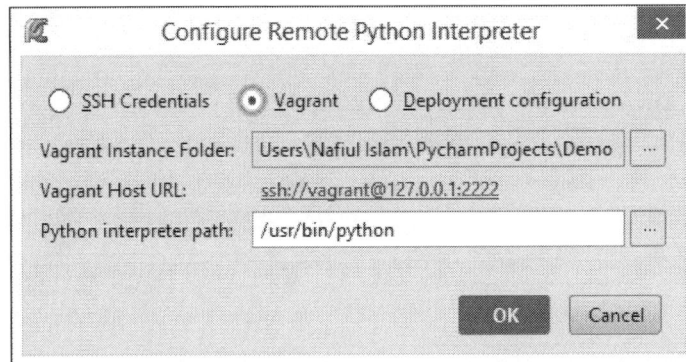

And now, if we set our project interpreter to the Python interpreter in Vagrant, the files will be run using the Vagrant interpreter, all within PyCharm.

The PyCharm console

The PyCharm console is another fundamental part of PyCharm. In essence, it's the Python REPL with autocompletion and variable watch (which we will get into later). Right now, let's take a look at what the console offers us:

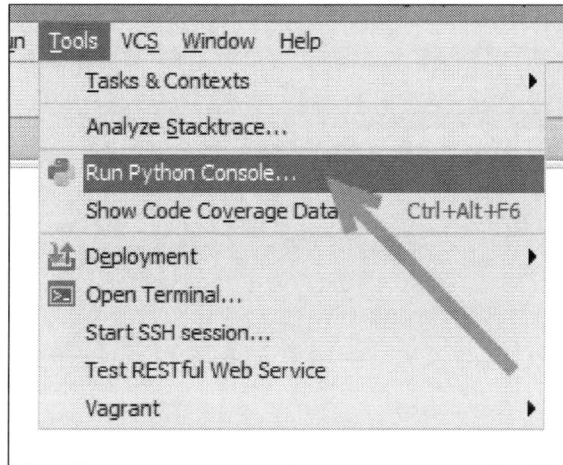

You can of course invoke the same action from the **Find Action** and **Search Everywhere** search boxes. This opens up the following:

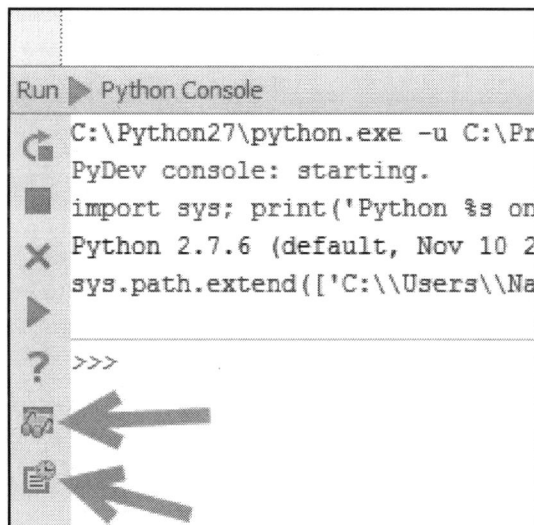

Most buttons are self-explanatory, except for the two indicated by the arrows. The first is what I like to call **variable watch**; in essence, this shows you all the variables in your console (by pressing it, you toggle it):

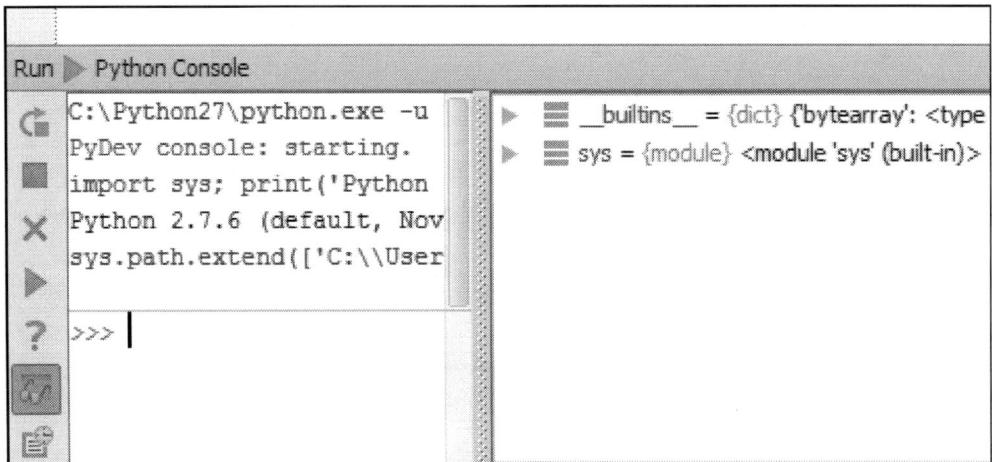

New variables and the changes in variables are shown in blue:

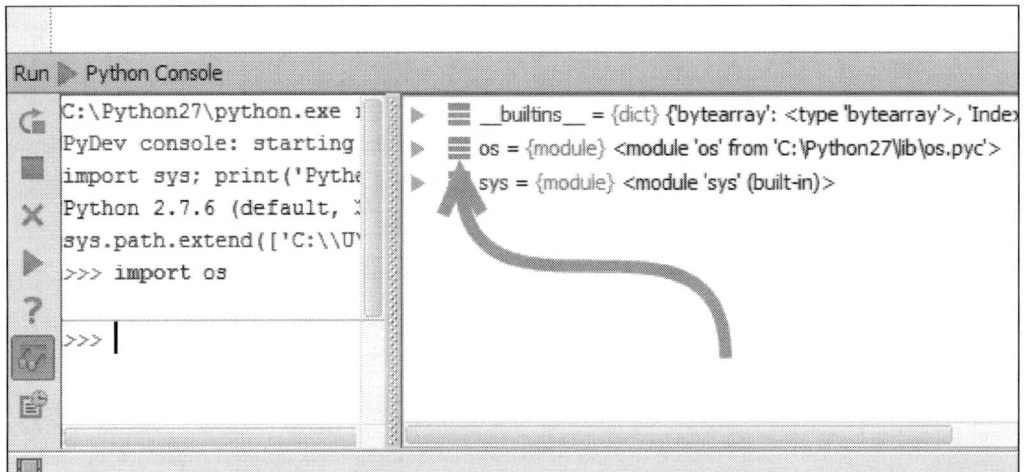

The Variable Watch button is even more powerful, but that's a topic for *Chapter 6, Debugging*.

The second button after variable watch is actually pretty useful; it's a history of all the commands you've entered into your console throughout the project, so even if you close PyCharm or even shut down your system, the history will have dutifully recorded all the Python statements that you have entered:

```
1   10                          import os
2   dir(map)
3   import hoogly
4   import os
5   print(demo.read())
```

Console configuration

Now let's head over to a few of the options that we have for our Python console:

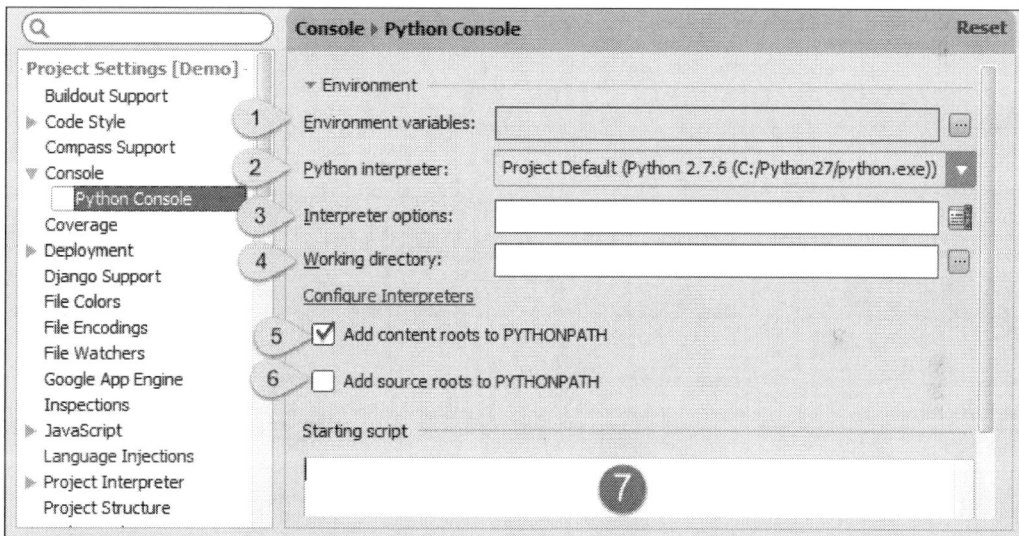

With reference to the preceding screenshot, with [1], we can define our environment variables:

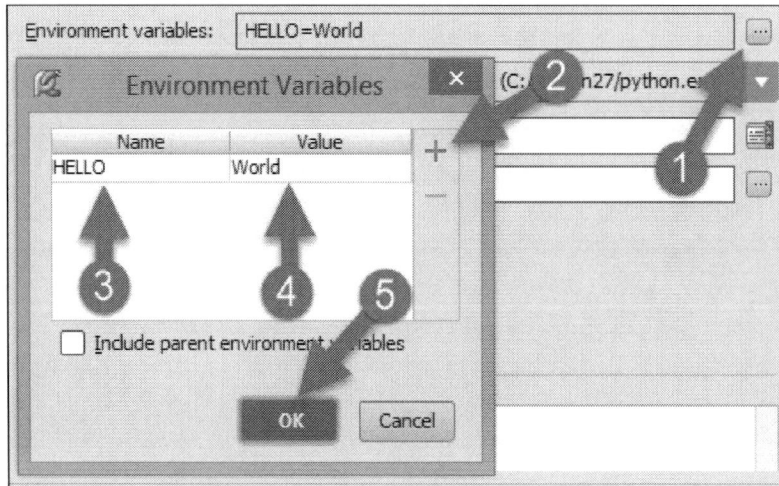

With this, you can now see the environment variables in the console (make sure that you restart your console):

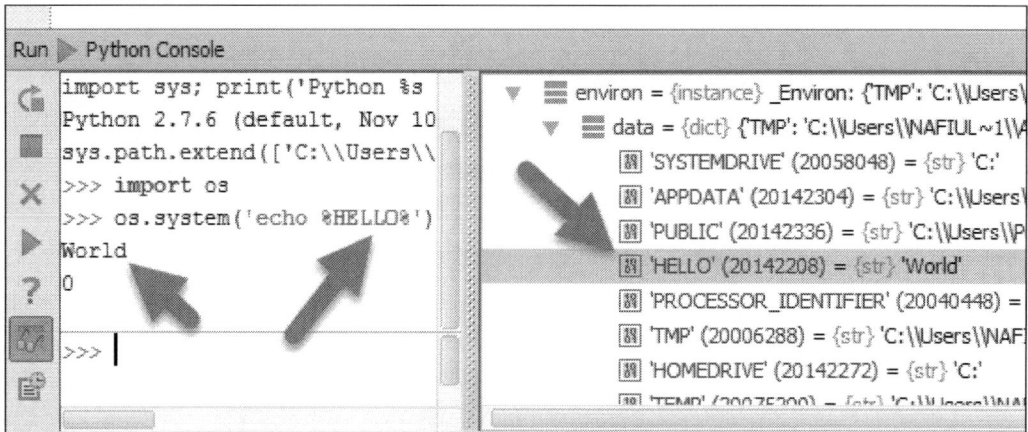

With that out of the way, you can set the path to your interpreter with [2], and provide additional arguments with [3]. The working directory can be specified with [4]. Enabling [5] simply adds your project root to the PYTHONPATH:

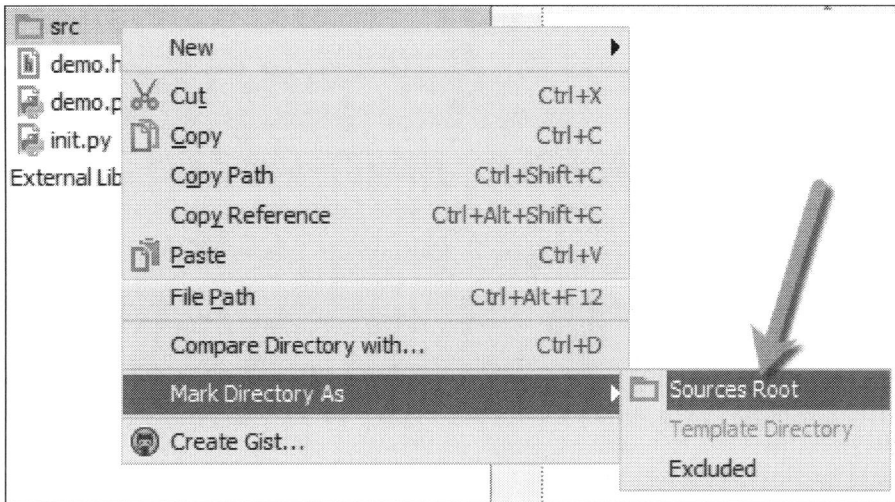

You can also add your source directories to your PYTHONPATH by enabling [6]. You can make a directory a source directory by doing this:

With that, when you open up your console with [6] enabled, you can see that PyCharm adds the directory to the PYTHONPATH, and hence, you can import files from that directory:

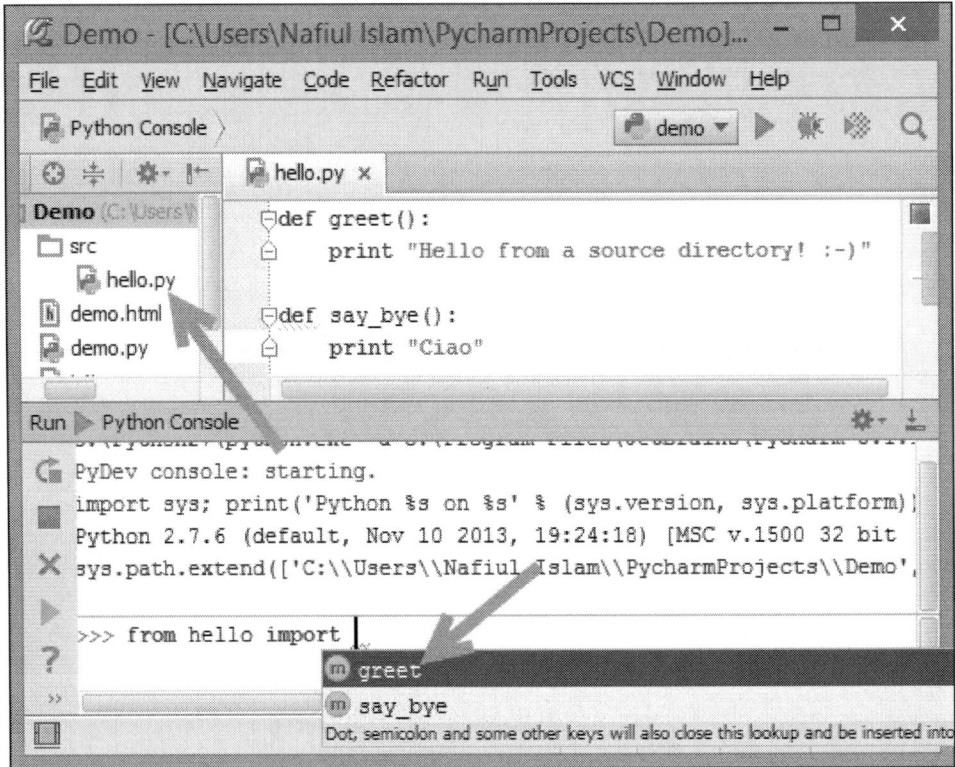

As you can see, you can also get code completion for the .py file inside the src directory.

Last but not least, we come to the **Starting script**, [7]. With this, you can specify the Python code that the interpreter will run at every launch. Note that you also get code completion here:

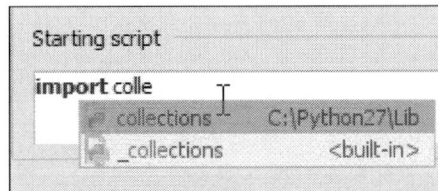

With this, you can see it imported:

> If you want to use IPython in PyCharm, all you have to do is install the IPython package, and PyCharm will automatically launch the IPython interpreter for you when you launch the console.

Summary

In this chapter, we learned a lot about managing the several interpreters, both local and remote, as well as taking advantage of PyCharm's top class support for code completion in the console. If you're curious about why code completion is better in the console than in the editor, it's because PyCharm knows the types of every single variable that you're using. Please note, however, that should you close PyCharm with the console open; the next time you open PyCharm, the console will launch too. This is totally fine for local interpreters, but should you configure a remote interpreter, launching PyCharm can take a pretty long time.

6
Debugging

"There is no freedom quite like the freedom of being constantly underestimated."

– Scott Lynch

When I first started programming, I used `print` statements. Having to write this book, I took a look at some of my earliest code samples, and it turns out that most of it was commented out `print` statements used for checking the value of variables. Note that I started off writing C using Notepad, and compiling all that through the command line, so no green run button and no IDE. I knew about GDB, but it was so hard to even set a simple breakpoint that I stuck to my `print` statements. Most of the bugs I had encountered so far had been obvious bugs staring at me in the face. After a few mishaps, I started to print everything that I could so that I could take a look at where the program was and what was happening, making sure not to underestimate bugs or the extent of my own stupidity.

In this chapter, we are going to be talking about PyCharm's powerful debugging tools and use them to understand, examine, and yes, debug our programs. We are going to:

- Take a look at how we can run Python scripts in running mode and debugging mode
- Understand the different components of the debugging toolset
- Use variables and watches to make sure we miss nothing
- Utilize frames to zoom in and out of different layers of a program—from your scripts right down to the Python standard library
- Evaluate expressions at breakpoints
- Use the Python console and Python prompt to gain a better understanding of program execution

Running, debugging, and setting breakpoints

You can run a .py file in two modes: running and debugging. If you run a program, then even if you set breakpoints (points at which PyCharm will stop program execution), nothing will happen. It's only when you run it in debug mode that breakpoints become effective. The way I like to run or debug my programs is through the **Resume Program** action:

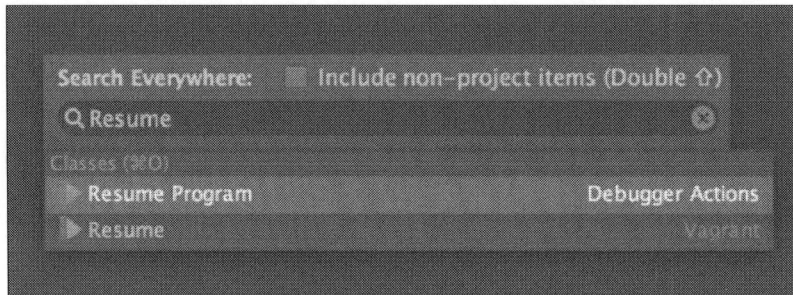

You can then choose any of the different ways to run/debug your program. By default, if you press *Enter*, you will go into debug mode, if you press *Shift + Enter*, the program will just run. You can also choose coverage by pressing the left arrow:

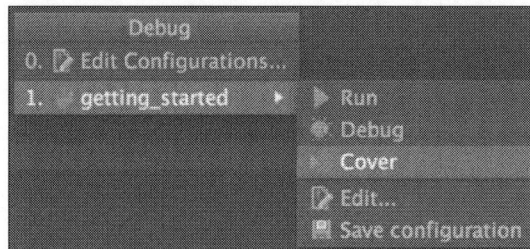

As soon as you start debugging, a window appears underneath and you have so many options that it's hard to make sense of it all. Let's focus on managing breakpoints for now. To the bottom-left of the window, you can see a bunch of buttons:

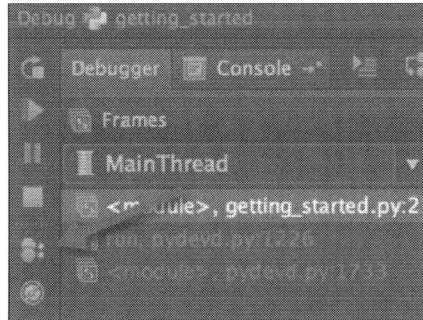

This is the View Breakpoints button. This allows you to see different types of breakpoints that are available to you:

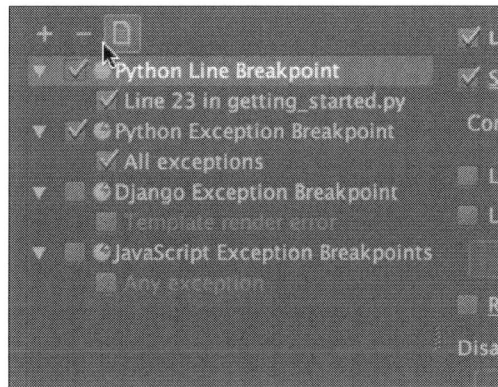

The breakpoint we set is a line breakpoint, but by default, in debug mode, program execution will suspend when you get an exception. You can actually disable this, but this only makes sense when you're looking for certain exceptions. Say, you only want to catch `TypeError` exceptions:

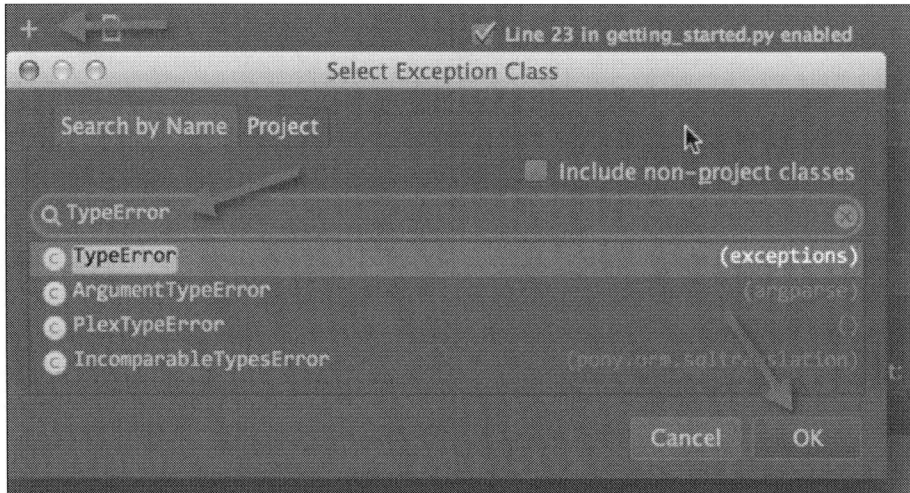

You add `TypeError` to your list of exceptions; you can also add exceptions that are only available in your project. So, with that added, we now have:

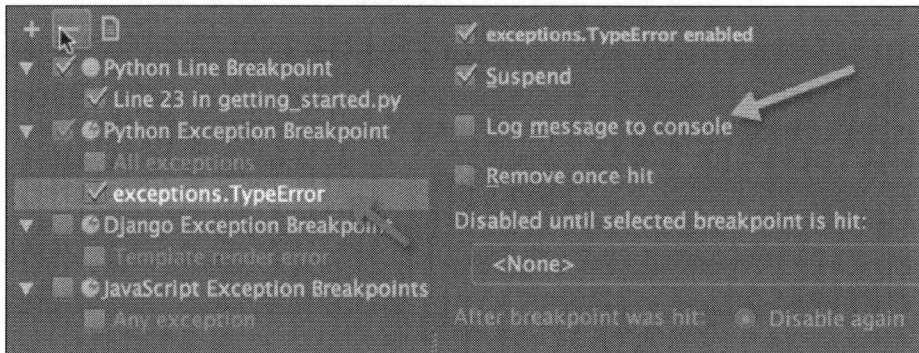

Unfortunately, you do not have the same fine-grained control as you do with line breakpoints, where you can evaluate expressions to pause execution. But, it still allows you to narrow your focus on certain exception types:

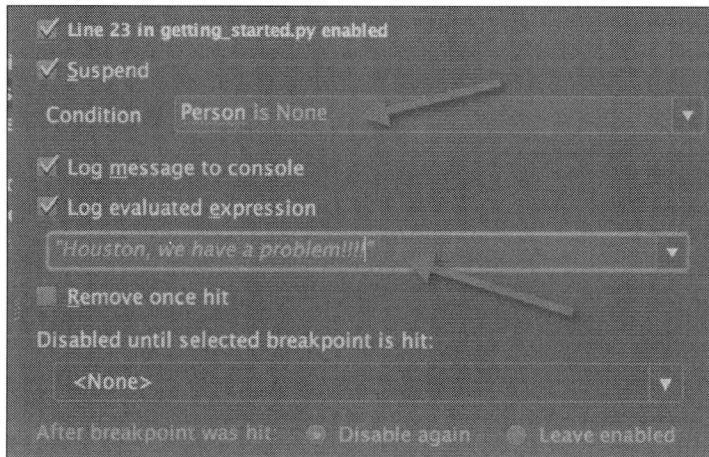

In the preceding example, the breakpoint will only execute if the `Person` object is `None`. If this condition is true, this will be logged to the console, and so will the expression. In this case, it will simply print the string.

You can of course toggle all the breakpoints in debug mode as well:

This will render your line breakpoints moot.

Debugging workflow

A friend of mine, who used Java in his day job, sent me a code snippet that he needed help with. He was new to Python and was still getting used to the differences between Java and Python. He mostly worked with databases, so he was exploring the different ORMs that were available. He tried SQLAlchemy, the Django ORM, and eventually, found that he liked a still very new ORM called **Pony**. At that time, the documentation for Pony was still in its infancy, so he sent me the code so that I could help him out. It looked similar to this:

```python
__author__ = "John Doe"

import string
import random

from pony.orm import db_session, commit, Database, Required

db = Database()


class Person(db.Entity):
    name = Required(str)
    age = Required(int)


vowels = 'aeiou'
consonants = str(letter for letter in string.ascii_lowercase if letter
not in vowels)


def gen():
    return random.choice(consonants) + random.choice(vowels)


names = [(gen() for _ in range(random.randint(3, 4))) for i in
range(100)]

db.bind('sqlite', 'data.sqlite', create_db=True)
db.generate_mapping(create_tables=True)

with db_session:
    for name in names:
        Person(name=name, age=random.randint(5, 21))

commit()
```

I ran this fine in debug mode, and got an exception in the console, saying that it was a `MappingError`, so I looked at the file and found out that the script did not bind to a database before generating mappings, so that was easy enough to fix— it needed to bind before generating mappings. But then came another problem, and that was `TypeError`:

So, it's saying that we have `TypeError`, and that it was expecting Unicode, but for what? This is where frames come in handy. Frames, located on the left-hand side of the debug menu, are like layers in an application. Frames showcase this callback sequence (or a function call stack), letting you jump between the files where the problem was caused.

In the preceding screenshot, you can see that the topmost item in the frame list is where the exception was raised; the list item shows you the function call, as well as the file in which the function exists. You can also see that the library files are highlighted in a dark yellow color (indicated by the red arrow), whereas your files are clear (indicated by the orange arrow). By using this panel, you can go back and forth in the sequence and see what went wrong. In this case, let's go back to our own file and see what the problem is:

```
Models.db.bind('sqlite', 'data.sqlite')
Models.db.generate_mapping(create_tables=True)

with db_session:
    for name in names:
        Models.Person(name=name, age=random.randint(5, 21))

commit()
```

So, it seems that the problem here arises when we try to initialize a `Person` object. Now, let's go back to the original exception, which said that it was a `TypeError` and it expected a Unicode object. Let's use our frames to dive into where the object was initiated:

We can see here that name is a generator, which feels wrong to me, because it should be a string or perhaps even Unicode. Let's go back to our original file and see what this is all about and also see what name is all about:

```
with db_session:
    for name in names:
        Models.Person(name=name, age=random.randint(5, 21))

+ name = {generator} <generator object <genexpr> at 0x104c1daa0>
```

So, if we hover over name, we can see that it's a generator object, but that doesn't sound right. I mean, a person's name isn't supposed to be a generator. Name comes from names, and let's take a look at what names is made up of:

```
names = [(gen() for _ in range(random.randint(3, 4))) for i in range(100)]
```

Debugger Console

Frames   Variables

MainThr...

Expression: ge

Result: gen()

You can use the **Evaluate Expression...** button to check what an expression is; this button even has autocompletion. Right now, you can use it to evaluate simple expressions such as checking out the gen function. You can even select an expression in Python, right-click on the expression and then choose **Evaluate Expression...**:

```
gen():
    return random.choice(consonants) + random.
```

Copy Reference
Paste
Paste from History...
Paste Simple
Column Selection Mode

Evaluate Expression...
Run to Cursor
Force Run to Cursor

You could also choose to evaluate this inside the console:

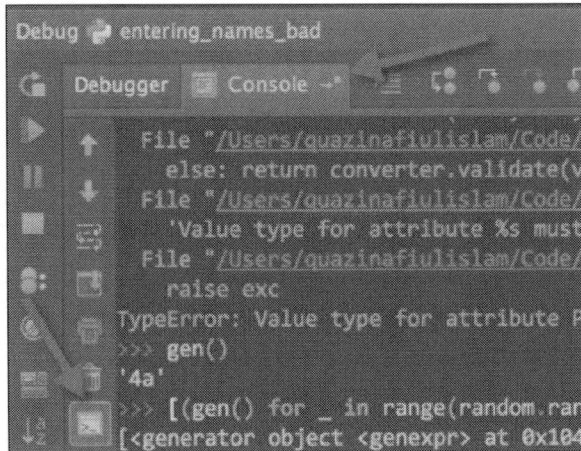

It turns out that these objects are all generators, and we need to fix that by getting rid of the braces around the expression to be added:

```
[gen() for _ in range(random.randint(3, 4)) for i in range(100)]
```

But, if we were to evaluate this, it would look rather weird:

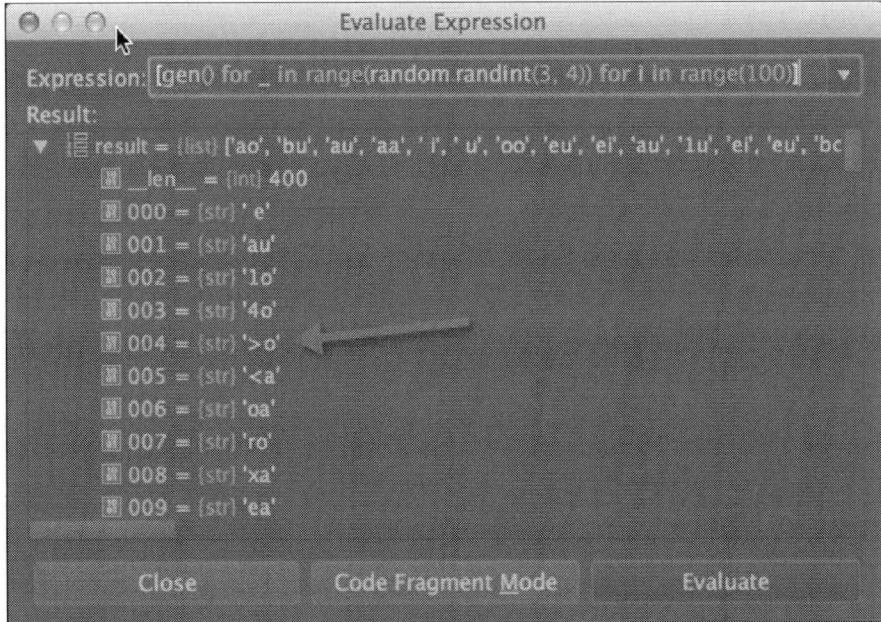

First, we're trying to generate names; names are usually not two letters long. Second, when was the last time you saw a name with a greater-than sign in it? Something fishy is going on here. So, the gen function is giving us all of this data, and hence, there has to be something wrong with the gen function. Let's take a look at the gen function then. It turns out that gen concatenates a consonant and a vowel to form a pronounceable syllable.

Taking a look at gen, we find that it makes function calls to `random.choice`, so I doubt there's a problem in the standard library. It uses two variables, vowels and consonants, and that means there's a problem in both or either of these two. The vowels variable is pretty simple, so there isn't much room for error. However, we're probably messing something up when we're generating consonants. Let's set a line breakpoint just before the declaration of the gen function and take a look at what the consonants variable is made up of.

```
9     import Models
10
11    vowels = 'aeiou'
12    consonants = (letter for letter in string.ascii_lowercase if letter not in vowels)
13
      consonants = (str)'<generator object <genexpr> at 0x10551daf0>'

16        return random.choice(consonants) + random.choice(vowels)
17
```

Ha! It looks like we've got a *stringified* (is that even a word?) generator. We need to use the string's `.join` function to get the job done. Let's do that now and change the line to this:

```
consonants = "".join(letter for letter in string.ascii_lowercase if
letter not in vowels)
```

Let's see if that works now and take a look at what the names look similar to:

```
17
18
19    names = [gen() for _ in range(ra
20
+ names = (list) ['zu', 'co', 'wo', 'no', 'hi', 'g
22    Models.db.generate_mapping(creat
23
24    with db_session:
25        for name in names:
26            Models.Person(name=name,
```

It seems like we're having a little bit of trouble here. I've heard of a nickname called zu, but I think the names are too small, so let's make them bigger:

```
names = ["".join(gen() for _ in range(random.randint(3, 4))) for i in
range(100)]
```

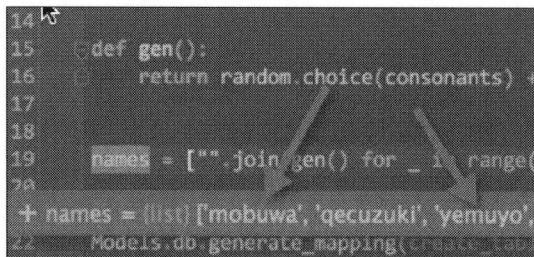

After making the change and rerunning the program, we get mobuwa and yemuyo as names. This is pretty neat! I might just use these names as example names; they are way better than John Doe.

After that final change, the script ran smoothly and the right data was inserted into the database. I was able to send this back to my friend, and told him where he went wrong—mostly with the string concatenation using generators.

Before we depart this section, I'd like to tell you that **Evaluate Expression...** and the **Console** work inside frames. This means that if you're trying to evaluate an expression in a different frame that you have currently selected in the debugger, the debugger will give you an error.

Finally, PyCharm also supports watches and the usual step-into/step-out procedures that are conventional in debugging.

Dealing with threads and processes

PyCharm has very good support for dealing with threads. Just like how we can change frames, we can also change threads if we so wish (that is, if we have more than one thread to begin with). Let's take the example of a simple downloader script called downloader.py:

```
# encoding=utf-8
from threading import Thread

import requests


def download(url):
```

```
        response = requests.get(url)
        if response.status_code == 200:
            print "Success -> {:<75} | Length -> {}".format(response.url,
    len(response.content))
        else:
            print "Failure -> {:>75}".format(response.url)



    if __name__ == '__main__':
        urls = "http://www.google.com http://www.bing.com http://www.
    yahoo.com http://news.ycombinator.com".split()

        for u in urls:
            Thread(target=download, args=(u,)).start()
```

> To run this code, you'll need to install requests though
> `pip install requests` in the command line.

This is a simple script that sends a `get` request to a `url` (there are four in total here), and each request is sent in its own thread. This simple script will demonstrate PyCharm's ability to debug threads. This is what the output looks similar to after an initial run:

```
$ python downloader.py
Success -> http://www.google.com.bd/?gws_rd=cr&ei=1N_HVePAH9HiuQTHsLigDQ
| Length -> 12559
Success -> http://www.bing.com/
| Length -> 58210
Success -> https://news.ycombinator.com/
| Length -> 27698
Success -> https://www.yahoo.com/
| Length -> 357013
```

It seems simple enough; we can now set a breakpoint after we check for a 200 status:

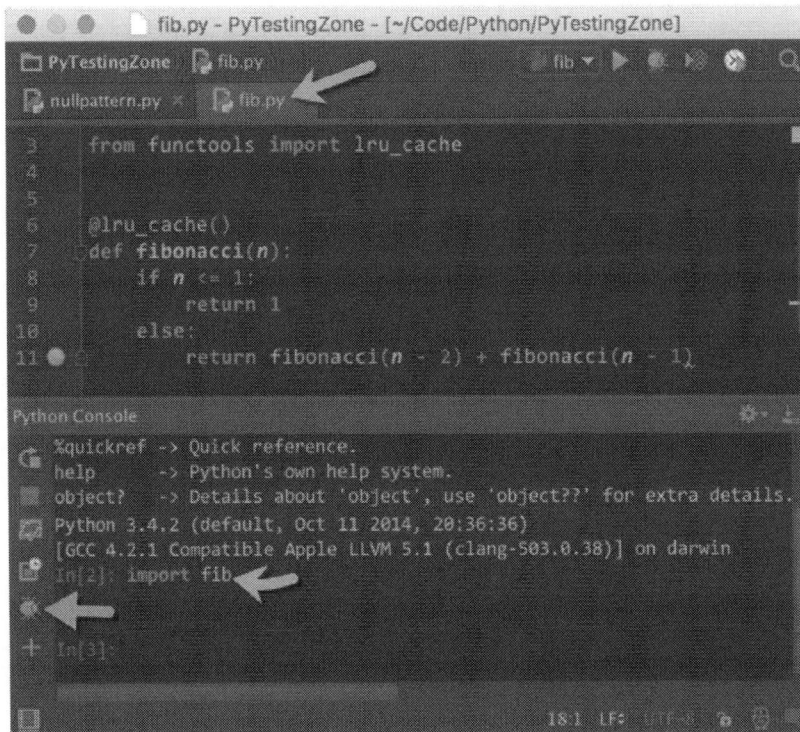

After we set the breakpoint, we can now debug the script, and we see that the debugger stops on every single thread.

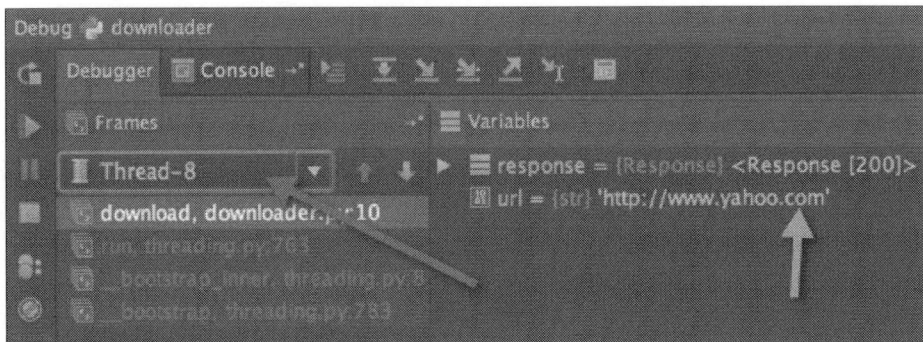

The drop-down menu, indicated by the red arrow, allows us to jump between threads. The orange arrow indicates the URL (since that is what is used to create each new thread).

We can swap to a different thread and see a different URL.

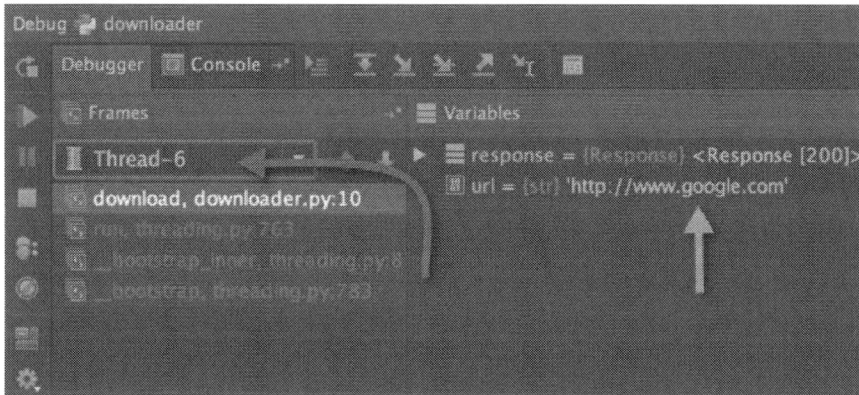

In the preceding thread, a request is being sent to `http://www.google.com`, whereas in the previous one, the request was being sent to `http://www.yahoo.com`.

Processes

Processes are handled similarly in PyCharm. We will make only a small change to the preceding code—importing `Process` instead of `Thread` and starting `Process` instead of `Thread`:

```python
# encoding=utf-8
from multiprocessing import Process

import requests


def download(url):
    response = requests.get(url)
    if response.status_code == 200:
        print "Success -> {:<75} | Length -> {}".format(response.url,
len(response.content))
    else:
        print "Failure -> {:>75}".format(response.url)


if __name__ == '__main__':
    urls = "http://www.google.com http://www.bing.com http://www.
yahoo.com http://news.ycombinator.com".split()

    for u in urls:
        Process(target=download, args=(u,)).start()
```

If we try to debug this by setting the breakpoint at the same place, we get process IDs instead of thread numbers since we're creating processes.

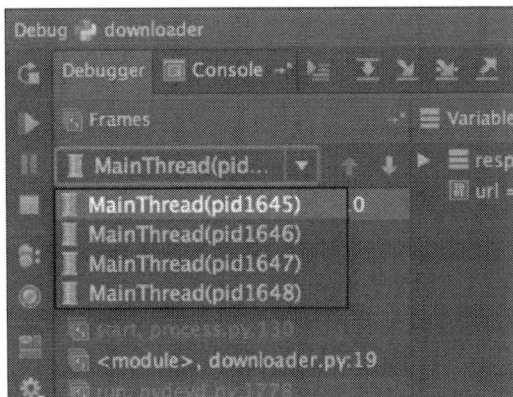

Debugging from the console

When playing around with new libraries in the REPL, it can be very useful to have a debugger to help you understand it better. You can directly connect your debugger to the REPL and hence, set breakpoints and break on exceptions:

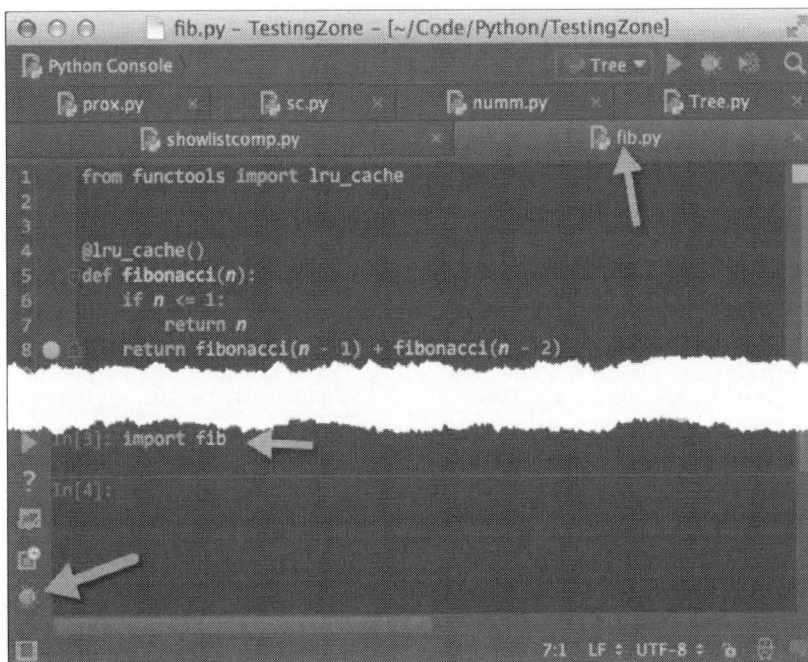

We're importing `fib` first (which is in our PYTHONPATH; in other words, in the root directory of the project), we set a breakpoint in the `fibonacci` function's recursive call, and we click on the button indicated by the green arrow. If we call the `fibonacci` function now from our REPL, we will see that the Python debugger suspends on the line indicated. So, first we import the file we want to test out in our PYTHONPATH, then we click on the debugger button in the console, and finally, we merely invoke the function where we have set a breakpoint.

Attach to Process...

PyCharm also has the ability to attach its debugger to separately running processes. This can be very helpful when trying to debug a command-line application that require changes in parameters or when trying to debug games. The PyCharm debugger simply looks for running the Python processes:

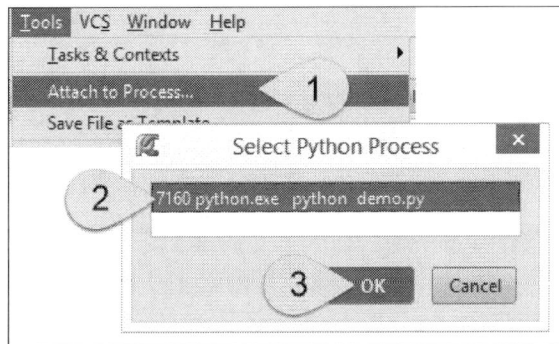

Profiling

Profiling is a new addition to PyCharm 4.5, and has a nice set of features, most notably, a graphic representation of the calls made. We are going to use the previously mentioned `downloader.py` file to demonstrate some of the new features.

```python
# encoding=utf-8
from threading import Thread

import requests


def download(url):
    response = requests.get(url)
    if response.status_code == 200:
        print "Success -> {:<75} | Length -> {}".format(response.url, len(response.content))
    else:
        print "Failure -> {:>75}".format(response.url)


if __name__ == '__main__':
    urls = "http://www.google.com http://www.bing.com http://www.yahoo.com http://news.ycomb
```

We simply right-click anywhere on the file and then left-click on **Profile 'downloader'**. With this, we will be taken to a new panel that shows us a call table.

Name	Call Count	Time (ms)			
compat.py	1	34	30.9%	7	6.4%
connectionp	Navigate to Source		.5%	6	5.5%
utils.py	Show on Call Graph		.7%	5	4.5%
_parse	223	15	13.6%	5	4.5%
__init__.py	1	5	4.5%	4	3.6%
__next	3256	4	3.6%	3	2.7%
__init__.py	1	4	3.6%	3	2.7%
__init__.py	1	108	98.2%	3	2.7%
_compile	378	5	4.5%	2	1.8%

We can also see that if we choose to, we can jump to both the source and the call graph. The call graph is a graphical representation of what functions are being called where and their impact; green means small impact and red means high impact. This is really quite useful since we can optimize slow code on the spot if the optimization is simple.

Furthermore, the call graph gives us a nice colorized hierarchical representation of function calls.

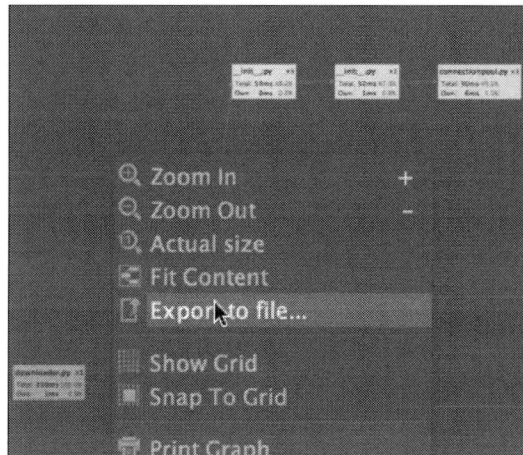

We can also export the graph files for others to see. If we right-click on any of the call blocks in the call graph, we can jump to the source.

Summary

I hope I was able to convince you of the value in PyCharm's debugging toolset. We looked at a lot of the tools that I find useful in my everyday work . We covered debugging tools and how we can use them in our own workflow.

I didn't discuss any of the common tools that are ubiquitous in any debugger, just the ones that I find make PyCharm special.

One thing I must note is that whenever you debug code, the script will run slower since PyCharm imports some helper functions before actually running your code. If you take a closer look at frames when you debug a program, you will see, at the very bottom, that a function from `pydevd.py` is called. Thus, if you're looking at execution times when you debug a program using PyCharm, you will find them a lot slower than when you actually run them in PyCharm or the interpreter.

We also looked at PyCharm's new profiler that allows to see a nice colorized call graph as well as giving you the ability to jump to source. If we so wished, we could also save the files for others to view.

Finally, make absolutely sure that you turn on the collection of runtime information when you debug since it will help you with type information, that is, better code completion.

7
The PyCharm Ecosystem

"Look well into thyself; there is a source of strength which will always spring up if thou wilt always look there."

– Marcus Aurelius Antoninus

This chapter dives into the inner workings of PyCharm. While having a little to do with PyCharm usage, it has everything to do with how PyCharm works, where to find help and report issues as well as the plugin ecosystem.

There are several key takeaways:

- **The IntelliJ ecosystem**: This section explores what kind of IDE PyCharm is. It explains how PyCharm shares common features with other IDEs

- **Support for PyCharm**: This section explores the different sites and tools that will help to solve PyCharm-related issues

- **Plugins**: This section explores the different plugins available in PyCharm, what kind of plugins to expect, and what makes a good plugin

The IntelliJ ecosystem

In the very beginning, there was IntelliJ, JetBrains' very first IDE. IntelliJ started off as a Java IDE but soon grew to incorporate other languages, both programming and document languages such as HTML. JetBrains has several IDEs for different languages such as RubyMine for Ruby, CLion for C++, and of course, PyCharm for Python. All of these IDEs are based on IntelliJ, in other words, PyCharm and others all are just plugins built on top of IntelliJ.

In fact, you can use the Python plugin in IntelliJ and the same feature set as the community edition of PyCharm. If you've already purchased IntelliJ, you don't need to purchase PyCharm or any other JetBrains IDE since all the language support can be installed through plugins.

If you've used IDEs other than PyCharm, you will notice that IDEs from JetBrains have very similar feature sets, for example, **Search Everywhere** and **Find Action**. In many cases, some IDEs may get common feature sets sooner than others and this has everything to do with build numbers.

The common features are made available at certain build numbers. The best way to stay updated with the latest build is to use PyCharm's **Early Access Program (EAP)**, and we can opt to take part in the program by changing our update settings.

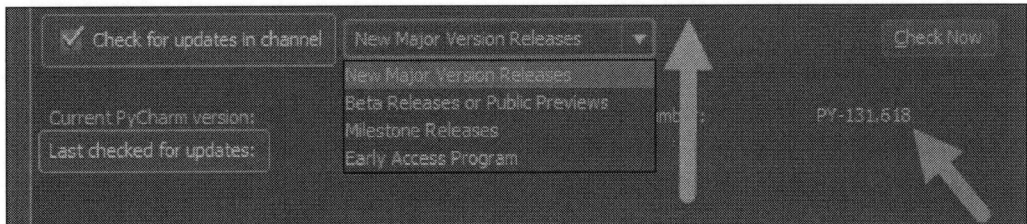

In the preceding screenshot, the green arrow shows update channels by increasing stability, with the most stable being **New Major Version Releases** and the least being **Early Access Program**. When reporting an issue, if you're using an EAP, be sure to place your build number (indicated by the red arrow) in YouTrack; otherwise, enter your version number (for example, PyCharm 3.0.2). Don't worry if you don't know what YouTrack means; it has its own section in this chapter.

EAP is the version JetBrains is currently working on. This version can be very buggy, and I would not suggest using it, use **Early Releases** or **Public Previews** instead; these give you new versions of the programs quickly, and they are quite stable.

One question that you might have nagging you is—what's the difference between PyCharm and IntelliJ with plugins? There is no difference! In fact, IntelliJ with plugins is probably superior because if you want to use Jython, it has better ways of managing your SDKs and libraries. However, PyCharm is much cheaper than the ultimate version of IntelliJ that allows you to install plugins.

Support for PyCharm

PyCharm has many places that you can get support from. The bundled documentation can often be the only thing that you need.

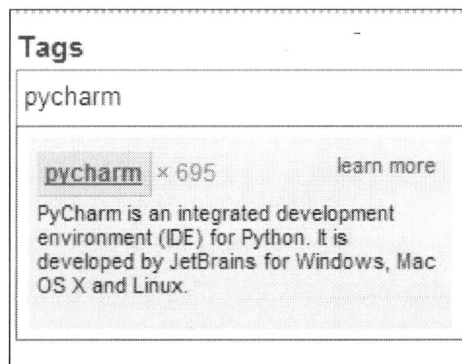

If you're stuck on a problem with regards to PyCharm, Stack Overflow is probably the best site for such a thing. I myself have received a lot of support on this site, and you can ask a question with the PyCharm tag.

There is also a PyCharm forum, `forum.jetbrains.com/forum/PyCharm`, which you can use if Stack Overflow fails to answer your question. I recommend Stack Overflow only because it is a far more active site, and the answers often come within 15 minutes of the question being asked.

Another site that I must recommend is the JetBrains PyCharm blog— `blog.jetbrains.com/pycharm`. It gives you all the latest news on all things PyCharm, and furthermore, gives you tutorials on how to use new features. This is especially important since they announce RC candidates in those EAP programs, which are far more stable than the other EAP releases.

YouTrack.JetBrains

All of the features and bug fixes that we see in PyCharm are actually from YouTrack.JetBrains, a place where users submit their bug reports and feature requests, and that is what we're going to be looking at next.

The complete URL for the site is `http://youtrack.jetbrains.com/`.

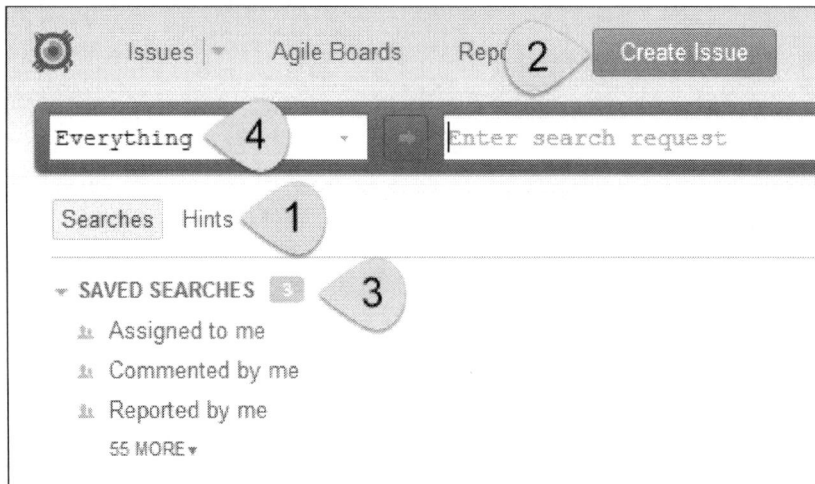

This is a site that you should definitely make an account on if you haven't already done so. It's the place where you submit bug reports and feature requests, and it's packed with a lot of tools that will help you showcase your problem regardless of the platform. You can already log in with Google, Yahoo, and OpenID.

With reference to the preceding screenshot, here are some details:

- **1**: This is where you should start. It's a guide to how to work with YouTrack, and it has a few useful pointers and video tutorials on how to use different features.

- **2**: You'll probably be clicking on this button a lot if you come here often! It creates an issue, ideally a bug report or a feature request. There are many more categories, but we'll skip the details.

- **3**: There are saved searches that are very useful for taking a look to see if anyone has replied to any of the issues you've created. You can always make more of them, and the guides in [1] will help you make them.

- **4**: This is the category view; ideally, we're only interested in the **PY** category for PyCharm. If you click on this and select **PY**, it will show you all the different issues that are relevant to PyCharm.

Now, if you've filed a bug report or a feature request, there are different priorities that the developers can assign to these requests. This gives you an indication of how quickly the problem will be resolved, and the following categories are listed in descending order of importance:

- Show-stopper
- Critical
- Major
- Minor
- Normal

Firstly, when reporting an issue, most of the time, you will need to take a screenshot. If you don't have one, don't worry; you can use the one that comes with YouTrack. This is an application that is made using Java, so you will need Java running on your system, however, it will work with almost any operating system out there.

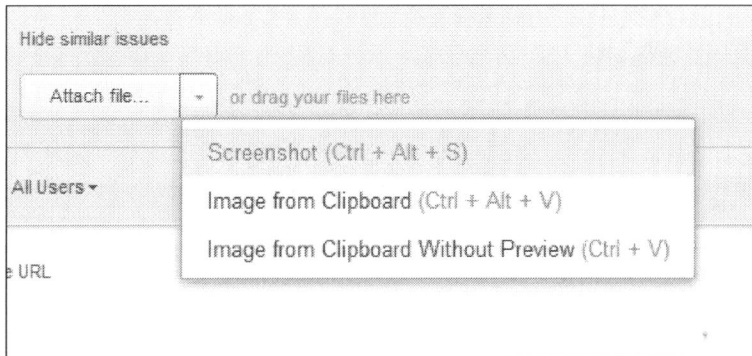

Another thing to note is that you can use wiki markup in your description to format code samples. If you click on the wiki markup link in the following screenshot, it will lead you to a site with all the information you need to make sure that the code highlighting works for the language you want to show a code sample of.

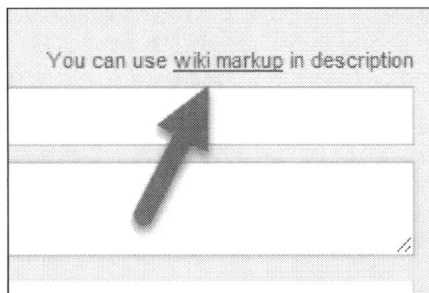

You can fill up the information on the right-hand side with the stuff we've already talked about so far, so that shouldn't be an issue.

You can also vote for a given topic on YouTrack, and as you might expect, the more votes you cast, the more likely a feature is to be added in a future release. However, this is not set in stone (so don't get your hopes up too high). Here's an example at `http://youtrack.jetbrains.com/issue/IDEA-63201`:

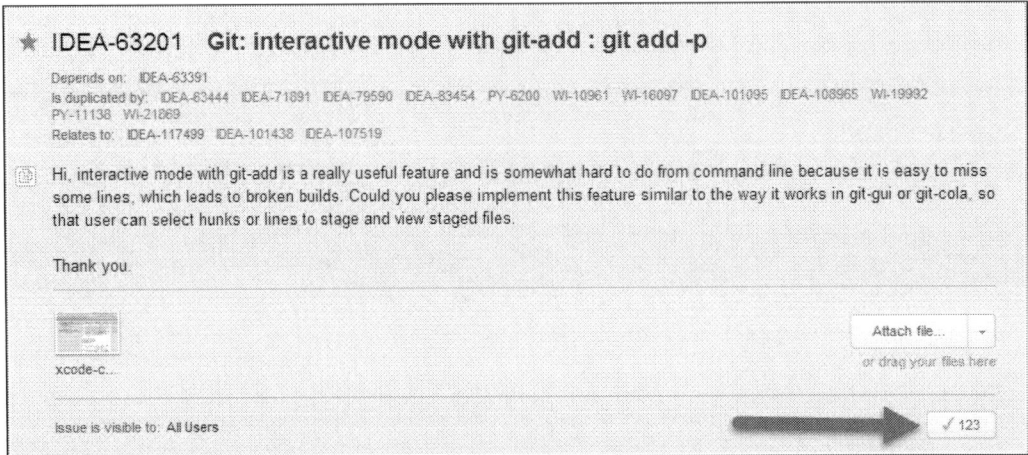

This topic has 123 votes (a very high number) and it was opened 3 years ago, but this feature is yet to be implemented.

Now, if your feature request has been accepted, you can take a look at it in the agile board:

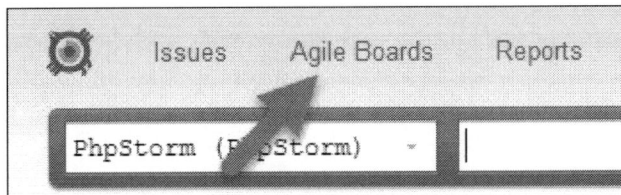

There are different parts of the board—you can take a look at the issues that have been verified, the ones that are being fixed, and the ones that have been fixed. This can give you an idea of how long it will take for JetBrains to finish the feature request or fix the bug.

What makes a good plugin?

The most important thing is—whether the plugin does what it is supposed to do. If a plugin works for you, then it's a good one; however, this section will take a different approach to plugins. We are going to list what the elements of a good plugin are, but what do I mean by that?

A good plugin solves a problem that you need it to solve, but at the same time, it must be stable, well-supported (updated often), and compatible with your version of PyCharm (and the underlying IntelliJ Platform). Without giving you an extensive dose of theory, let's take a look at a couple of examples. We can get to the plugin repository through **Preferences** (Mac) or **Settings** (Windows/Linux):

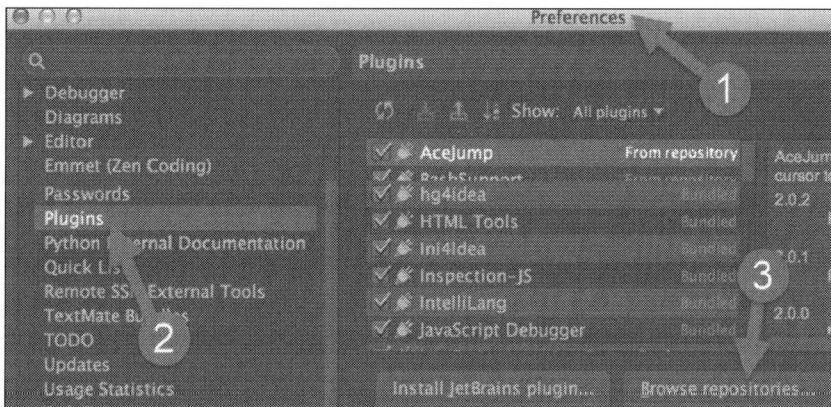

The first thing that hits you when you explore the plugin repository is the star system. Surely, that's useful, but it's not the best indicator of whether something functions properly (and we'll get into that later). But for now, let's take a look at IdeaVim, which, in essence, is Vim emulation for PyCharm (as well as for the rest of the IntelliJ family):

So, IdeaVim has a good rating, but notice that even though it does have a good rating, it's been updated recently (at the time of writing this chapter), indicated by the **Date** column. This is very important because there are many plugins that target a different version of the IntelliJ Platform (a lot of language-specific plugins), and so, even though they have a high rating, installing them on your version of PyCharm would cause errors (I speak from experience). A recent date is a good indication that it supports the latest versions of the IntelliJ Platform, but you can double-check by visiting `plugins.jetbrains.com`:

And then searching for IdeaVim:

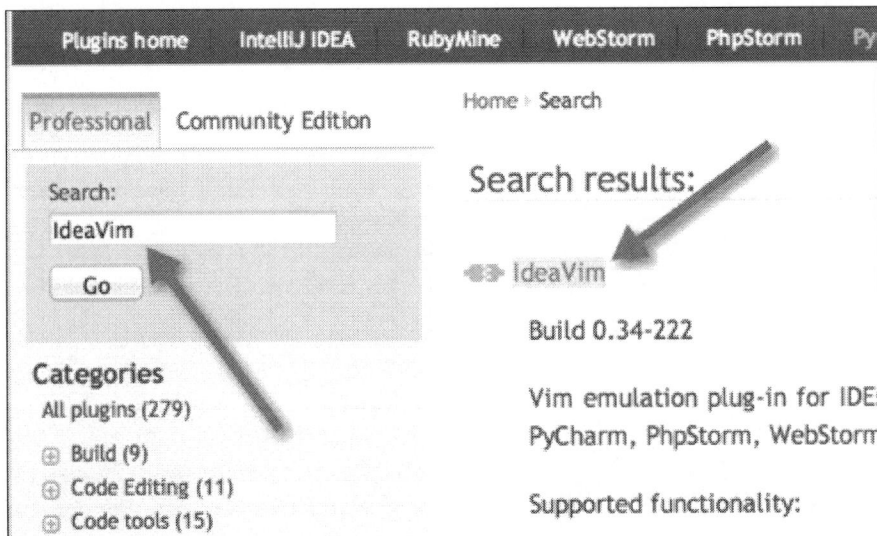

After you're done with that, you can scroll down the IdeaVim page and take a look at its different versions, the latest is always at the top:

Downloads: **398220**
Rating: ☆ ☆ ☆ ☆ ☆
Participated in rating: **148**

Comment and rate

Version	Since Build	Until Build	File/URL	Size (Kb)	Date	Details
0.34	120		Download	860.47	2014-04-29 21:58:24	details
0.31	110		Download	831.28	2013-11-12 04:24:15	details
0.16.60	107.100		Download	1069.45	2011-05-18 11:43:20	details
0.15.59	106.500		Download	1069.49	2011-04-26 12:30:29	details
0.14.54	103.1		Download	1068.97	2011-04-01 14:01:28	details
0.12.7-9.x	93.1		Download	1061.76	2010-03-30 16:05:04	details
0.12.5-8.x	92.9000		Download	704.33	2009-12-04 02:15:37	details
0.12.1-8.x	80.8280		Download	1062.7	2008-10-15 20:45:19	details

So, you can use IdeaVim with any version of the IntelliJ Platform after build 120. Another thing to notice is that the vendor for this plugin is JetBrains, the creators of PyCharm. As a rule of thumb, anything that is created by JetBrains is good and well supported. However, let's take a look at a plugin that by JetBrains and another one that was updated quite some time ago:

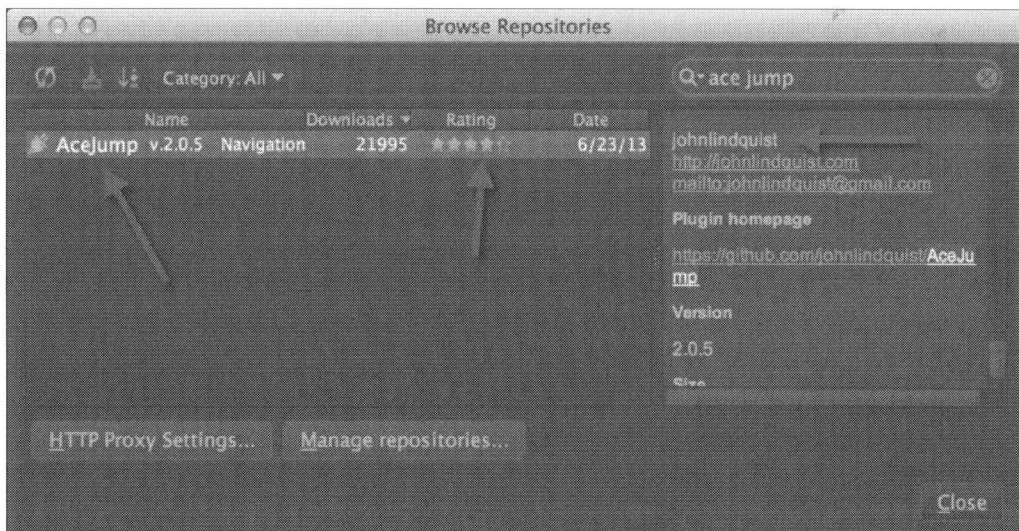

Browse Repositories

Category: All ▼

Q ace jump

Name	Downloads ▼	Rating	Date
AceJump v.2.0.5 Navigation	21995	★★★★☆	6/23/13

johnlindquist
http://johnlindquist.com
mailto:johnlindquist@gmail.com

Plugin homepage

https://github.com/johnlindquist/AceJump

Version

2.0.5

Size

HTTP Proxy Settings... Manage repositories...

Close

This particular plugin, AceJump, has a good star rating. However, the other reason for this being a good plugin is because John Lindquist worked at JetBrains before and maintained this plugin well.

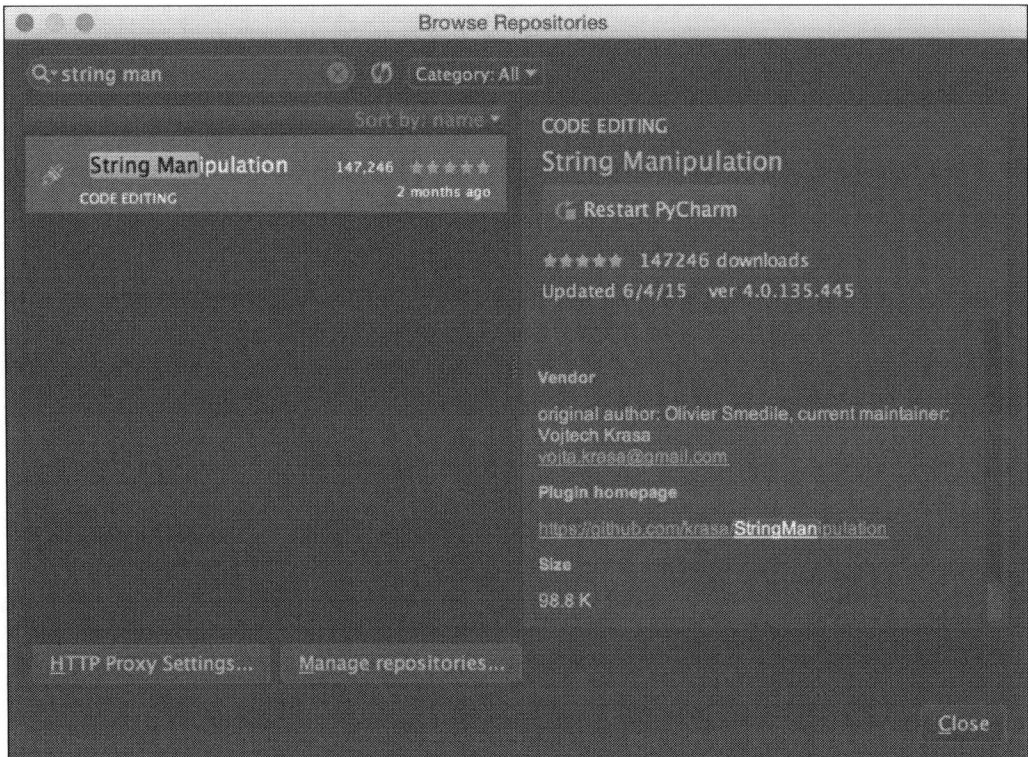

Another great plugin that hasn't been created by JetBrains is called **String Manipulation**. It basically gives you a lot of quick fixes when dealing with strings. It's recently updated, and has a high rating, although its creators do not have an affiliation with JetBrains.

Summary

In this chapter, we gained an idea of what makes PyCharm work the way it does, its support systems, as well as its feature/bug tracking system. We also got a taste of what makes the IntelliJ Platform so powerful — plugins.

PyCharm supports many plugins that are language-specific such as Markdown or Bash. It also supports productivity plugins such as Key Promoter, which gets you used to shortcuts quickly. It has plugins for all kinds of needs, but you might be asking — how do you write a plugin? With Java or JVM languages (preferably Kotlin)? If you want to get started on plugin development, this is the place to start from `http://confluence.jetbrains.com/display/IDEADEV/PluginDevelopment`.

8
File Templates and Snippets

"Are we there yet?"

– Everyone, including you

Coding is a ton of fun, but sometimes, it can be rather repetitive. Snippets (live templates) in PyCharm help you do away with a lot of the receptive parts. However, PyCharm goes further; it even allows you to make file templates so that once you make a new file, for example, a `.py` file or a `.js` file, you can have some boilerplate code written for you. You're already using file templates in PyCharm if you haven't changed its default settings. This chapter is all about coding speed, so hold on to your hats!

In this chapter, we are going to take a look at:

- File templates
- Snippets (live templates)
- Surround templates

File templates

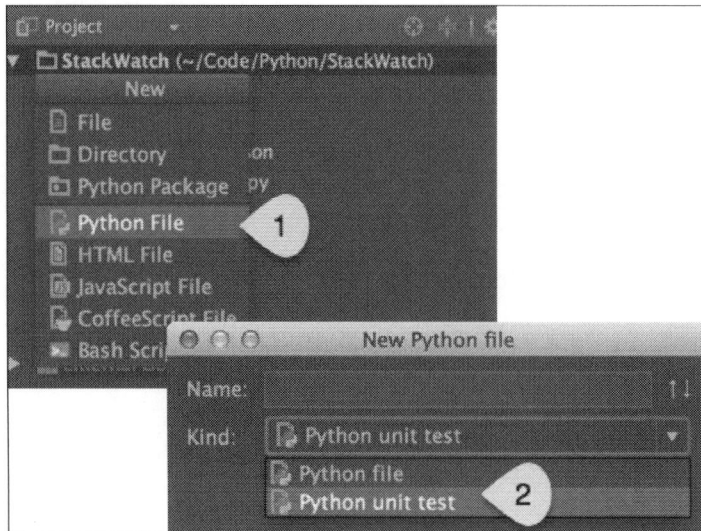

Let's make a new file in PyCharm. The two options that you have, **Python file** and **Python unit test**, are file templates. You might have more than what is shown here, but in essence, when you make a new file template, it shows up as an option when you make a new file. So, let's take a look at what's inside these two templates:

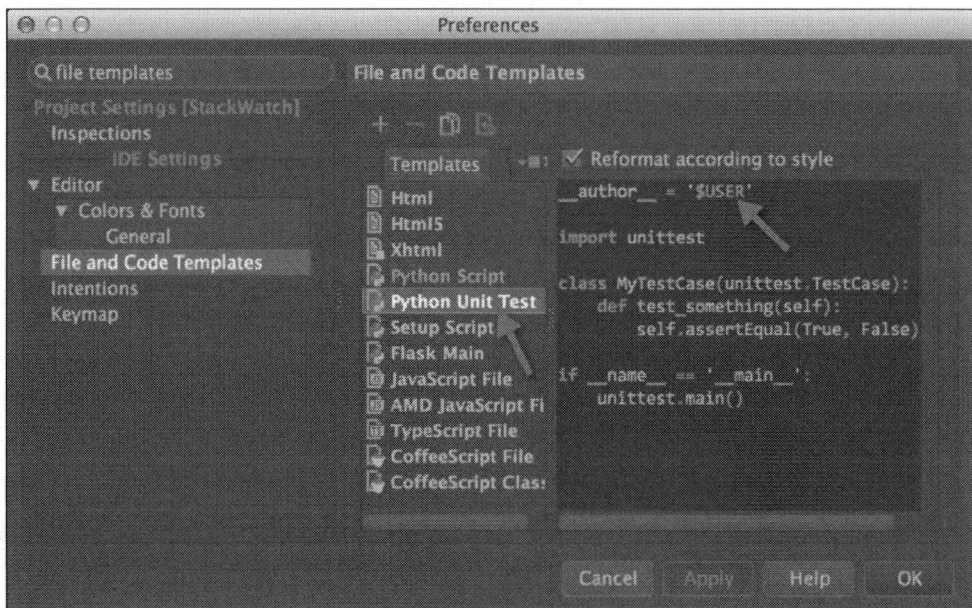

Understanding variables

As you can see in the template (in the preceding screenshot) there is some code to initiate the file. In this case, it's **Python Unit Test**. You can also see that (indicated by a red arrow); there are some special variables that you can use inside the template. The file templating engine PyCharm uses is called **Velocity Template Language (VTL)**.

Some of the variables are given to you by default. So, $USER is derived from the username that the user has registered to PyCharm with. If you registered with an abbreviation of your name, you might want to change the $USER variable, and you can do it like this:

```
#set ( $USER = "THE AMAZING SPIDER MAN" )
```

You can change preconfigured variables and make new variables using #set. The documentation on **File and Code Templates** provides a good account of the default variables available, but if you want to explore more of VTL, which is an Apache project with tons of documentation, refer to `https://velocity.apache.org/engine/releases/velocity-1.5/user-guide.html`.

Making new templates

You can make new templates with the (+) icon. You can also copy the existing ones with the copy icon if you want to make slight modifications. Now, it is fairly simple to create new templates with variables in them. But, say, you registered with the username CHEEZIE; although this is a great name for the Internet, a pseudonym is often inappropriate in more formal circumstances.

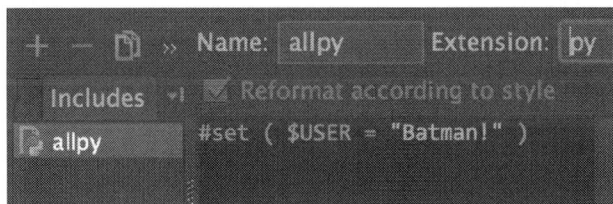

We saw that we can set $USER with #set, but we don't want to be doing this for every script that has a reusable variable in it. We can use this by using the **Includes** tab.

We can set the include template here and simply include it at the top of our file in our Python script using #parse:

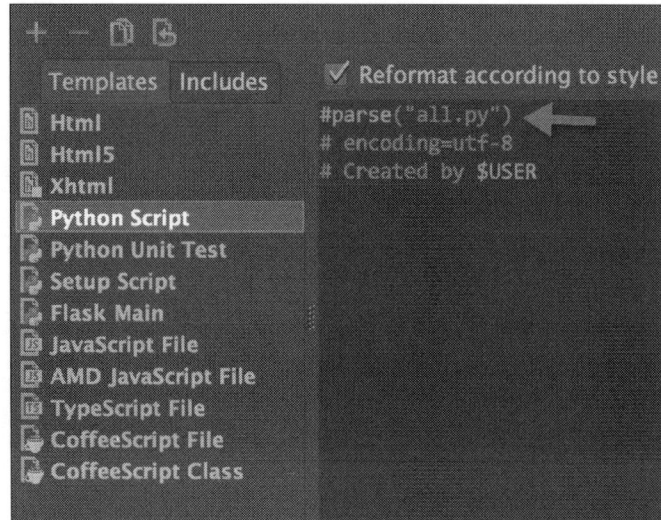

However, we cannot create your own group. Some other templates such as **Setup Script** and **Flask Main** are only available under certain conditions. For example, **Flask Main** is used as a template when you first create a Flask project using PyCharm.

In most cases, the basic tools that file templates provide you are often more than adequate and can speed up a lot of repetitive tasks for you. You probably won't use this feature very much, but you will certainly use snippets, or as PyCharm likes to call them, live templates, which we will be discussing next.

Snippets (live templates)

Live templates are a wonderful part of PyCharm. They are very helpful when there is a repetitive pattern that you need to type over and over again. PyCharm 3.4 introduced a couple of new snippets into the mix, so let's see how we can make our own by inspecting the snippets that are already available. Let's take a look at the `main` snippet that comes bundled with PyCharm 3.4:

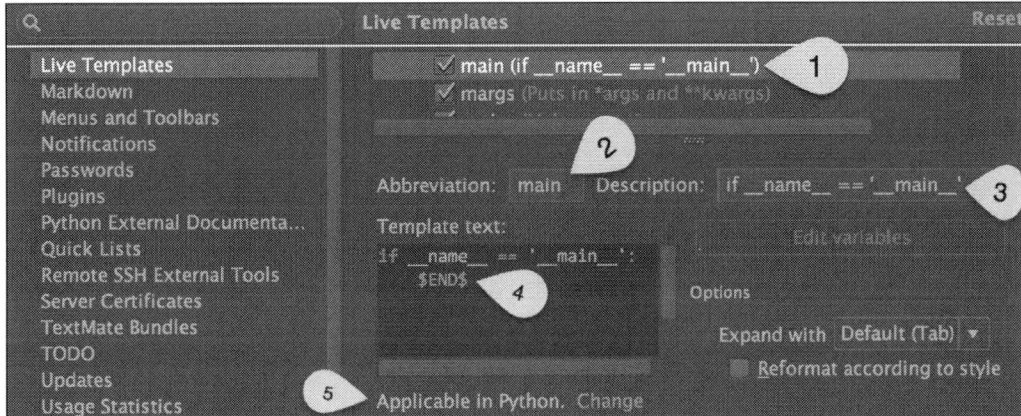

We can see that [1] is the snippet in question and it has its own abbreviation `main`, and this is what we invoke with [2]. The description for snippet [3] is what will be shown when you try to invoke **Insert Live Template** (*Command/Ctrl + J*). You can change the abbreviation to suit your fancy so that you can invoke it using whatever you like. The most important parts of the screenshot to discuss are [4] and [5].

`$END$` [4] is a special template variable, and it is where the cursor will be after the snippet has been inserted (after you've put in any variables that the template requires). `$END$` is a reserved template variable, and there are a couple of others that we will get into. This particular snippet is under a particular template group, Python [5]. This means that this template can only be invoked inside a `.py` file.

Variables in **Live Templates** are very similar to that of file templates, but with **Live Templates**, you have a lot more control. So, let's take a look at a List comprehension snippet in PyCharm, compl:

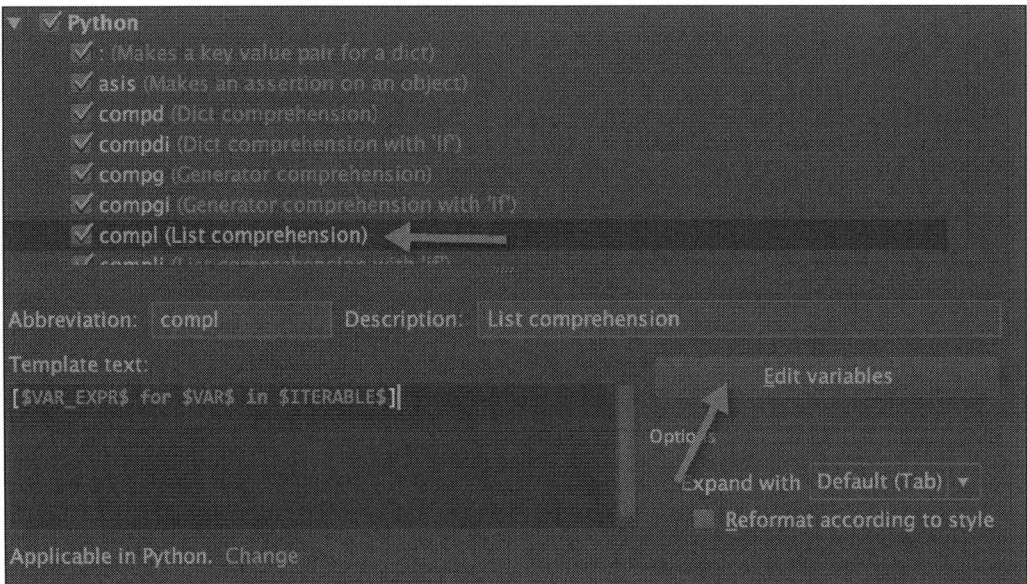

So, the variables are there and you can use them as they are, but we need to take a look at the customizations made to the variables to appreciate the power of this snippet:

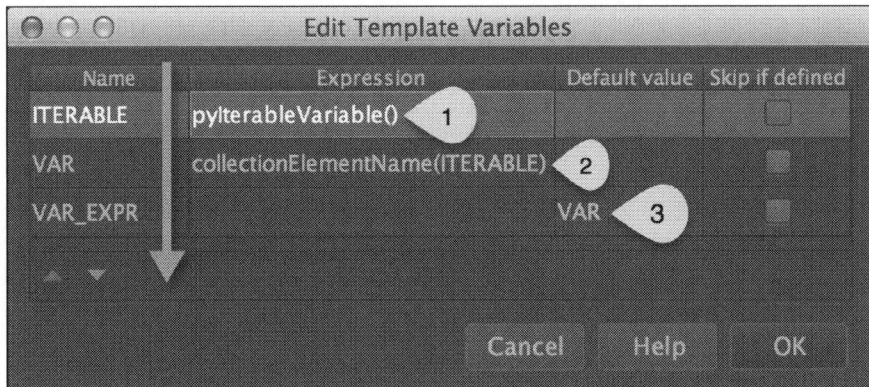

The order in which the variables are arranged in this list is the order in which your cursor will be placed, so in this case, your cursor will initially be placed in the position where the ITERABLE variable sits.

So, ITERABLE is `pyIterableVariable()` [1], and this means that the only type that is allowed in the code completion dialog box is an iterable, meaning a generator or a list, set, and so on:

```
1    a_list = "cheese cake coffee tea biscuits".split()
2    a_dict = {
3        "Cold Play": "Viva la Vida",
4        "Bastille": "Pompei",
5        "Alt-J": "Breezeblocks",
7    }
8
9    not_an_iterable = 21  <----
10
11   a_set = {1, 2, 3, 4, 5, 6}
12
13   [ for  in a_dict]  <----
            a_dict
            a_list
            a_set
```

Note the completion that you get. The variables are only iterable. This is actually a very powerful way in which you can minimize any mistakes that you make when writing Python.

But you can do more than just saying something will be an iterable. In the Edit Template Variables screenshot, you will see that there is another expression, `collectionElementName(ITERABLE)` [2], and this takes the first variable as an argument to the expression, essentially making a function call. This function turns a plural noun into a singular noun, so take a look at the following screenshot:

```
names = 'Bob Joe Jack Gill Ham Sam Bill'.split()


[name for name in names]
                   names
                   name
```

So, we have a list called **names**, and that gets turned into a singular version, **name**, by the logic in the snippet. There are many more in-built functions, which can be seen in the drop-down box in the expression column of each variable.

You can have default values and they can be variables that you have defined before, or you can have hard coded variables using strings, so we can modify the `main` snippet that we discussed earlier:

1. Let's change the name to `ifname` so that we invoke it using `ifname` instead of `main`. You can do this by changing the abbreviation.

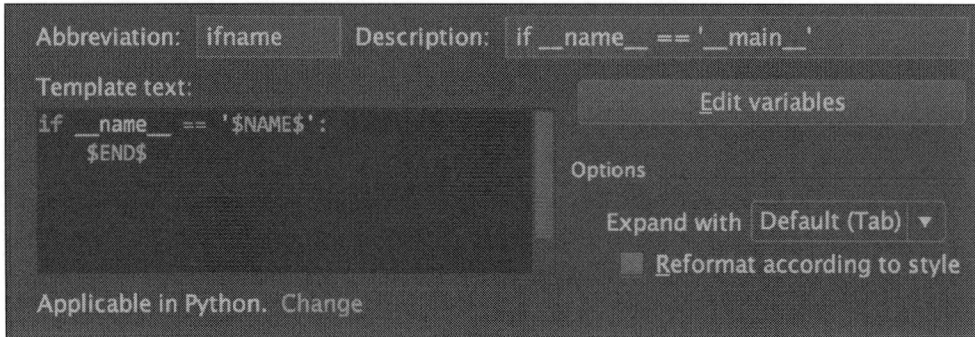

2. Introduce a variable instead of `__main__`.

3. Give **NAME** a default value of `__main__`:

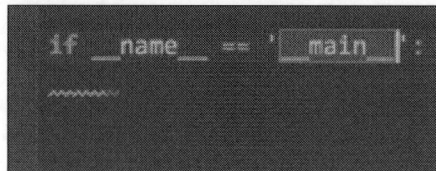

4. With this, when you invoke it, you will automatically get `__main__` as the default argument, but you can change it if you like.

Although this is a simple example, it does demonstrate a lot of the things that we talked about.

Surround templates

Surround templates allow you to take advantage of the **Surround With** action.
An example of an in-built **Surround With** (*Command/Ctrl + T*) template is
the **try / except** block:

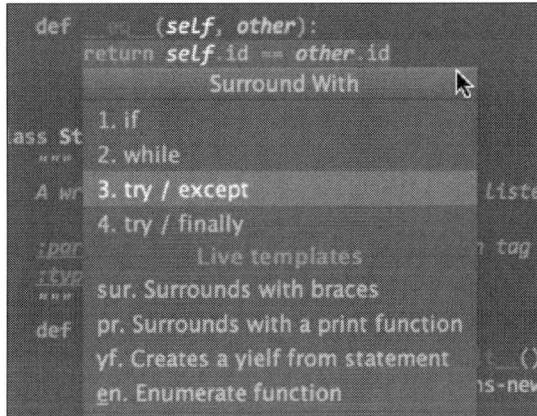

You can see that there are a few live templates that I can use since I've made them
myself. The key to using surround templates is using the SELECTION variable. Here is
a simple demonstration:

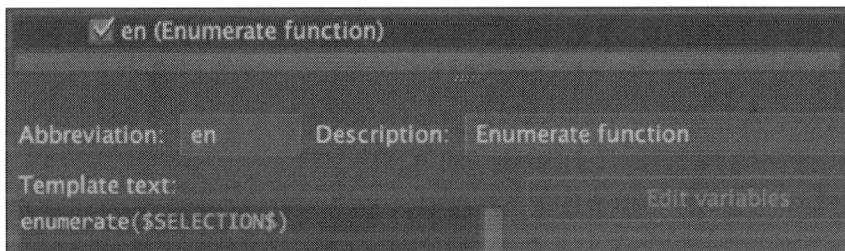

Summary

In this chapter, we learned about one of the most important parts of PyCharm. Both file
and live templates are excellent for storing up bits of code that we reuse throughout
our development, and can make our development a lot less error-prone by making
sure that all the variables that we input into a snippet fall under a certain expression.

To take full advantage of PyCharm's live template system, it would be wise to take a
quick look at the VTL's syntax.

Version Control Integration

9

"As a project drags on, my git commit messages get less and less informative."

– Randall Munroe

A lot of my friends use IntelliJ IDEs and hence, have forgotten how to use most Git command-line tools. I can't blame them; the interface that we have is very simple to use, and most of the common commands are available to us in a neatly packed menu. That isn't to say that this layer of abstraction like many others is leaky. In this chapter, I will take a quick look at most of the tools and talk about some limitations. Version control is in no way a simple topic and hence, I won't explain its topics; I'll merely show you how to use the tools available in PyCharm. We will mainly go over:

- Initializing version control
- Ignoring files
- Adding remotes
- The VCS menu
- The **Changes** panel
- Change lists

Initializing version control

PyCharm supports different version control systems. In the following examples, we will be using a Git repo to elaborate on different features since it's the modus operandi of most development. As most of what we cover in this chapter is VCS agnostic, this will not matter; however, each tool has its own submenu in PyCharm, which we will go over. After we've created our project, we can initialize VCS right away:

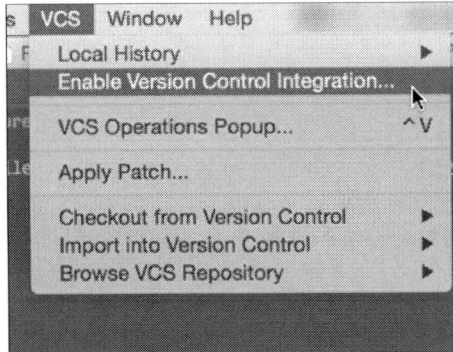

This will give us a popup of all the types of repositories that we can initiate:

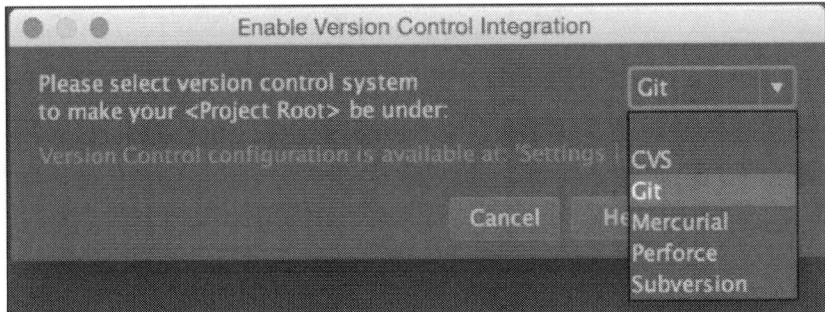

Ignoring files

In my project, I have my virtualenv set up in my `.venv` folder, and I certainly don't want to include it in my commit, so I have to make sure to ignore it. So, let's head over to **Settings...** and do the following:

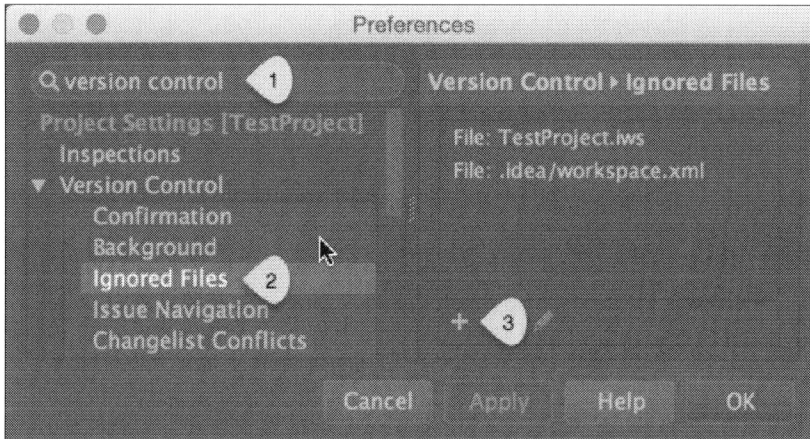

Inside, we can choose to add either files or folders. Come to think of it PyCharm also generates project metadata and stores this data in the `.idea` folder, and I'll need to ignore that as well. After clicking on [3], we get the following window:

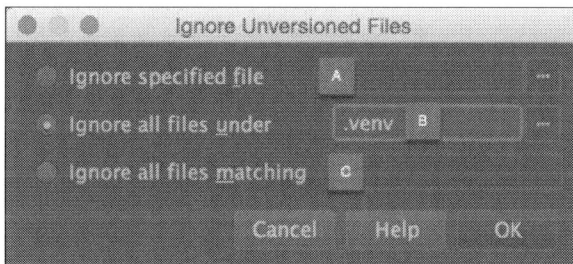

We can choose to ignore files, folders, or even patterns. For example, you can ignore all the compiled Python bytecode files by adding `*.pyc` in (C). In the preceding screenshot, we just ignored all the files under `.venv`. This works across VCSs.

Git users are in for a special treat. There is a special plugin called `.gitignore` that allows us to create a `.gitignore` file and get code completion in the `.gitigore` file:

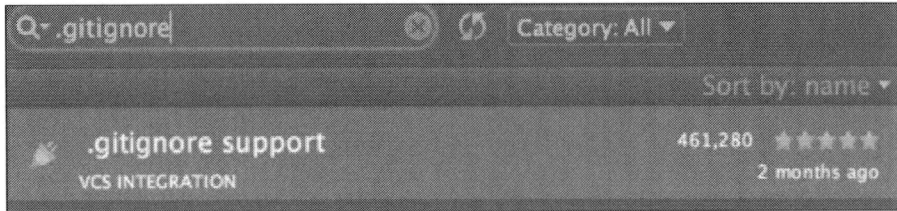

This plugin allows you to create a new type of file called the `.gitignore` file, which, as you would might guess, allows us to ignore files, folders, and patterns:

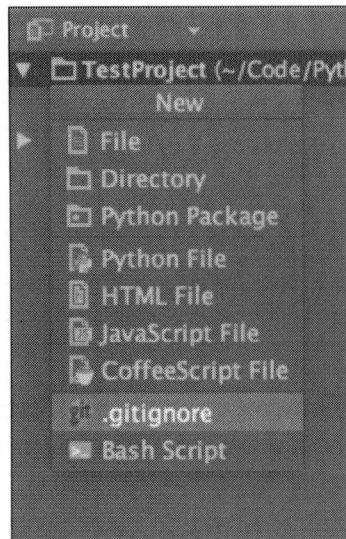

Inside the file, we will be able to get code completion for the files, folders, and patterns in our project's directory. This is a third-party plugin and also supports other `.ignore` files.

Remotes

Adding remotes is straightforward; you have to use the command line or make a file for your respective VCS systems. This is currently a feature request in YouTrack, so it will be worked on at some point. However, PyCharm understands remotes, so if we add a GitHub remote from Git (git remote add origin `git@github.com:gamesbrainiac/TestProject.git`), PyCharm would understand that we've added a remote when we go to commit and push:

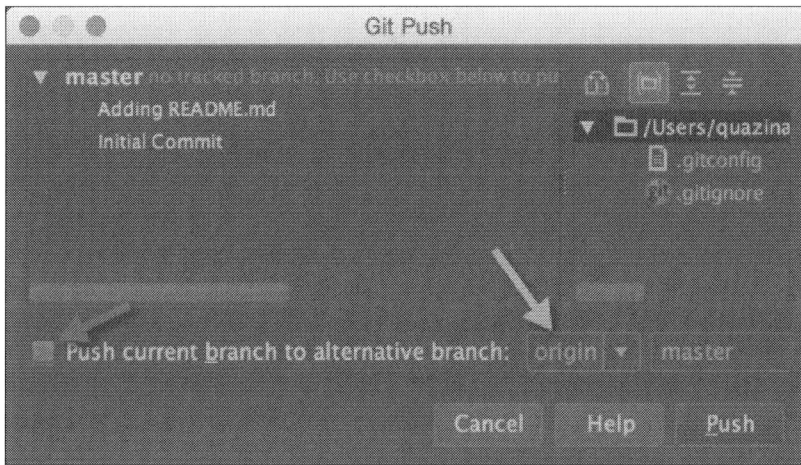

We can add multiple remotes via the command line, and PyCharm will allow us to pick which one we want to push. Make sure to check the **Push current branch to alternative branch** checkbox, or else PyCharm will tell us that there's nothing to push.

However, all of this is done for us by the built-in GitHub plugin in PyCharm if we click on **Share Project on GitHub**:

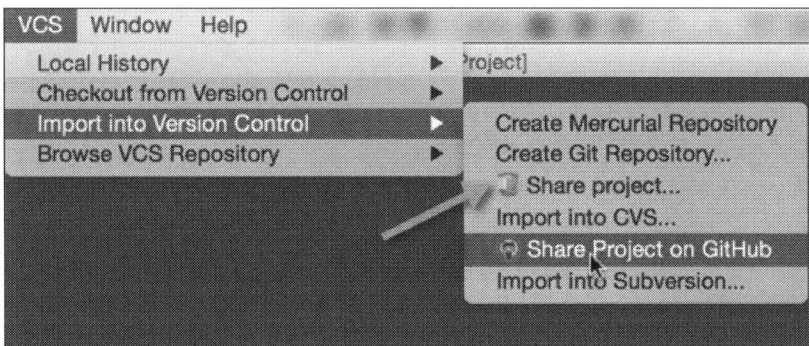

If you're a Bitbucket user, you may also choose to use its plugin, which gives you similar functionality:

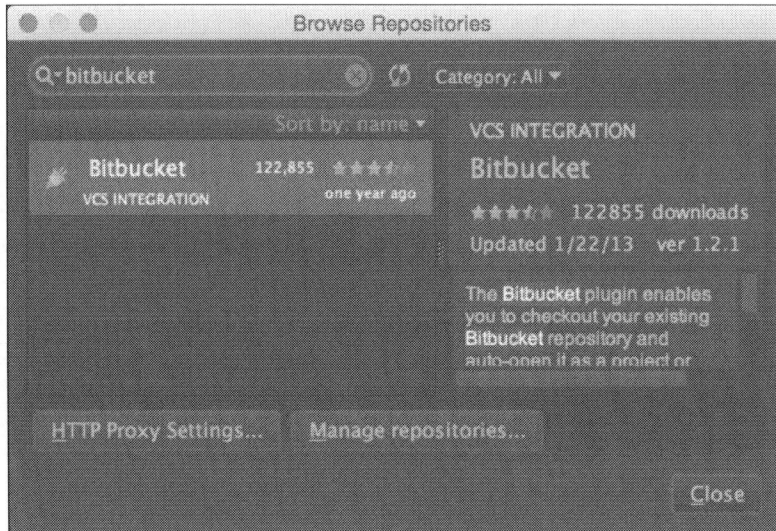

Be warned though; this plugin has not been updated for quite some time, and has a few quirks. The orange arrow in the second last screenshot is pointing to the action for sharing on Bitbucket.

The VCS menu

The **VCS** menu allows us to see all the possible actions available to us, and can be easily invoked:

This will cause a new menu to pop up:

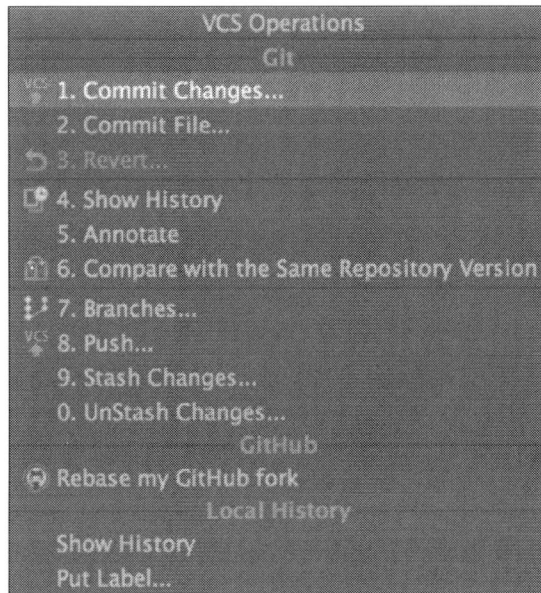

This menu also has search and allows us to do most of the things that we want to do, from committing to reverting. History actually opens up the **Version Control** panel, which allows you to see a log of all the changes that our actions have been translated into.

The **Console** tab (indicated by the orange arrow) will show you all the commands that have been entered and the **File Readme.md History** tab (indicated by the red arrow) will show you a list of all the changes that have been made, and their associated hash values. **Annotate** will give you a side panel that shows you all the hashes of the commits, and **Branches...** allows you to check out branches and tags.

If you know Git, then all of these options will register with their command-line equivalents. Now, we will move onto the **Changes** panel, which gives you a more graphical representation of what's been happening to our project.

The Changes panel

The **Changes** panel gives us a bird's eye view of the status of our commits and the branches we have as well as the difference between the commits. There are so many features that we cannot go over all of them, but we will be looking at most of them.

Changes is a panel, just like **Project**, and we should able to access it once we've initialized version control in our project:

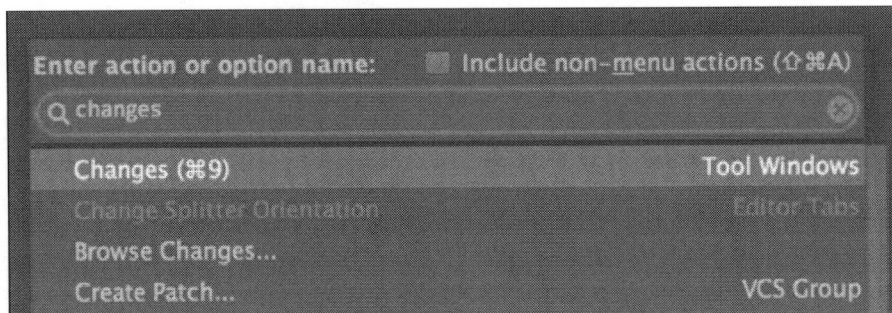

The **Changes** panel has two tabs: **Log** and **Local**. The **Log** tab allows us to dive into the changes that have been made, providing powerful search tools. It also gives us the ability to quickly see the changes between different versions of the commits.

But, before we dive into this awesome panel, we need a project that can showcase how powerful it can be, and this is why we are going to be cloning the Python requests, an open source library by Kenneth Reitz, which has been around for quite some time and hence, has many different commits for us to look at.

The first thing that we're going to do is clone the Python requests so that they give us a large library with lots of commits. Then, we are going to take a look at all the changes that have been made over the lifetime of the project using the **Changes** panel. We can clone a Git repo directly within PyCharm by heading over to the **Quick Start** screen and choosing to check out from version control:

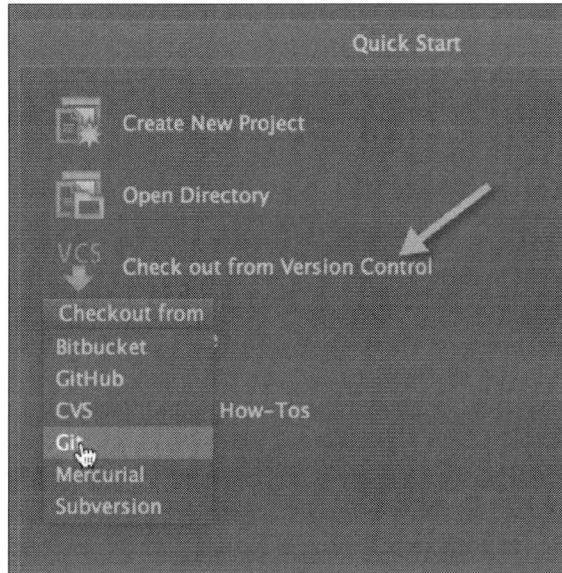

And then, we enter the Git repo's URL:

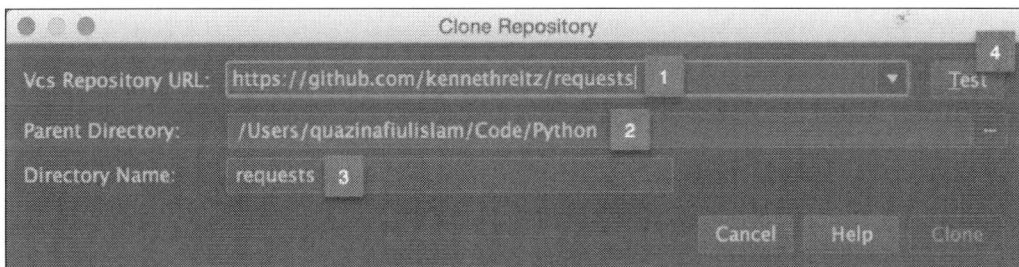

Here, [1], [2], and [3] are pretty self-explanatory. We can use [4] to check whether the repo exists before cloning to avoid errors later on.

The first thing that we are going to do is take a look at how a particular file, index.rst, has changed over the course of the project's existence and we are going to use the **Changes** panel to do it. The first thing that we do is select index.rst as the structure that we want to observe:

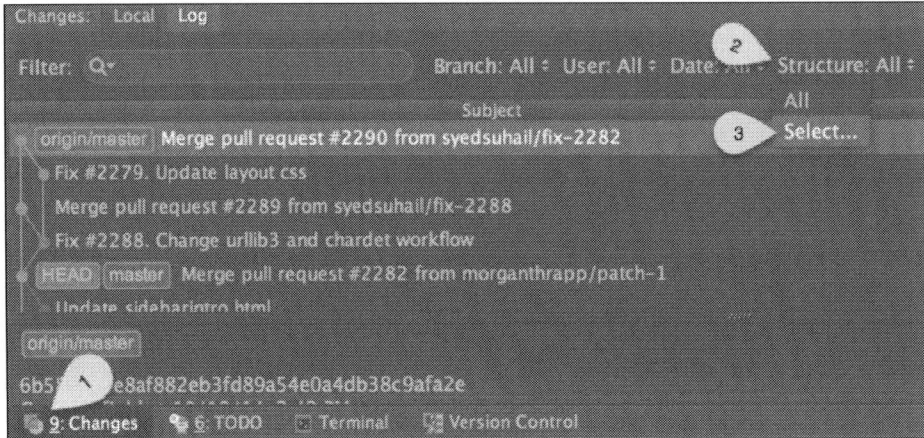

We first get to the **Changes** panel by clicking on [1] or we can use **Find Action**, as shown before. Then, we select **Structure** [2]. It is an example of a filter that we can apply just like **Branch**, **User**, or **Date**.

Structure allows us to select multiple files and/or directories that we wish to observe. We may not, however, select the root directory because it is pointless to do so as it would list all the changes that we get as the default view when we first open up the **Log** tab.

So, let's add the index.rst file as the structure that we want to watch:

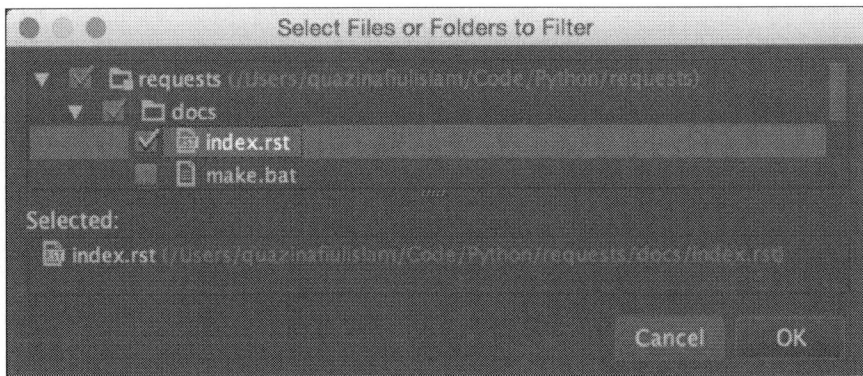

Once this is done, we will see a list of all the commits that have changed the `index.rst` file. Furthermore, we can filter these commits based on their messages:

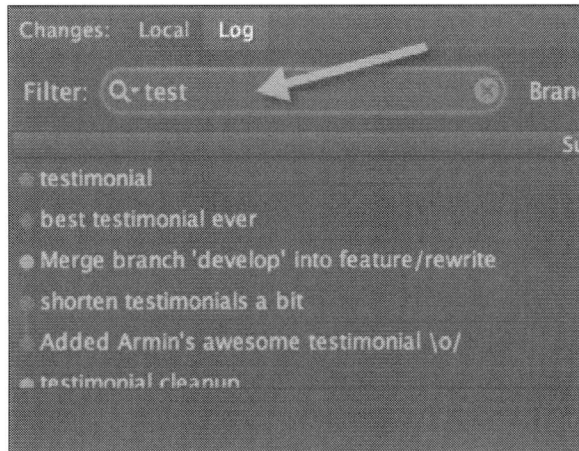

Here, we can see that in one of the commit messages, Armin Ronacher's testimonial was added. Let's take a look at it by selecting the commit. Then, we will look at the changed files.

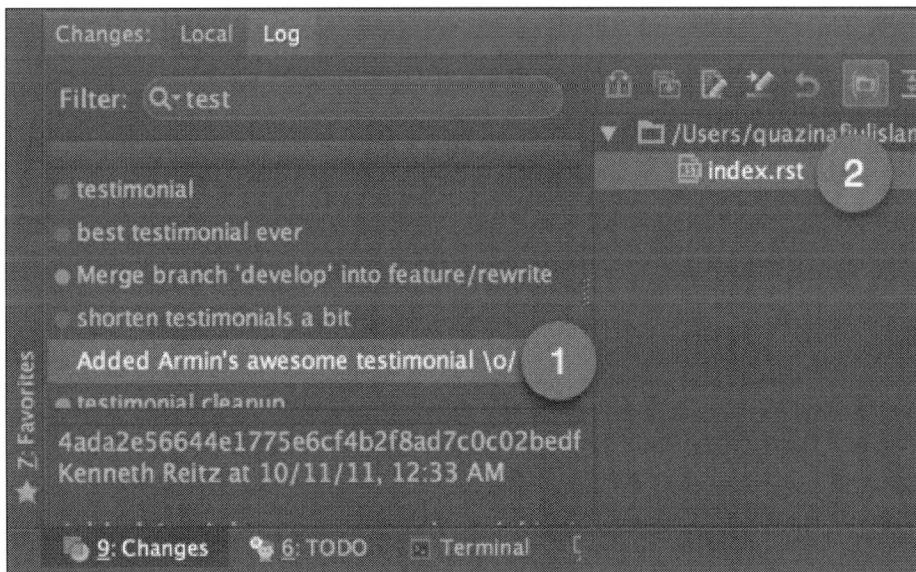

Once we've double-clicked on [2], we can take a look at the changes made to
`index.rst` in the commit:

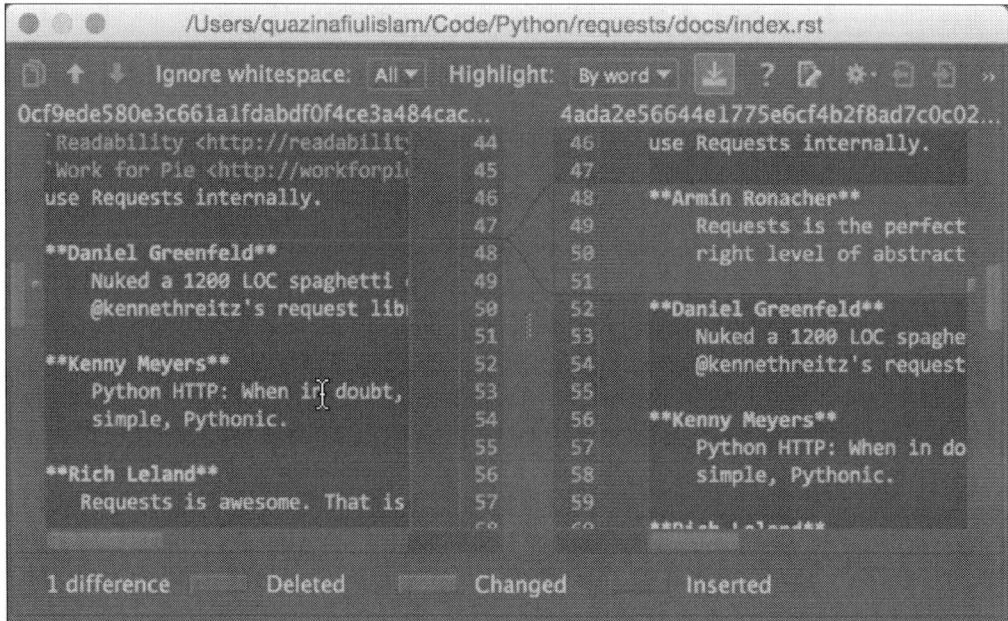

We can also see the changes between different commits by selecting the two
different commits:

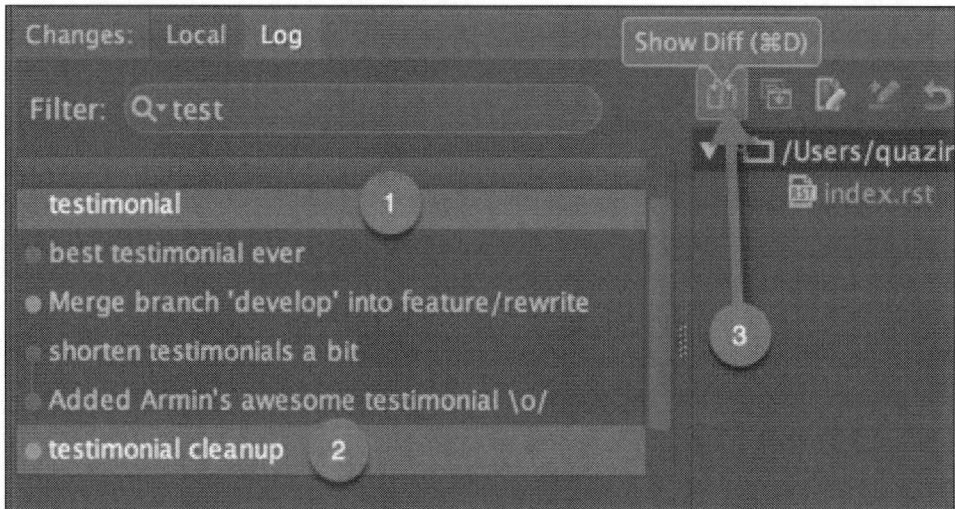

Other filters such as **Branch** and **User** have code completion:

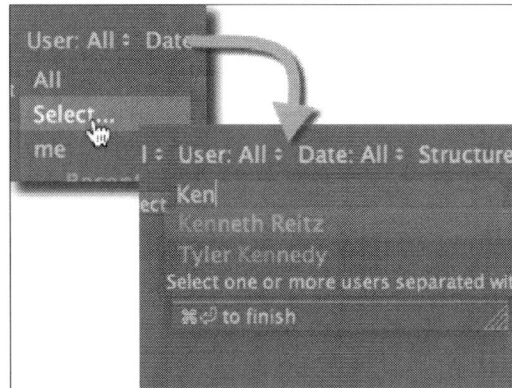

Here, we can even enter multiple names on separate lines to get changes from different users. All the recent filters are saved too.

Changing Diff colors

If we wish to change the **Diff** colors, all we have to do is alter the colors in **Colors & Fonts**:

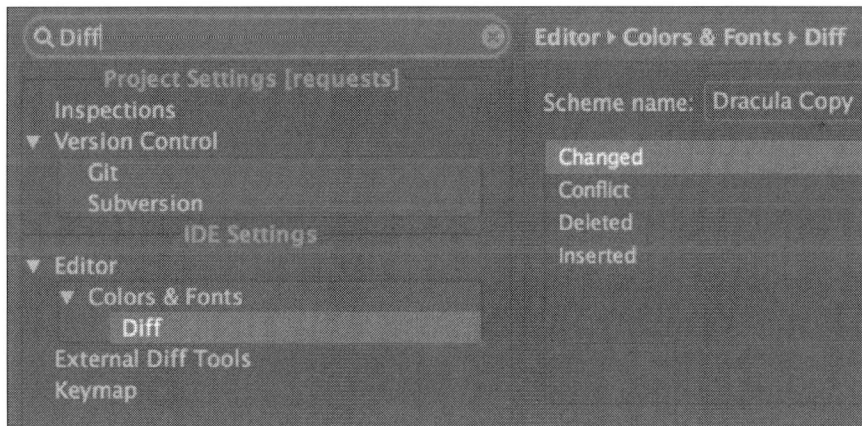

Change lists

Often, we want to group the changes to the project together. By default, PyCharm puts everything in our **Default** change list. But what if we wanted to just commit changes to a certain file or a group of files? In the **Changes** panel, we can select a bunch of files, and move them to a separate change list:

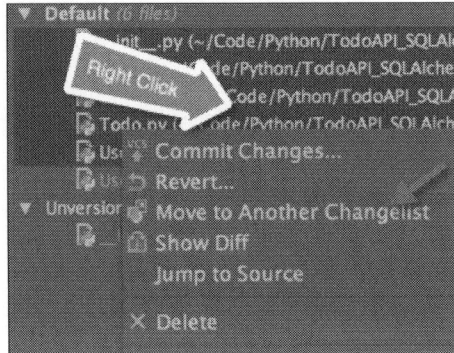

We've set the change list to become the active change list, meaning that the changes we made will get added to this change list. However, note that this is in no way a partial commit, it is file-specific. We cannot pick out individual commits and add them to a change list. Once this has been done, when we go to commit, we should see two different change lists—one being **Default**, and the other being the new change list that we've just made.

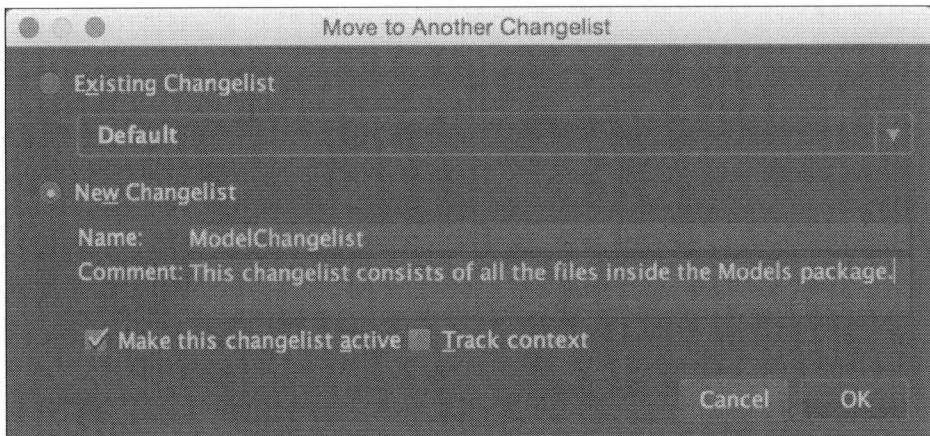

We can also move files between change lists by dragging and dropping.

Change lists also give us the ability to configure what happens when we commit from a particular change list:

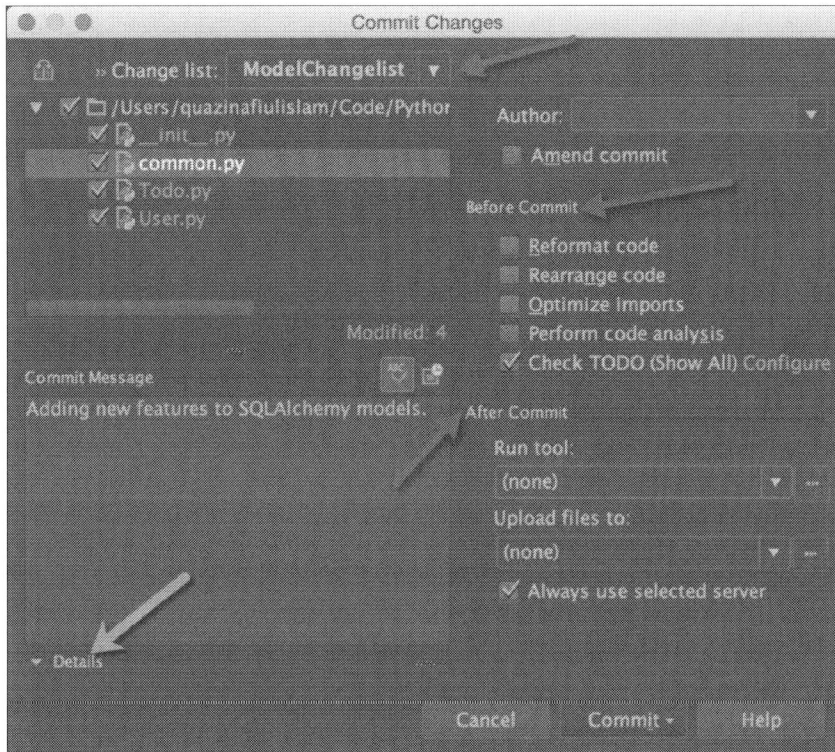

The **After Commit** and **Before Commit** menus allow us to do specific things before and after each commit list is committed. The **Details** tab, indicated by the orange arrow, allows us to see the exact changes that are going to be committed on a file-by-file basis.

Summary

In this chapter, we looked at what's possible with PyCharm's VCS and what isn't. PyCharm has super support for Git and GitHub, but lacks a little bit elsewhere, which can often be made up for with additional plugins. PyCharm's VCS is not a leaky abstraction over a VCS, such as source tree, but still has some powerful search and filtering tools.

10

HTML and JavaScript Tools

PyCharm's support for JavaScript is exclusive to its professional edition. These sets of tools are common across other IntelliJ IDEs (see *Chapter 9, Version Control Integration*). This chapter is by no means exhaustive because most of the support for JavaScript in PyCharm comes from plugins. If we were to dive into all the plugins available for IntelliJ IDEs, we would've written several books on the topic. So, to keep this short and sweet, these are some of the most used features that any JavaScript developer would find useful. Here is a quick run-down of what we're going to cover:

- **JavaScript support**: This section of the chapter is the largest and covers many features that developers would find useful. We are going to look at JavaScript code completion, NodeJS support, library support (for libraries such as jQuery and `underscore`), transpiled language support, and code quality tools such as JSLint. This section is rather large, so it's been broken down into much smaller subsections for your convenience.

- **HTML and CSS**: This section deals with support for HTML, CSS, Emmet, and live editing, as well as transpiled CSS languages such as SASS and Less and transpiled HTML languages such as HAML. We are also going to take a quick look at watchers and how they can make the task of compiling these files much simpler.

JavaScript support

JavaScript is all around us, and with the advent of NodeJS, it has become (much to my chagrin) undisputedly the most prolific programming language. PyCharm has several JavaScript-specific features to deal with the influx of JavaScript needs. However, it's impossible to cover everything with regards to JavaScript support, and many of the features will appear as you work in PyCharm. So, let's look at some of the best tools that PyCharm has to offer for JavaScript. We will start off with the simplest—code completion.

Getting the most out of JavaScript code completion

JavaScript is a difficult language to provide code completion for. Luckily, PyCharm has powerful tools to make code completion a lot better in JavaScript.

Using JSDoc

There are two things that make JavaScript code completion in PyCharm outstanding—smart type completion and support for documentation, including TypeScript stubs. If you don't know what that means just yet, let me demonstrate. JavaScript has support for JSDoc; this means that the documentation and the types will help out in code completion. Let's start off by making an **Immediately Invoked Function Expression**, and in it, let's create a function called `greetNames`:

```
(function () {


    function greetNames(names) {
        for(var i = 0; i < names.length; i ++) {
            console.log("Hello, " + names[i])
        }
    }


})();
```

While writing the preceding code, PyCharm will provide several completion suggestions for the function, and when `names` is made a parameter, `names.length` should automatically come up as a viable option. However, in JavaScript, we often want specific suggestions as in many cases, PyCharm offers us a host of possible code completions that we do not want. One way to fix this issue is to include a JSDoc stub. With stubs added, our code looks similar to this:

```
/**
 * This function greets all the names in an array of names
 * @param {Array} names
 */
function greetNames(names) {
    for(var i = 0; i < names.length; i ++) {
        console.log("Hello, " + names[i])
    }
}
```

In the stub, we specify that `names` is an array, and so, when we go for suggestions, PyCharm will offer up `length` as one of the very first suggestions, and this is because PyCharm understands that `names` is an array. If we get the quick documentation on names, we see that PyCharm sees `names` as an array.

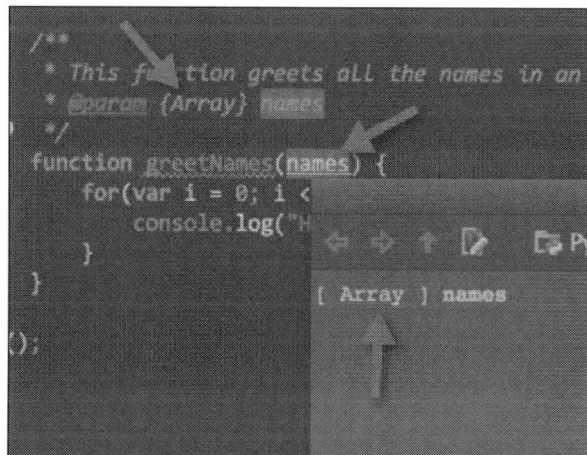

This kind of documentation will also help when we make the function call.

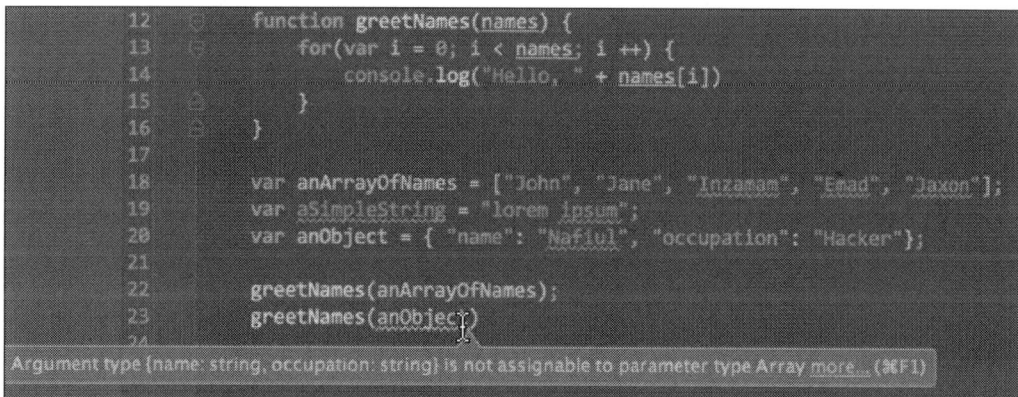

This can become very useful when dealing with large code bases. Also, note that PyCharm understands the type of the `anObject` variable as well. Inserting a JSDoc stub will come automatically if you want it to. Go to the line above the function declaration, type out /** and then hit *Enter*. PyCharm will automatically create the @param lines for you.

Using libraries

When writing client-side JavaScript, we almost always use third-party libraries. This can often be difficult for PyCharm to understand when you have a lot of them. Furthermore, if we're using the minimized JavaScript files, PyCharm will not be able to give us the kind of code completion that we expect if we had written these files ourselves with the proper documentation stubs. This problem is remedied by including library support in a specific JavaScript file. Inside the JavaScript file, we can right-click anywhere and choose to add a supported library; in this case, we are going to add support for jQuery.

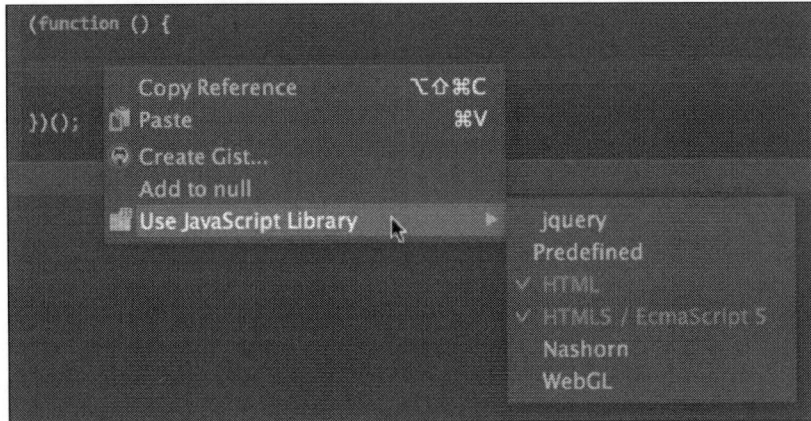

This will allow PyCharm to offer code completions based on jQuery's official documentation.

PyCharm is not limited to just jQuery or just the most popular set of libraries, it can support a wide range of libraries because of the TypeScript stubs made by the TypeScript community. In order to add support for a library, we simply need to head over to the **Libraries** section inside the **JavaScript** preferences.

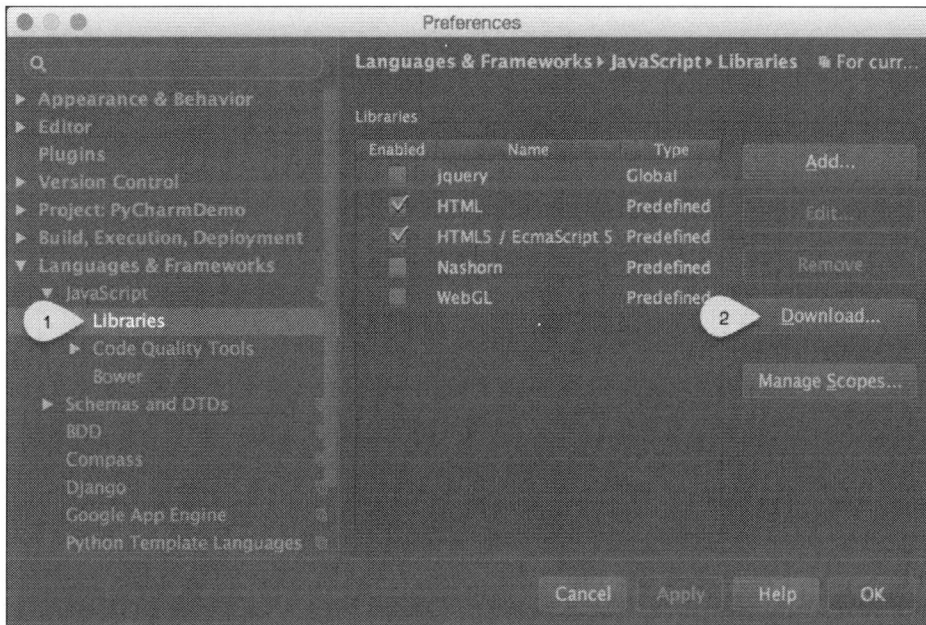

There is of course official library support, but more interestingly, we can also download support for lesser-known libraries (such as underscore) because of the TypeScript stubs.

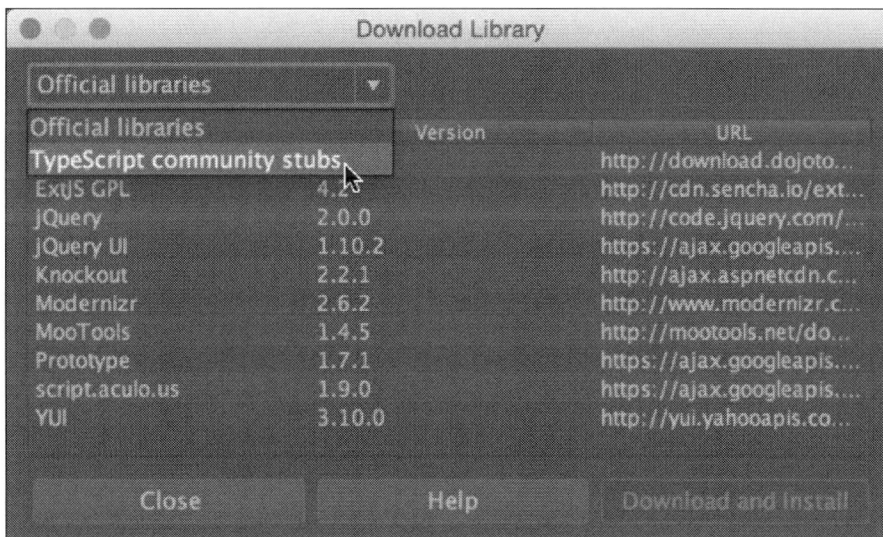

In this example, we are going to try and download support for `underscore.js`.

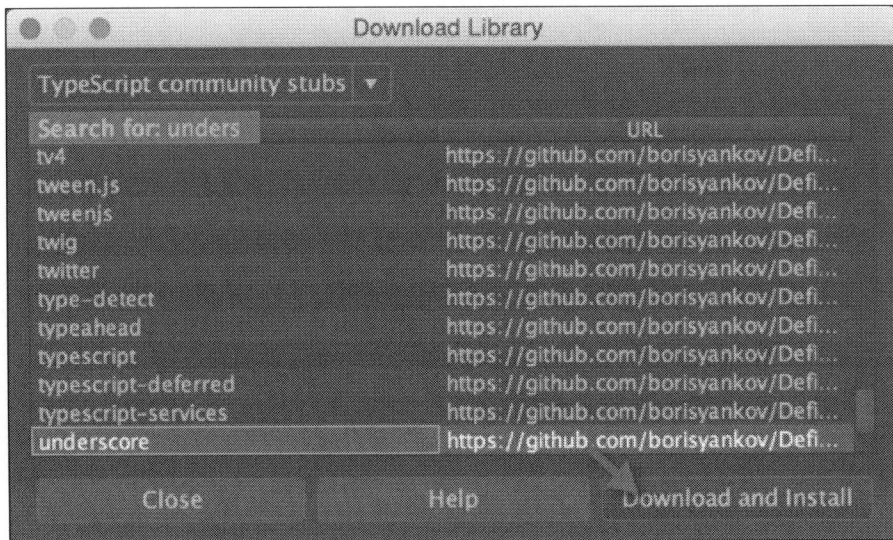

Once we've successfully downloaded the stub file for `underscore`, it will appear as a library that is supported by PyCharm:

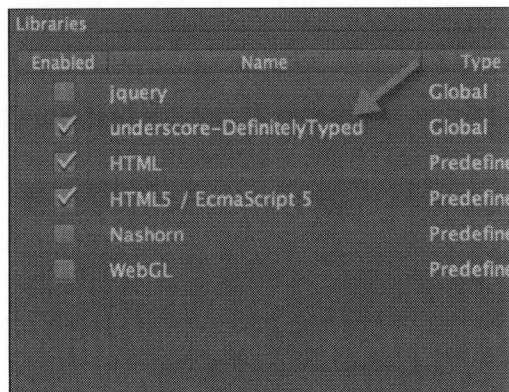

It is best to disable the **Enabled** box, and only assign library support to the files when you need it, otherwise, your suggestions will get overly cluttered.

We can now choose to include `underscore` as one of our libraries inside the file:

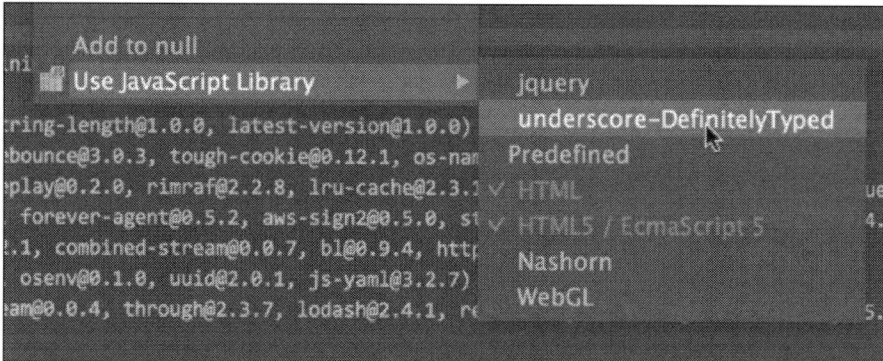

So, if we want to use `underscore` functions now, we get code completion as well as type checking (because TypeScript is a statically-typed language):

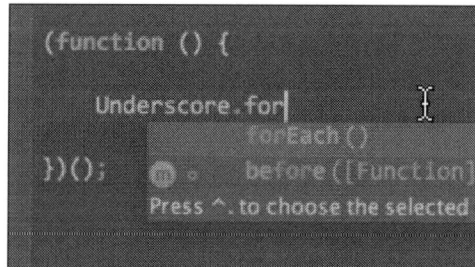

In most cases, I prefer using TypeScript stubs over the community or official documentation simply because the stubs are of very high quality and always provide type information that can be very handy when managing large projects.

Transpiled to JavaScript languages

PyCharm supports TypeScript and CoffeeScript (not the iced version though). Support extends quite far: code completion, syntax highlighting, and the automatic creation of map files are supported. Furthermore, automatic watchers to turn these files into .js files are added when you initialize a TypeScript or CoffeeScript file. Although no templates exist for automatic TypeScript or CoffeeScript creation, simply creating a file with a .ts or .coffee extension will cause PyCharm to recognize those files and provide the required code completion/syntax highlighting for those languages.

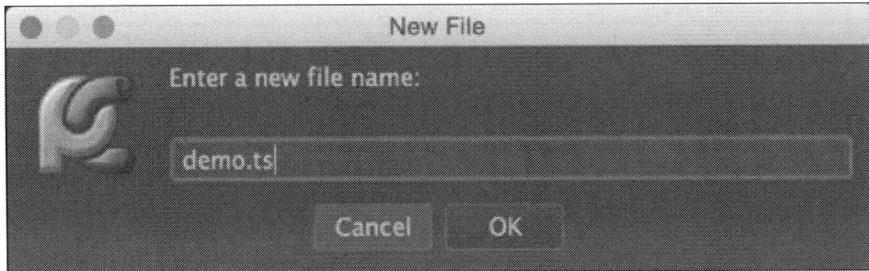

As soon as we create the file, PyCharm will prompt us to add the watcher that compiles this TypeScript file into a JavaScript file. It will also generate a map file to aid with debugging.

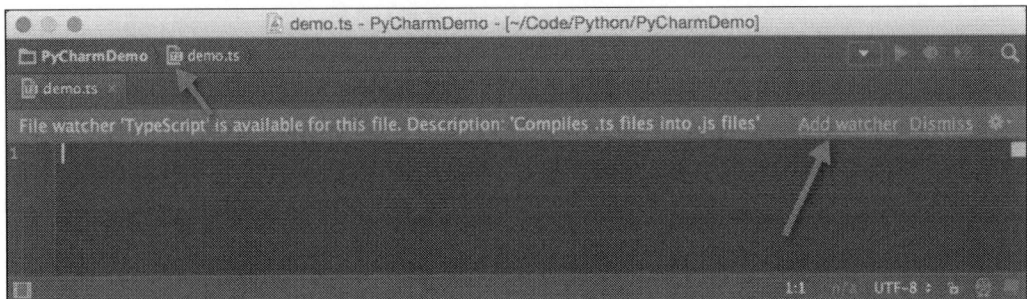

We can configure the watcher in the dialog window that pops up when we choose to add the watcher.

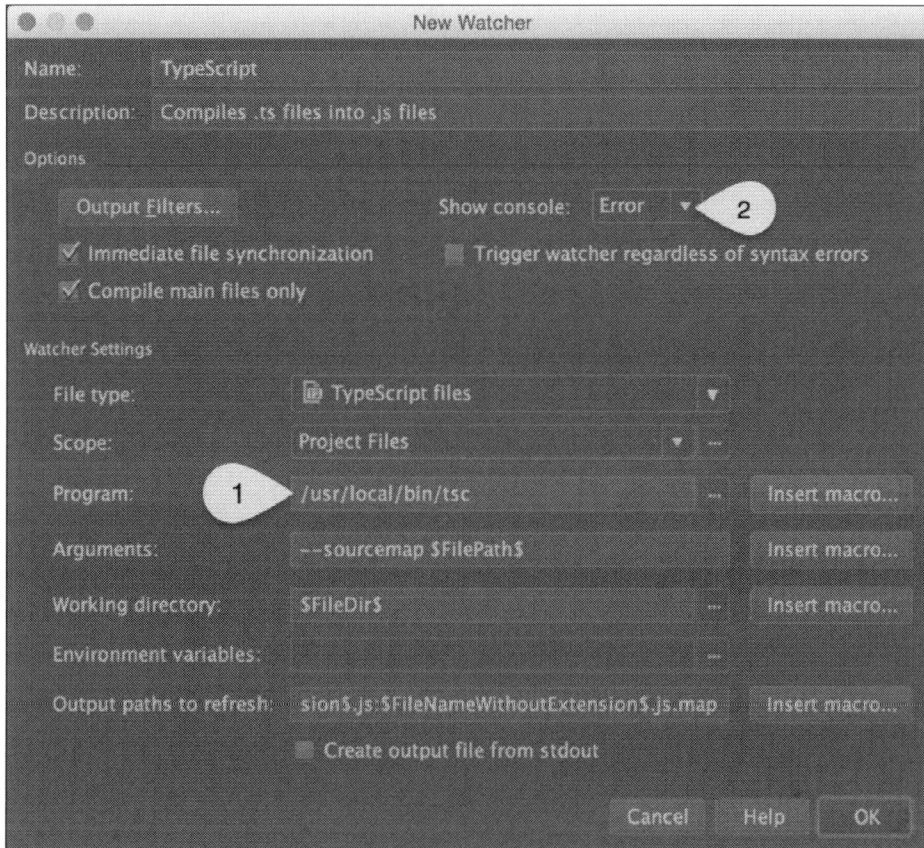

This may seem intimidating at first, but you really don't have to do anything other than say **OK** to all of this. We will go into depth about this later when we will talk about watchers. For now, the two most important parts of the whole dialog window are [1] and [2]. Number [1] indicates the TypeScript executable that will be used to compile your TypeScript file; make sure that you have TypeScript installed, and if you don't have it, simply install it by using the following command:

```
npm install -g typescript
```

Number [2] indicates when the console will be shown. As you write in your TypeScript file, PyCharm will automatically run the executable every single time you make a pause or save the file (this can be changed, however) and produce two files, a .js file and a .map file (which helps while debugging).

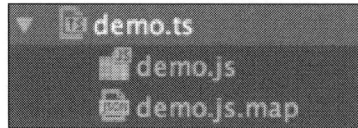

If the compilation causes an error, only then will you see the console pop up at the bottom of the PyCharm's window.

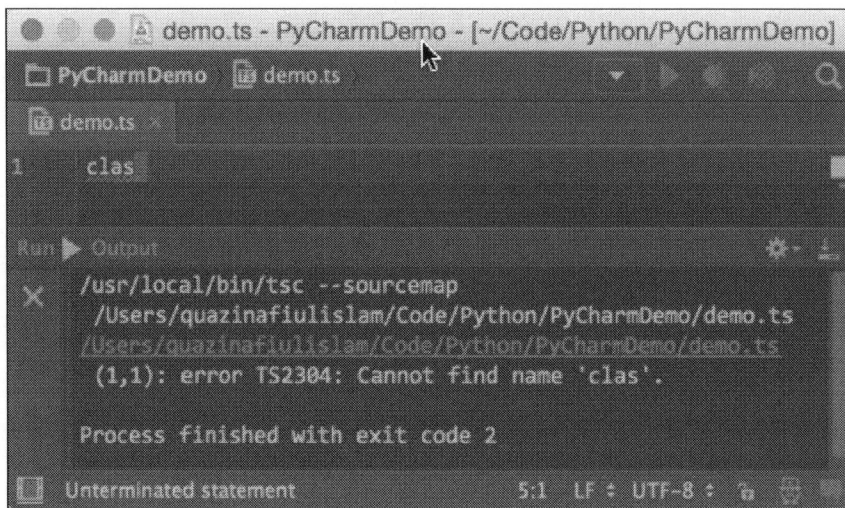

Notice how the window shows you what command was executed, and what the console output was. When we finally finish typing out class, the console will disappear.

This support is identical for CoffeeScript, with the only difference being that CoffeeScript will have a separate executable. However, ES6 support (using traceur) is a little different. In this case, we need to make sure that we have traceur installed; you can do that with the following command:

```
npm install -g traceur
```

To support ES6, we need to tell PyCharm that we want to use ES6 as our JavaScript standard. To do this, all we need to do is change the version number of ECMAScript that PyCharm is using.

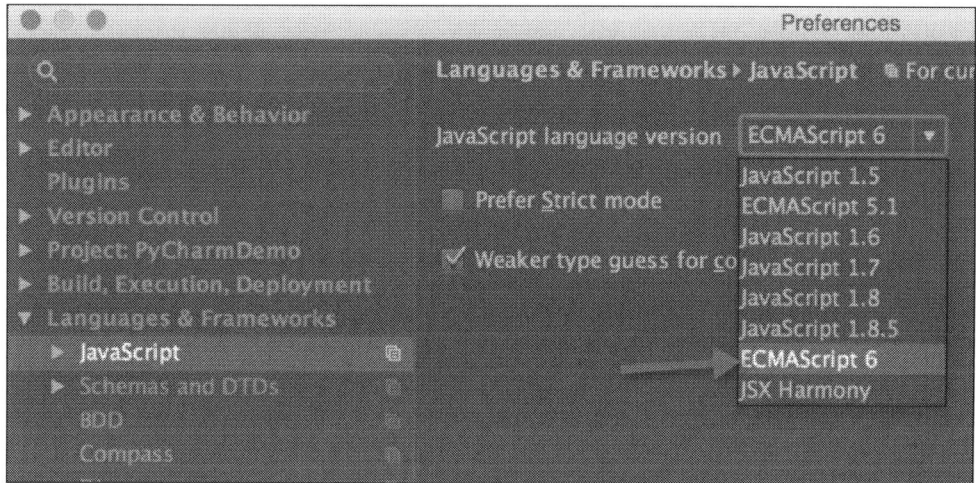

Unlike last time where we created a specific extension, to use ES6 all we need to do is create a new `.js` file, and PyCharm will ask us to add a `traceur` watcher for it.

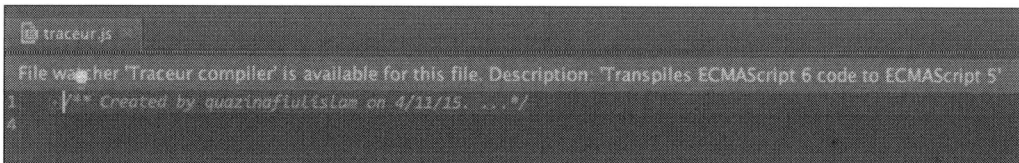

And once we add the watcher, the same thing will happen as it did for TypeScript, a dialog window will pop up, asking for an executable and other options.

Support for libraries and frameworks

Support for third-party frameworks is done through plugins. There are so many plugins that aid JavaScript development that it is impossible to cover them all. However, this section talks about the highlights of both the client- and server-side frameworks that are supported.

Client-side frameworks

Through plugins, PyCharm has excellent support for both client-side and server-side JavaScript frameworks. Think of PyCharm Professional as the PyCharm community + WebStorm (an IDE for building JavaScript applications).

On the client-side of things, PyCharm has support for AngularJS, and the support extends to having quick fixes for directives, the creation of controllers, and syntax highlighting for AngularJS templates.

PyCharm also supports Bower out of the box.

Server-side frameworks and NodeJS

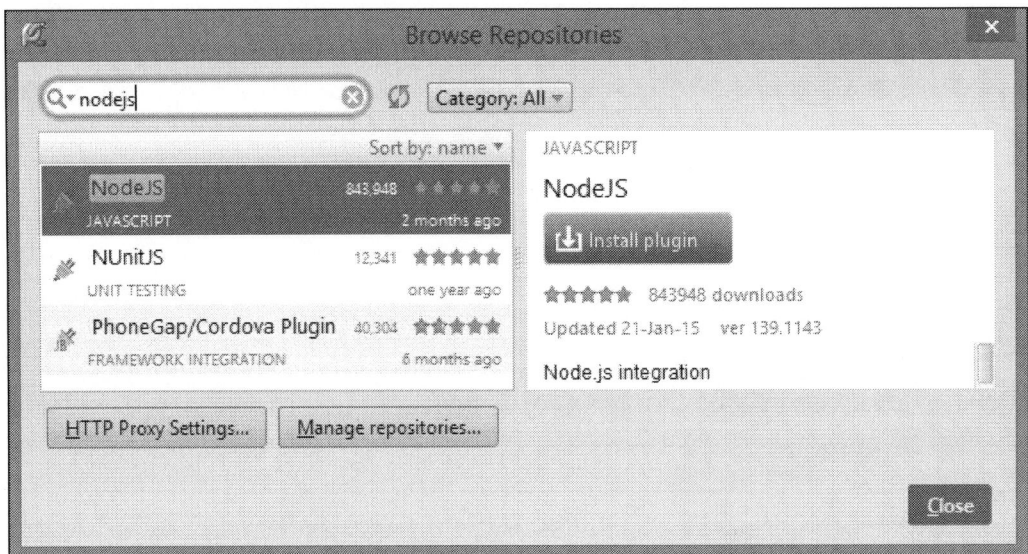

PyCharm can support NodeJS through plugins. If we install the NodeJS plugin, we will not only gain node support, but also gain access to custom project creation, with the Express framework. The NodeJS plugin also comes with support for managing the node modules (through npm) you have installed in your project.

JavaScript Code Quality Tools

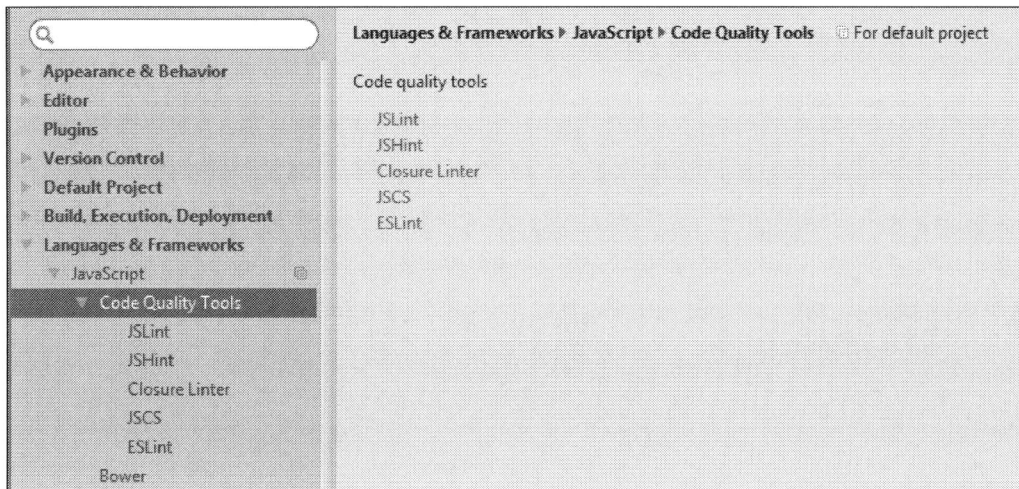

PyCharm supports a wide range of linters and other quality tools. However, please note that some tools require you to install node on your machine as well as point the node package that does the linting or the hinting for you.

HTML and CSS

HTML and CSS are well supported in PyCharm. This section is by no means exhaustive, but does provide a detailed account of the tools that will help you stay productive. PyCharm provides tag completion for HTML, but it has so much more than this that tag completion is the least exciting feature in its feature set.

Emmet

Emmet is essentially shorthand HTML and CSS. You type the abbreviations of what you want, hit *Tab*, and PyCharm will automatically convert that shorthand into the desired tags and subelements.

For example, if we were to type in `div.container`, we would be creating a `div` tag of the `container` class. In other words, the following:

```
div.container
```

turns into:

```
<div class="container"></div>
```

with your caret automatically placed inside the `div` tag.

This section won't teach you the basics of Emmet; the Emmet documentation site does a much better job: `http://docs.emmet.io/`

However, PyCharm has its own twist on Emmet, and this includes extra support for XML tags as well as automatic insertion of vendor prefixes that can be customized inside the Emmet subjection of the **Editor** settings. Depending on what CSS selector you're using, you can have PyCharm autocomplete browser prefixes for you and customize what browser prefixes you support. The default prefixes are updated with every PyCharm update.

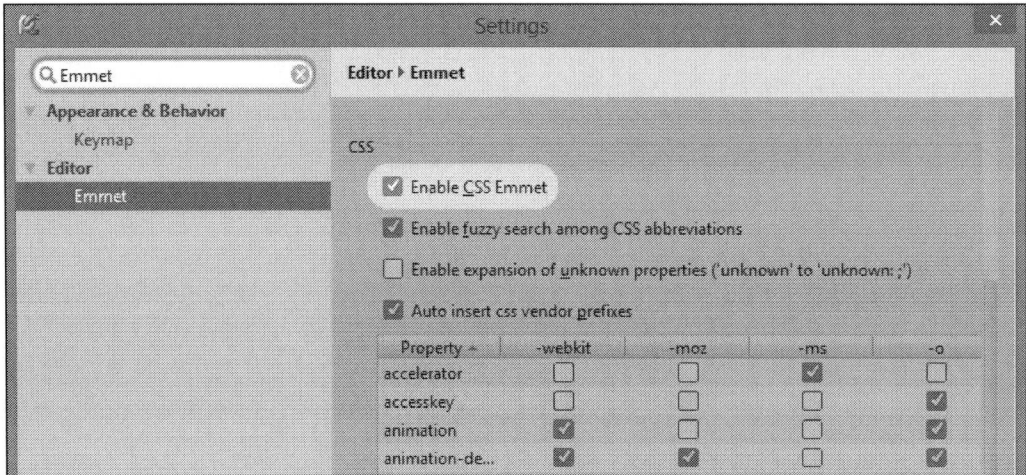

What Emmet for CSS essentially means is that now when we type in an attribute, such as `animation-delay`, we will get browser-specific attributes written for us as well.

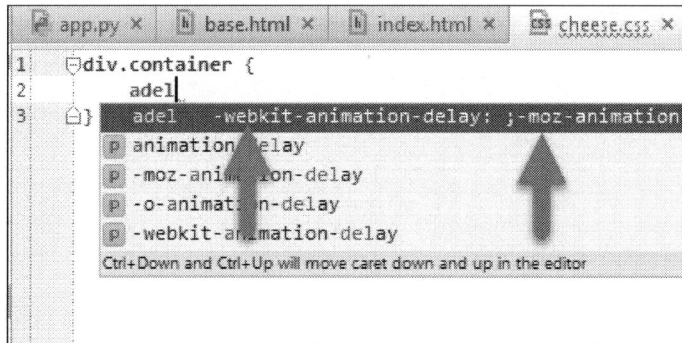

Emmet also supports surround templates. For example, we can make a selection, invoke **Surround With...**, and use Emmet abbreviations to surround the relevant HTML.

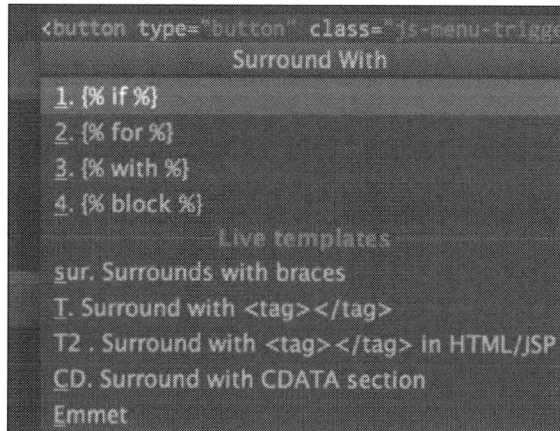

Live debugging

Live debugging is one of the best PyCharm features. It renders your HTML and CSS in real time, meaning that the changes you make inside your editor are reflected in your web browser. It also channels Chrome's JavaScript console directly to PyCharm's console, meaning that you can control your web browser directly from within PyCharm.

Installing the plugin

However, before we are allowed to use live edit or live debugging, we need to make sure that we have the **JetBrains IDE Support** extension installed.

Once this is installed, if we debug an HTML page, PyCharm will automatically figure out how to set up the connection between Chrome and itself. I wouldn't recommend messing with the settings of the extension, but I'm going to show you how to mess around with it anyway.

In most versions of Chrome, we see the JetBrains extension after we've turned on developer mode. In doing so, we gain access to the **Options** menu.

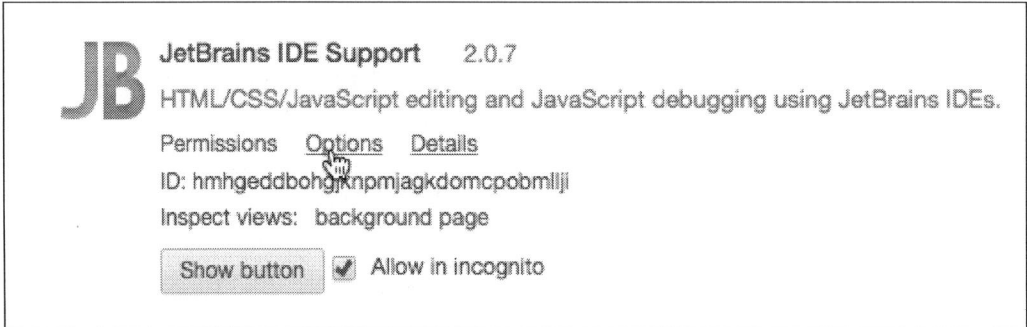

JB JetBrains IDE Support   2.0.7

HTML/CSS/JavaScript editing and JavaScript debugging using JetBrains IDEs.

Permissions   Options   Details

ID: hmhgeddbohgjknpmjagkdomcpobmllji

Inspect views: background page

Show button   ☑ Allow in incognito

Inside **Options**, we have a few things that we can change. First of all is the port number. JetBrains uses a pretty specific port number, so don't change it unless you absolutely need to (in case you see a connection refused error pop up somewhere in PyCharm).

However, there is an option that allows you to whitelist a few sites that you want to make cross-site requests to (in case your security options are preventing a request to a specific site).

Debugging the file

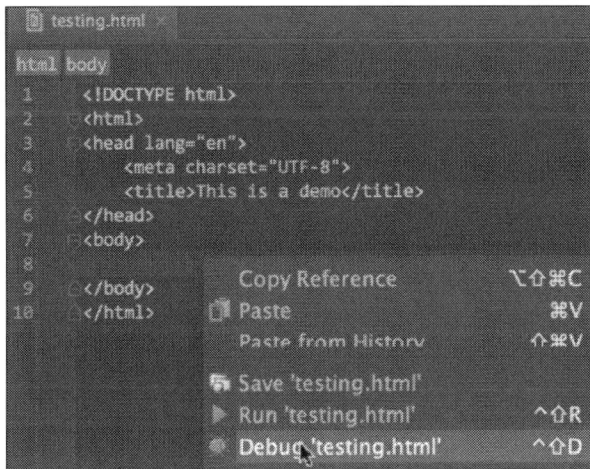

Unfortunately, I can't show you the pure awe that you feel when using live debugging, I simply can't convey it through a book (because it's something that's happening). But here are a few things to note:

- At the start, you will see a notification in Chrome, saying **JetBrains IDE Support is debugging this tab**.

- Any change to the HTML file will be reflected in the browser. In case it isn't, you can always use the **Reload in Browser** command.

- CSS changes are also reflected instantaneously, even with SASS and SCSS files, since PyCharm incrementally builds them.

- You can run JavaScript inside the console that pops up in PyCharm, and see it reflected in the console inside Chrome. Try it! Just run `alert("I am from the future");` into the console and see what happens.

- Whatever you select with your cursor in PyCharm will be directly reflected in Chrome.

- Make sure to disconnect after your debugging session, otherwise, the port used by PyCharm stays open.

- You can set breaking inside your JavaScript files as well as your transpiled to JavaScript files and debug the script when it's executing from PyCharm.

This is such a neat feature that I always debug when I edit. This may just be because I'm never really sure if my styles work the way I want them to, but it's good fun anyway.

File watchers

File watchers are language and framework agnostic, but I feel that they are most relevant when working with HTML, CSS, JavaScript, and transpiled languages. Previously, we talked a little about file watchers in this chapter as I wanted to showcase the simplest way of setting up a watcher that suits most needs. However, the file watchers in PyCharm are very powerful and allow you to leverage macros.

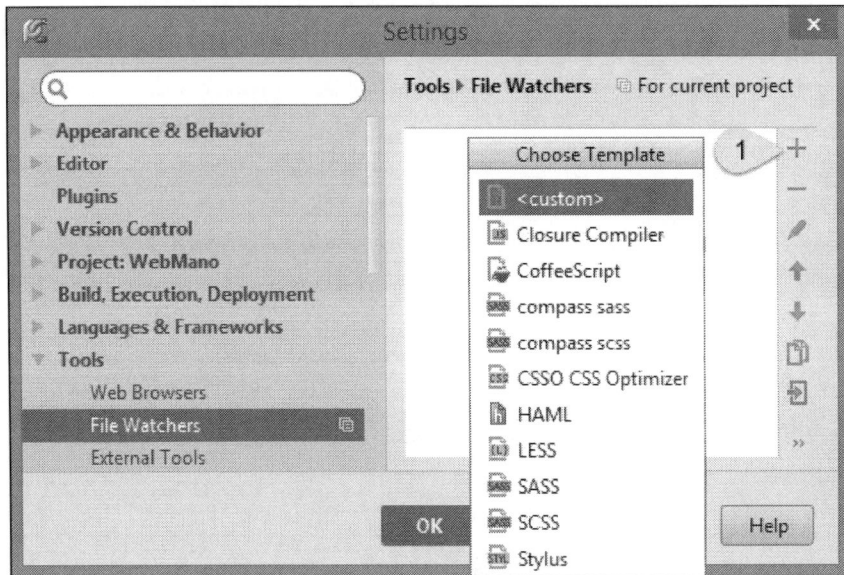

File watchers essentially run a tool on a kind of specified file after that file has been changed. For example, most of the preceding templates are for transpiled languages such as CoffeeScript and LESS. However, some of them carry out different tasks such as the CSSE CSS Optimizer template. Let's start off by looking at a sample template.

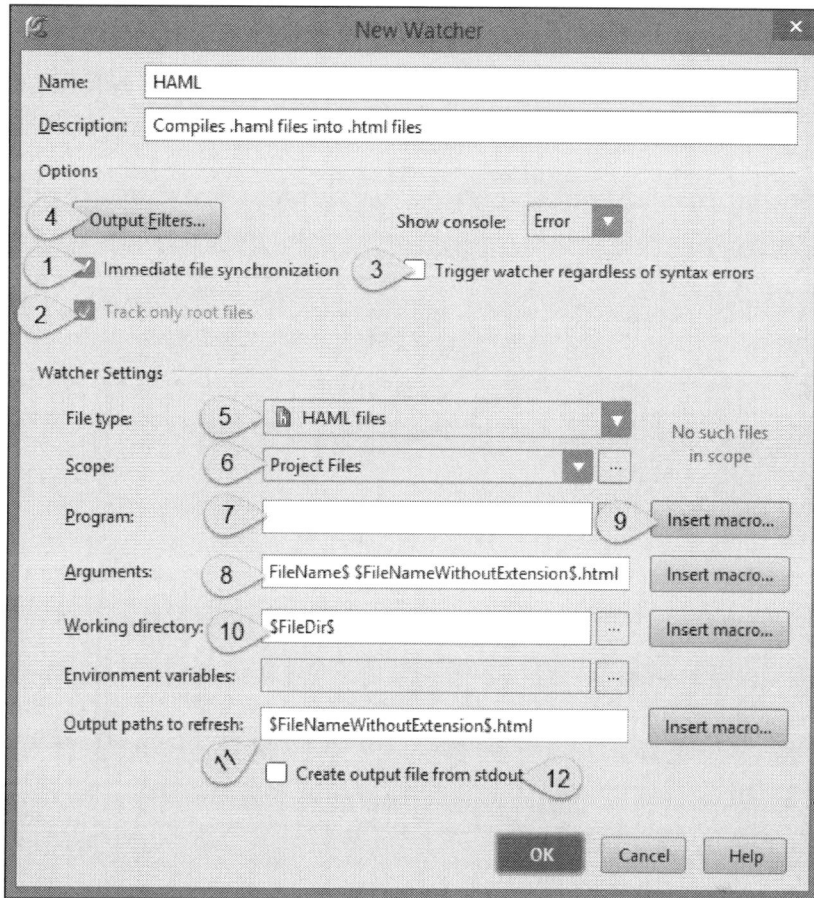

- **Immediate file synchronization**: This means that the file watcher will run the desired task if there is a change in the file; it does not matter whether the file is saved or not. This is enabled, by default, on most templates, but if your tool takes time to run, then disabling it would be best.

- **Track only root files**: This is a more subtle feature. Root files are files not included in any other file. In other words, the files that the HAML watcher is watching are the files that aren't imported anywhere in any other file. You might think that this is rather useless, but consider a language such as SCSS, which can import other SCSS files. We have a main SCSS file that we are actually going to import into our HTML. This means that when any file that is imported is changed, the watcher only runs on the main SCSS file. This saves a lot of compile time.

- **Trigger watcher regardless of syntax errors**: This is self-explanatory. However, I highly recommend that you keep it turned off since the console popping up and then automatically closing down again can be rather annoying since screen space is eaten up.

- **Output Filters...**: This allows you to use PyCharm to recognize the output from the watcher. For example, the TypeScript watcher can recognize the file path and the line numbers on which the error has occurred because of the output filter that it has enabled by default.

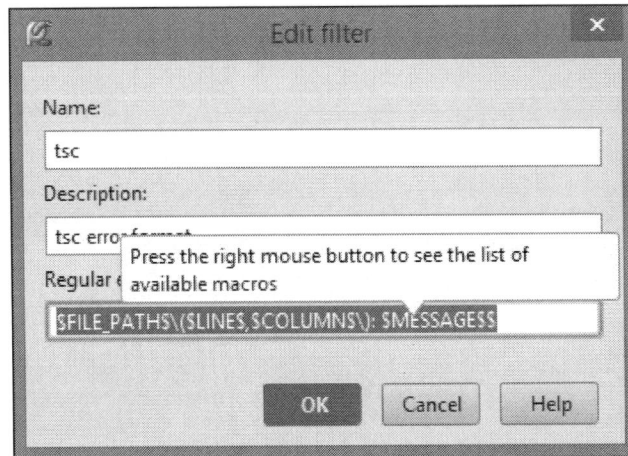

Due to this output filter, PyCharm can make links from the output console to the error in question. The `$<ALLCAPS>$` variables are macros. These macros are used to recognize where the file is and the line and column number of the error message.

- **File type**: This indicates the file type. You can only watch files with extensions recognized by PyCharm. So, in order to add a watcher for a file that is not normally recognized by PyCharm, you need to add recognition for that file by navigating to **Editor | File and Code Templates**

- **Scope**: This specifies the scope of the watcher. Although the default is what you always ought to be using, there are many other options as well that you can explore, for example **Open Files**.

- **Program**: This links program/executable to the program that is doing the task.

- **Arguments**: Don't ever change this if you don't know what you're doing, it's easy to get it wrong. These are basically the arguments that are fed into the program. Notice how macros are used here again to specify a generic way of passing in parameters.

- **Insert macro…**: This allows you to insert macros and preview them as well. Please note that it has a few quirks, for example, the Python interpreter is pointed to as $JDKPath$.

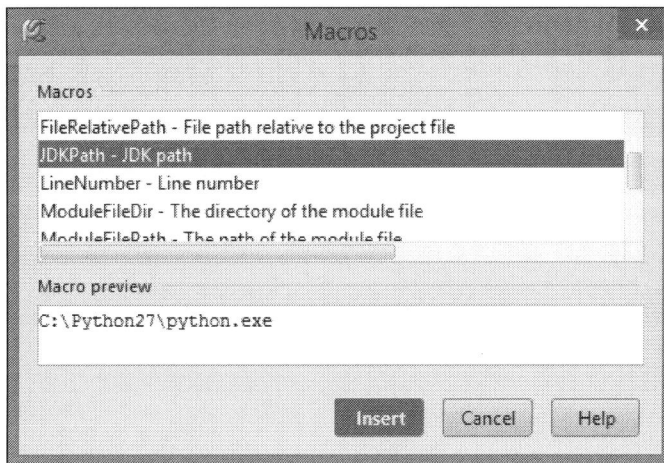

- **Working directory**: This also takes in macros but also accepts hardcoded file paths. This is the directory of where the output file will go.

- **Output paths to refresh**: Once again, a macro is used here to refer to the compiled file. If the files were not refreshed, then live debugging would not seem to work since the compiled files would not be refreshed.

- **Create output file from stdout**: Only use this if the output of your program gets directly printed into stdout.

Summary

This is by no means an exhaustive account of PyCharm's web development prowess, but it does showcase its unique features that I myself have come to deeply appreciate. We focused on code completion and support for transpiled languages in JavaScript and took a look at the tools that will boost our HTML and CSS productivity. Live debugging is probably the best tool of the lot, and something that you should take full advantage of. File watchers were also covered in detail as they offer a very powerful way of handling task management and can be a good alternative to Gulp and Grunt.

11
Web Development with PyCharm

In this last and final chapter, we are going to look at the database and framework support that PyCharm provides out of the box. PyCharm allows you to connect almost any kind of database, and will automatically download JDBC drivers for you to act as an interface. It also has support for multiple web frameworks such as Flask, Django, Pyramid, and GAE. This chapter introduces you to some of the best tools that PyCharm has to offer for web development. However, this chapter does not go into great depth; instead it opts to showcase the most useful features. Here is an outline of what we're going to cover:

- **Database tools**: This section will deal with connecting to databases and using PyCharm as a complete interface to the database. Please note that, for now, PyCharm only supports RDBMSes.

- **Web frameworks**: This section will look into the different web frameworks that PyCharm supports, starting with common tools and then eventually heading off to framework-specific subtopics.

Database tools

PyCharm supports interfacing with almost any database. Once you give PyCharm a created database, it can give you the schema of the database, generate a diagram of all the tables and how they are connected, and provide you with SQL writing tools that have code completion.

Adding a data source

In PyCharm you cannot create databases, but provides facilities to manage and query them. Once you are granted access to a certain database, you can configure one or more data sources within PyCharm that reflect the structure of the database and store the database access credentials.

Connecting to a database

Adding an existing database is a simple process of configuring the hostname and port and providing the authentication details required for the connection. It might take a while to initially configure the database since PyCharm will need to download JDBC drivers in order to do so. To add a database, we must first select a type.

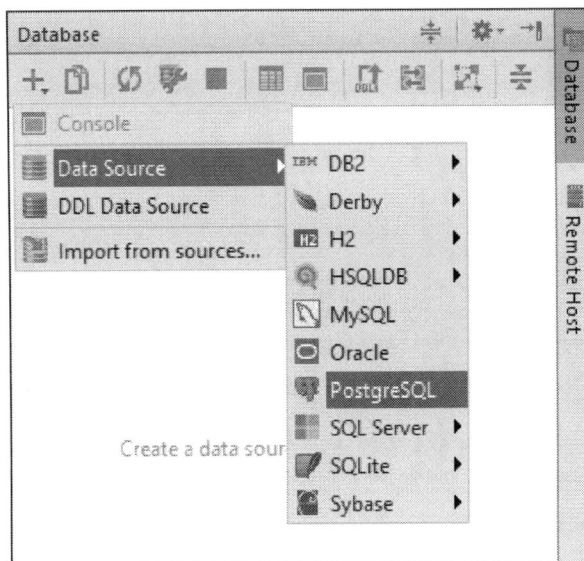

In this case, we are going to connect to an existing **PostgreSQL** database.

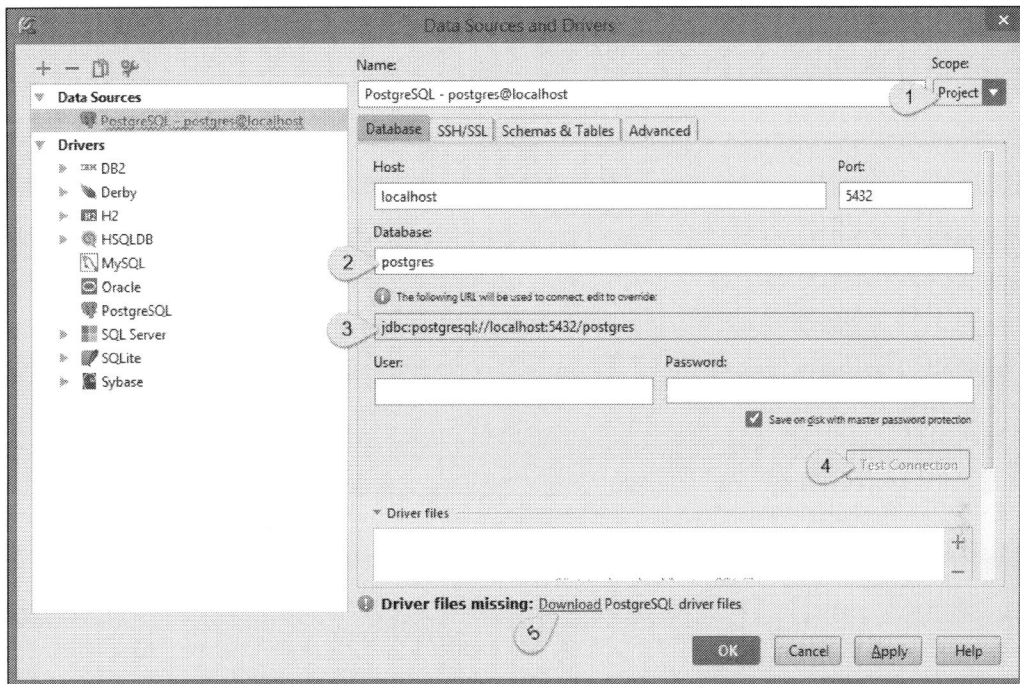

When adding a database, we can set its scope. When we set the scope to **Project** [1], we tell PyCharm that this database is only relevant for this particular project. If we set it to **IDE**, the database will be available on every single project in our database panel.

[2] is the name of the database we want to connect to and [3] will be generated automatically as the connection URL. The reason that we cannot test the connection using [4] is because PyCharm does not have the downloaded drivers; we can fix this by just clicking on the link in [5].

Once we download the files, we should be able to see that PyCharm is using the PostgreSQL drivers in the **Driver files** subsection.

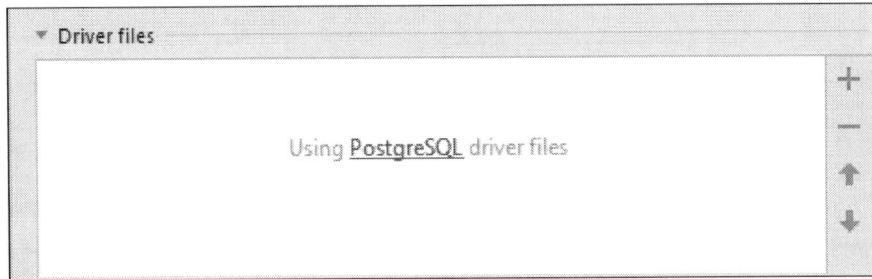

After installing the drivers and setting the credentials, we should now be able to test our connection.

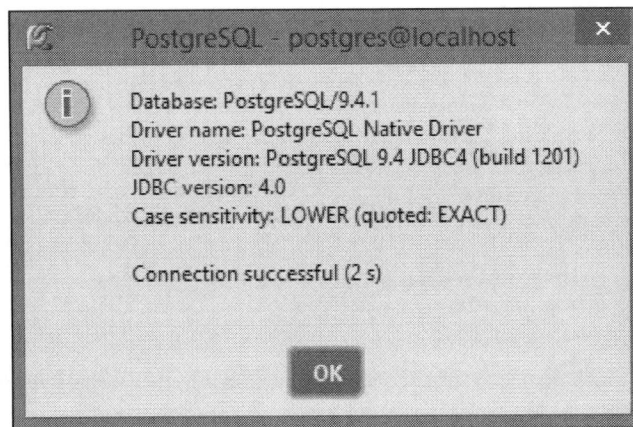

Adding files

We can even add .ddl files or sqlite databases (.db files) just by dragging and dropping them into the database panel. We can then query the files as if they were any other database.

Using the SQL console

Using the SQL console in PyCharm gives us many features, including code completion, error detection, diagram generation, and much more. Let's start by firing up the console for the newly added database.

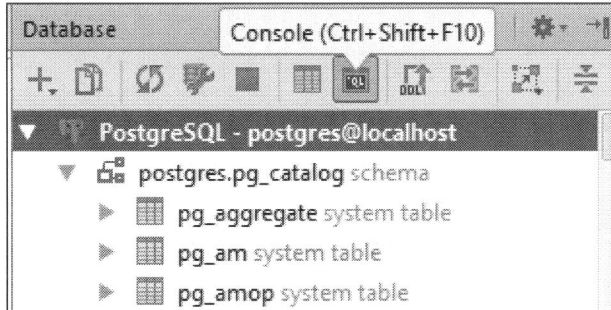

The console allows us to input SQL into the database, and the first thing we are going to do is create a schema called demo.

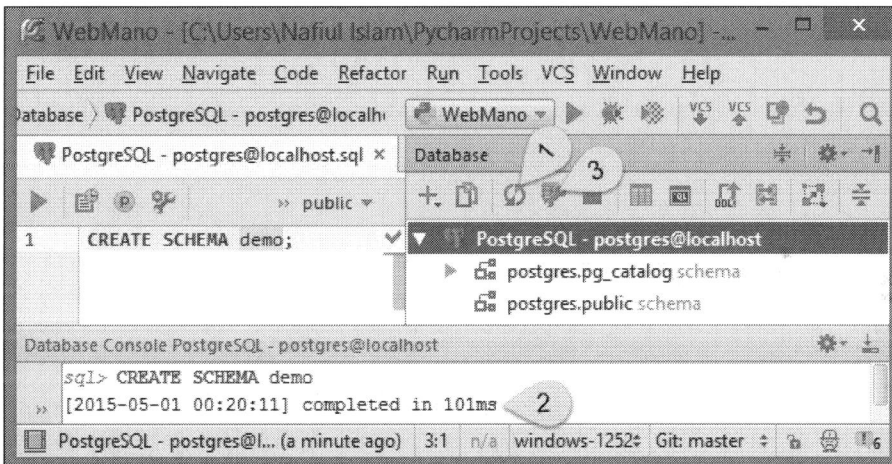

Once we run the SQL, we should expect to see the changes reflected in the database panel on the right-hand side since the statement was executed as shown in [2]. Our first point of call might be to synchronize using [1], but even that will not solve the problem because PyCharm offers you better code completion by only taking into consideration the schemas that you want considered.

The solution is to change the list of schemas that PyCharm does take into consideration using [3], which will allow us to once again configure our database.

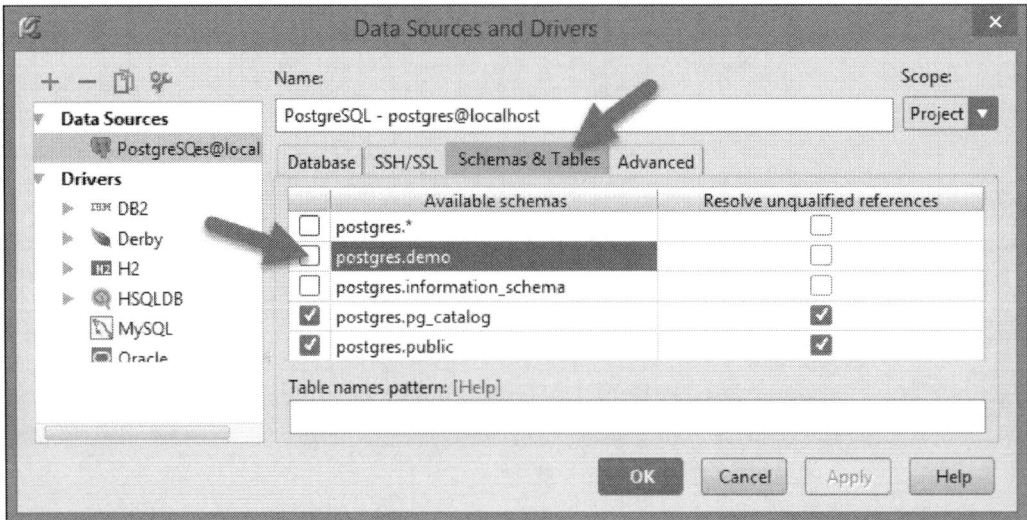

Underneath the **Schemas & Tables** tab, we must enable the `postgres.demo` schema. Once enabled, we can set the schema as our default schema. If we disable all the other schemas except for the `demo` schema, PyCharm will only provide us with code completion from the `demo` schema. This makes code completion a lot faster, and as a result, makes PyCharm a lot more responsive. This feature also extends to tables.

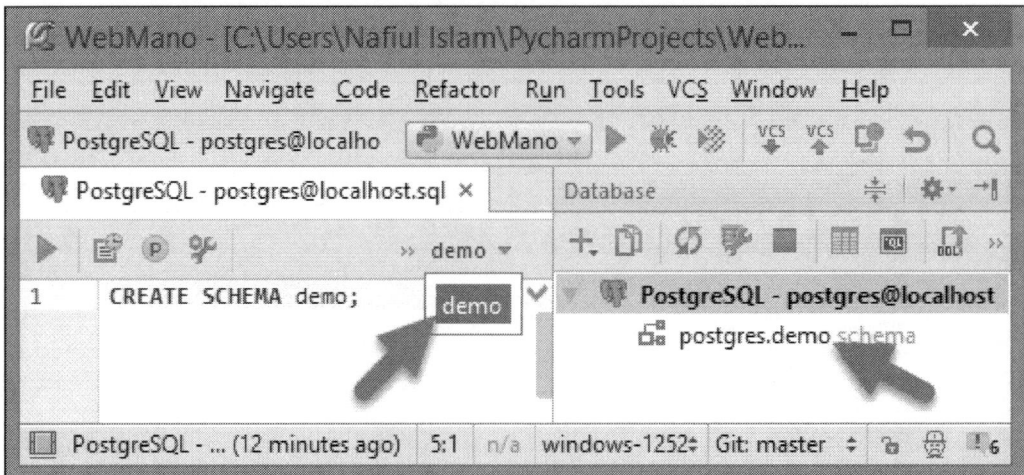

We can now begin creating a table called `students` under the `demo` schema.

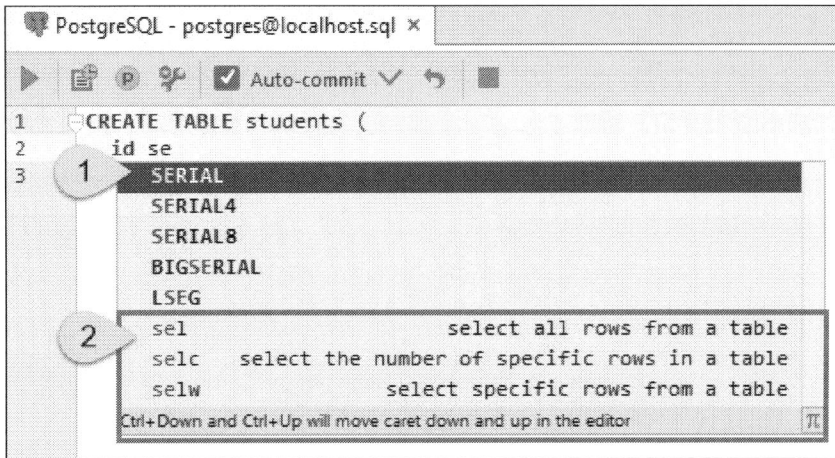

Note how PyCharm offers us possible types in [1]. We can also see that there are a few snippets available to us in [2]. PyCharm also provides table-specific completions and catches silly mistakes.

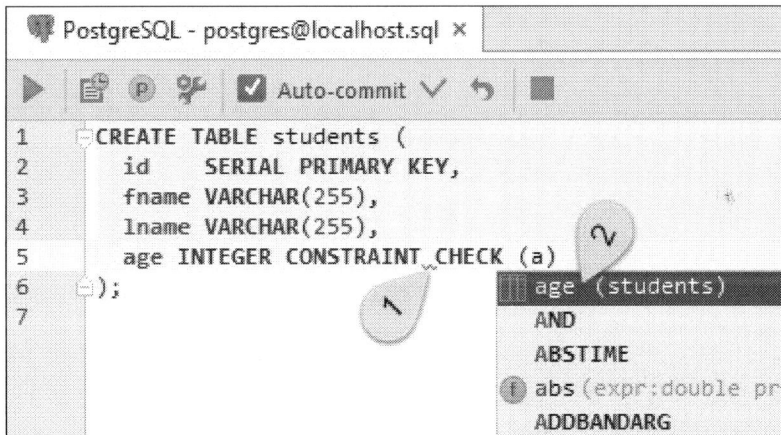

In [1], we forgot to add a name for the constraint, and in [2], we are provided with `age` as a possible completion. Note that other completions such as function calls are also suggested.

The complete schema looks similar to this:

```
CREATE TABLE students (
    id    SERIAL PRIMARY KEY,
    fname VARCHAR(255),
    lname VARCHAR(255),
    age   INTEGER CONSTRAINT minimum_age CHECK (age > 4)
);
```

It is a very simple table, but with it, we can illustrate a few points. First, the console only allows you to execute one selection or a statement at a time. This means we have to select the SQL we want to execute or place our cursor on a statement; otherwise, the green button will remain grayed out and *Ctrl + Enter* will result in nothing happening.

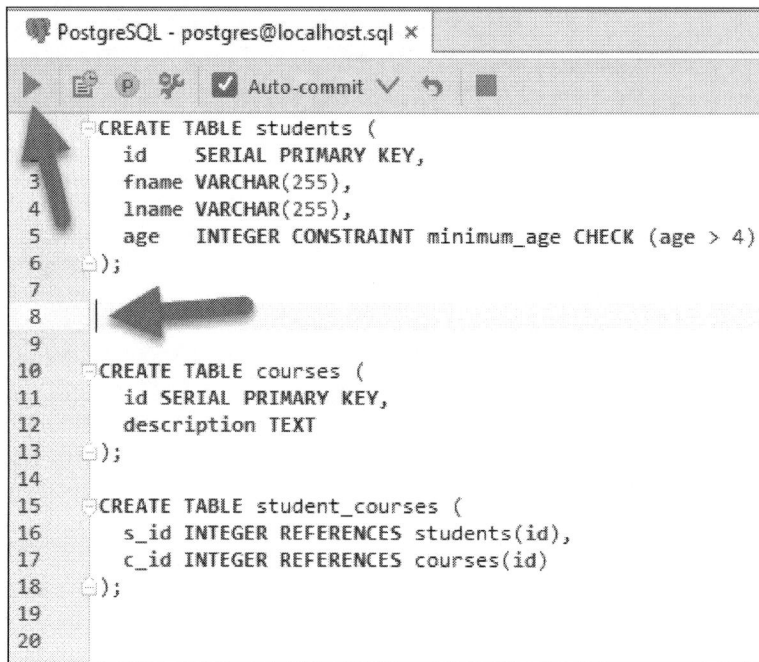

This means that if we have multiple statements as in the preceding screenshot, we need to select all of them; otherwise, only the statement we currently have our cursor on will execute. Once we have selected the statements we want to be executed, the results will appear in the console.

Parameterized statements

PyCharm allows us to reuse statements using parameters, and is particularly useful when we want to enter a sequence of statements. In this case, we want to create three students, so we are going to parameterize the statement using question marks:

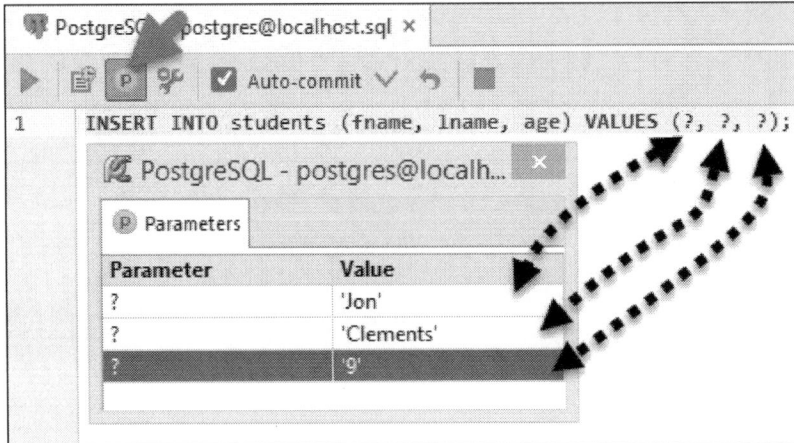

Opening up the parameters window (indicated by the red arrow) will allow us to enter different values for the three parameters. Please note that this window might pop up on the right-hand side as an attachment to the database console.

Console history

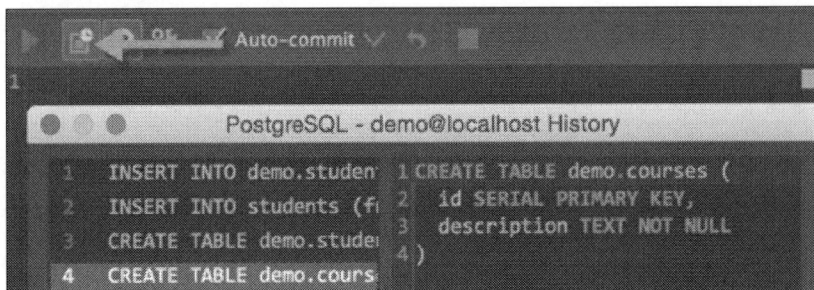

We can reuse any of the statements we've entered into a console session. The console sessions are saved for each project; so even if we were to close PyCharm, the history would remain intact.

Database diagrams

If we want a bird's eye view of how the tables in a certain schema are related to each other, we can use PyCharm's database visualization tools.

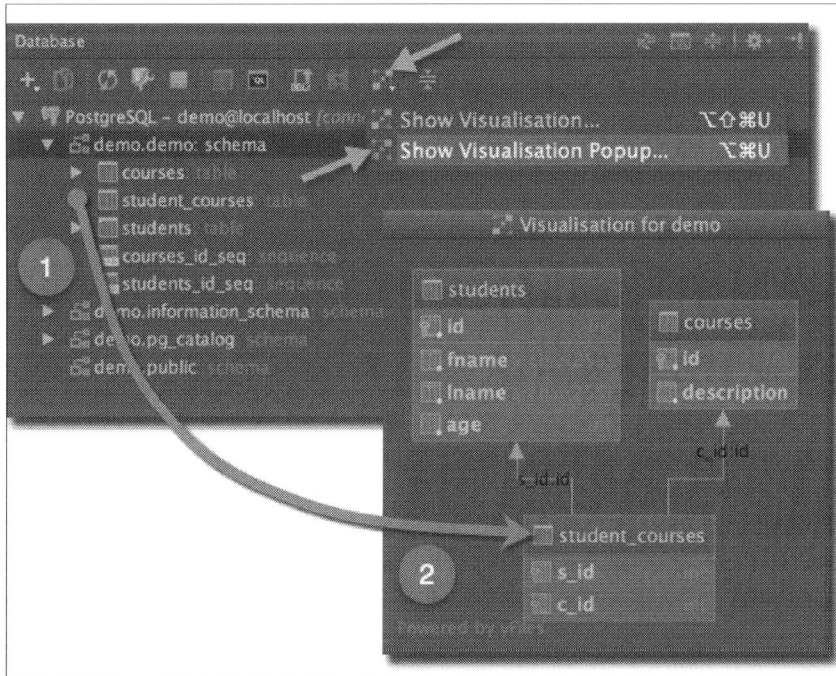

In the preceding screenshot, we first selected the schema and then we visualized the tables in the schema; if we wanted to see the relationships between just a subset of the tables in the schema, we could just select those tables and then visualize only those tables in the selection in addition to the tables that they're taking a reference from. So, if we were to visualize student_courses, we would get a visualization of all three tables, because student_courses is related to the other two tables as well.

Exporting data

PyCharm allows us to export pretty much anything from a database, ranging from the contents to a single table in JSON or CSV to the DDL required to construct all the tables in a schema. There are so many options here that we can only dive into a few, and talk about some of the unexpected behavior we see.

Copying DDLs

DDLs allow you to recreate tables. If we were to select a schema, table, or a subset of tables in a schema, PyCharm would be able to generate the DDL required to create all the tables that fall under the schema or our selection of tables. So, for example, if we copy the DDL for our `courses: table`, we simply select the courses as our table and copy the DDL.

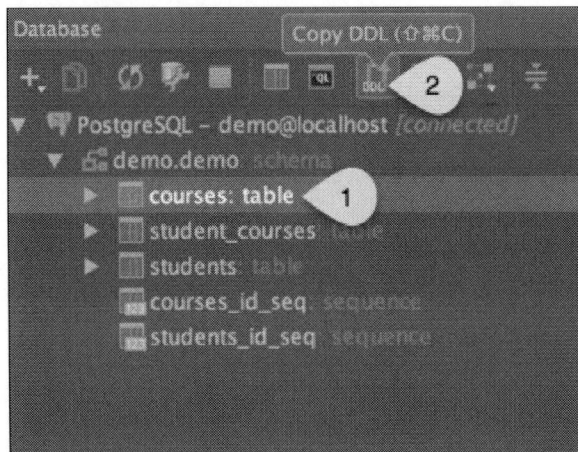

The resulting DDL will be the following:

```
CREATE TABLE courses (
    id SERIAL PRIMARY KEY NOT NULL,
    description VARCHAR NOT NULL );
```

We can do the same thing by selecting a schema, table, or a set of tables within a schema. However, note that the SQL generated may differ from what was originally entered.

Exporting the table contents

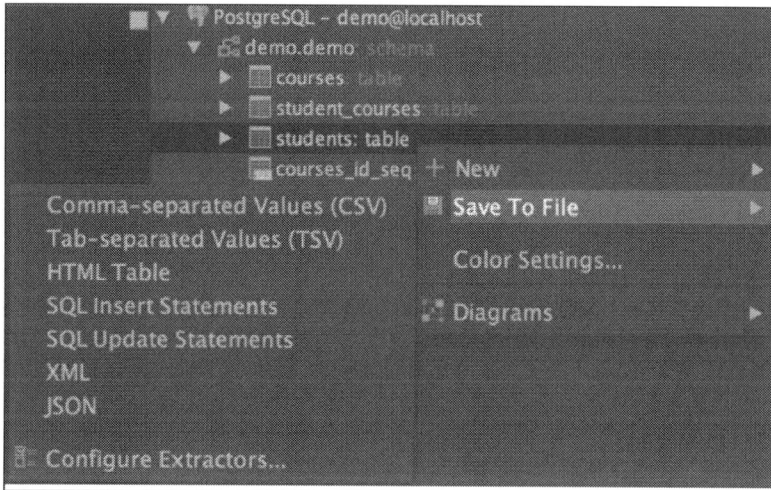

We can export the data in our tables in a myriad of ways. As shown in the preceding screenshot, we can export pretty much every file type imaginable from CSV to JSON. Furthermore, we can customize how we export CSVs, TSVs, and HTML tables in configure extractors.

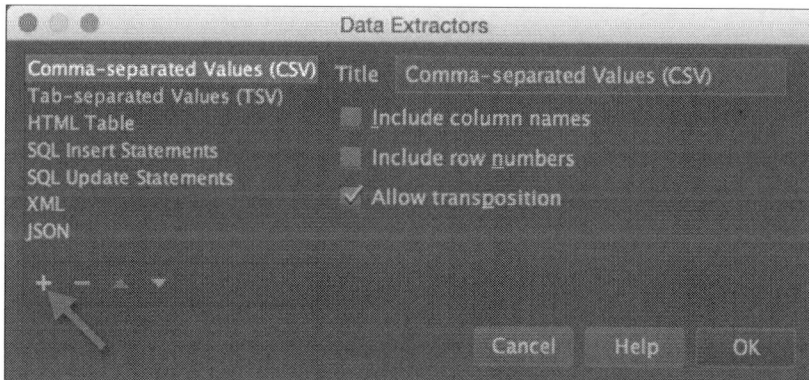

We can even configure new formats of export (based on the current formats that already exist) as separate options using the + icon indicated by the red arrow.

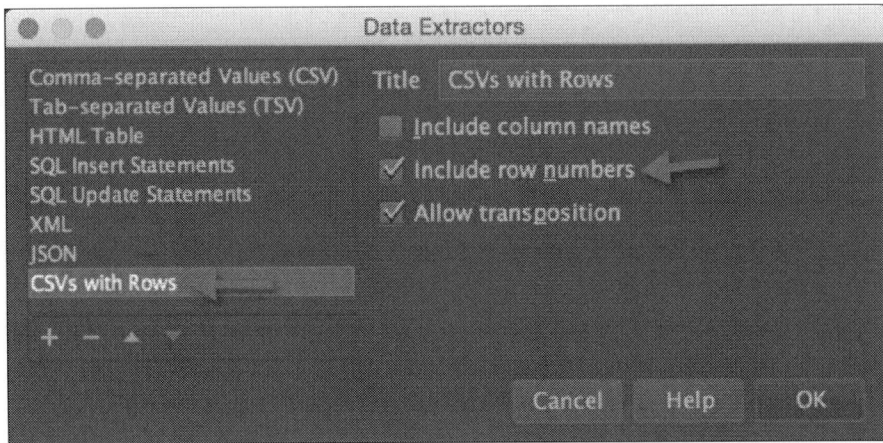

Web frameworks

PyCharm supports a wide range of Python frameworks. All the frameworks share common features such as setting the templating directory and mapping views to those templates; however, they also have their own unique feature sets, such as Django having very good code completion for its ORM. In the following subtopics, we will discuss common and specialized features for the different frameworks that PyCharm supports.

Although SQLAlchemy is not a web framework, PyCharm supports it just like it supports Django's ORM, giving you good code completion and being able to generate model dependency diagrams.

Common features

All the frameworks share some common features such as project creation. Here are a few of the common features that will help you with development in any framework.

Support for templating engines

Most frameworks will serve templated files. PyCharm supports a multitude of Python-based templating engines. Setting the templating engine and the `template` folder allows us to get code completion inside our templates. We can demonstrate this by first creating a Flask (or any other framework, for that matter) project. All we need to create a Flask project is an `app.py` file like this:

```
from flask import Flask

app = Flask(__name__)


@app.route('/')
def index():
    return "Hello World!"


if __name__ == '__main__':
    app.run()
```

The preceding code is very simple. It creates a simple Flask application using `Flask(__name__)`, then assigns it to the variable `app`, registers a route for the `/` path, and finally, runs it using `app.run()`. The `route` function simply returns `Hello World`. We are going to change the `index` function to render a template. The first thing we're going to do is create **Template Folder** in our current directory and mark it as a `template` directory.

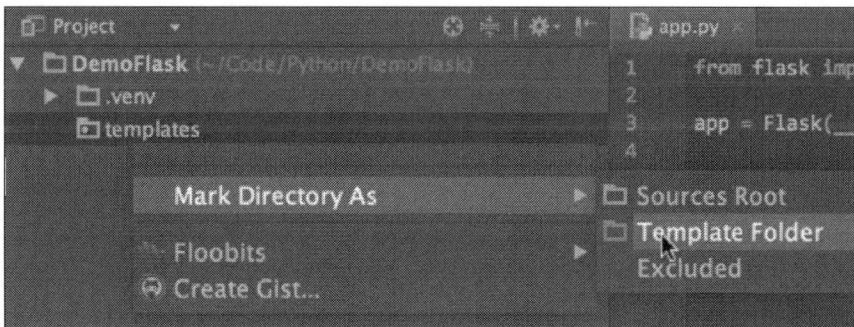

Once we've set this, we need to set the templating language as well.

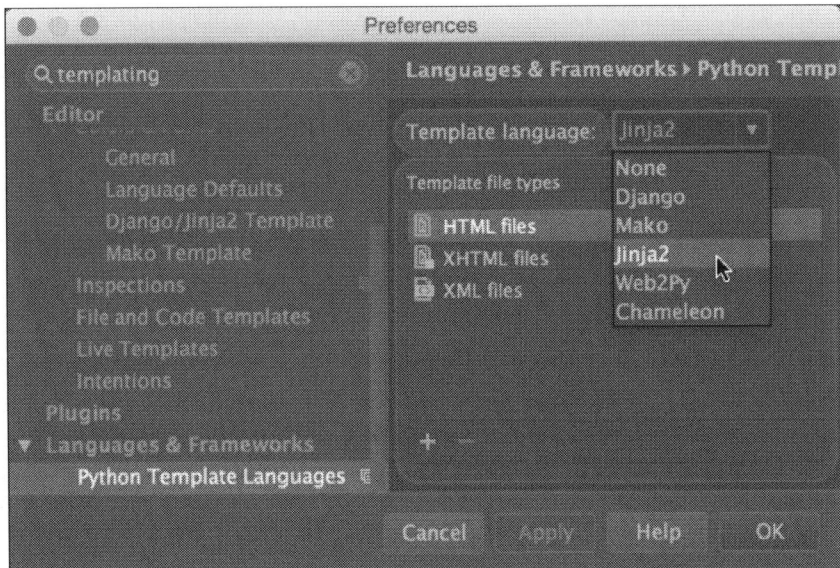

Flask uses Jinja2 by default, but we can use other templating languages as well such as Mako. We can now create an `index.html` file and get code completion for variables, but before we do that, let's modify our `index` function to render a template.

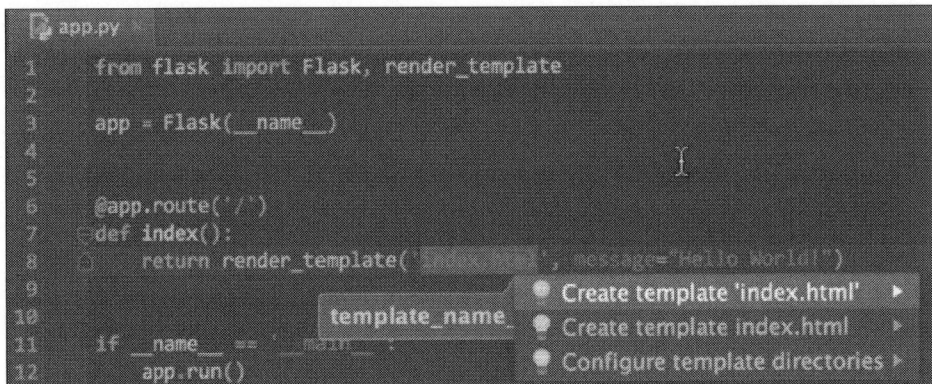

In the preceding example, we are using `render_template` to render the Jinja2 template file in question. Once we input `index.html` as our first parameter, PyCharm understands that such a template file does not exist in our `templates` directory and allows us to use a quick-fix for it (*Alt + Enter*). If we choose the **Create template 'index.html'** option, PyCharm will create the `index.html` file inside our **Template Folder**.

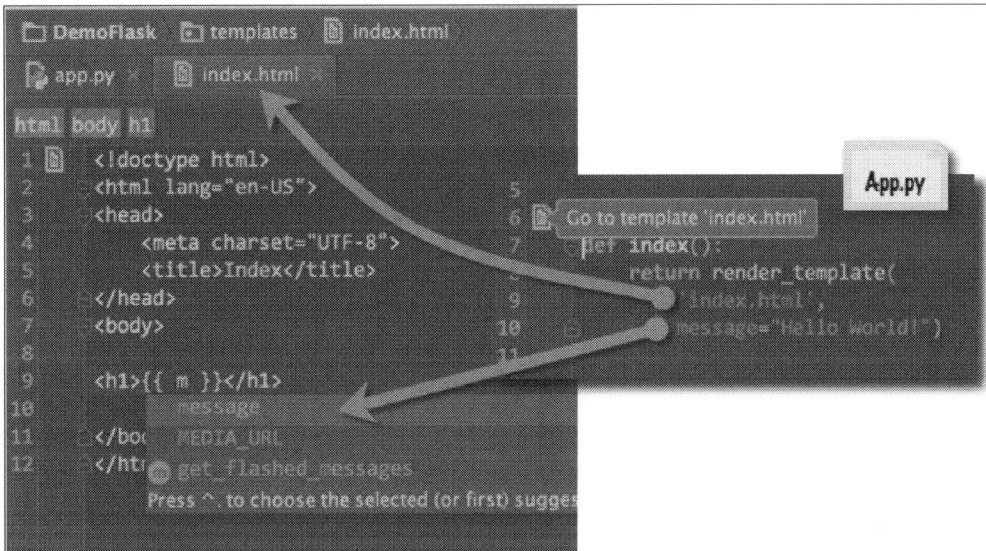

Furthermore, this template file will be linked to our view file and we will be able to get code completion for the variables we pass onto the template. In this case, we can see that message is popping up as an option when we type in `m`.

Customized project creation

PyCharm allows us to create projects for the different frameworks, with boilerplate code. For example, if we choose to create a Pyramid by navigating to **File | New Project... | Pyramid**, we will see a lot of customized options in **More Settings**.

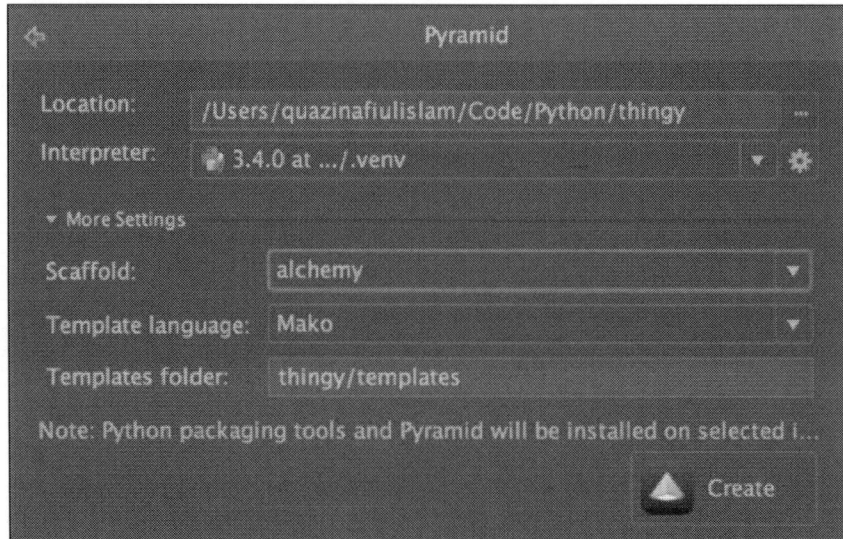

This means that PyCharm will automatically set **Templates folder**, create all the boilerplate files and download as well as install all the libraries necessary for the project we wish to create. This is very useful for quickly creating a project, especially on a Windows system.

If we were to create a Google App Engine application, the project creator would ask for our app ID in the creation window. All the **Project Creators** are customized to their individual frameworks with some common options such as the templates folder.

However, it is worth noting that all this will create files and install packages for you; it does not mean that the files themselves will be adapted to our choices. For example, if we were to create a Flask project using Mako as our templating engine, it would not mean that Flask would render Mako templates, it would still render using the default Jinja2 templating engine. We would still need to configure Flask to use Mako as the templating engine instead of the default one.

Debugging in templates

PyCharm allows you to set breakpoints inside our templates. This means that when we are debugging (not just running) our application, PyCharm will stop at the template's breakpoint. We don't need to do anything other than click on the line on the left-hand side to enable a breakpoint.

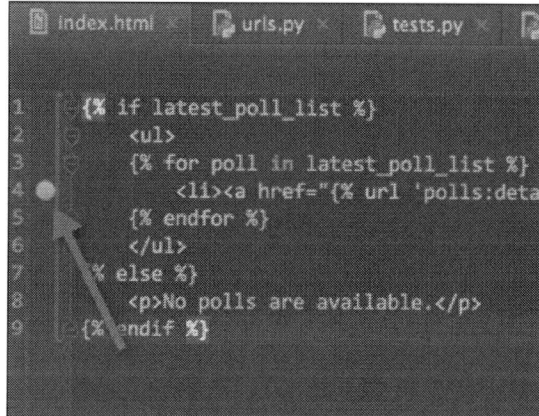

Django

Django is by far the best supported Python framework in PyCharm. Most of the support lies in code completion (and will therefore become self-evident), so this section looks at the tooling for Django.

Setting up Django

For a Django project that was not created by the PyCharm project creator, we have a little bit of configuration that we need to take care of.

First off, if we have an old Django project, PyCharm will offer to convert it.

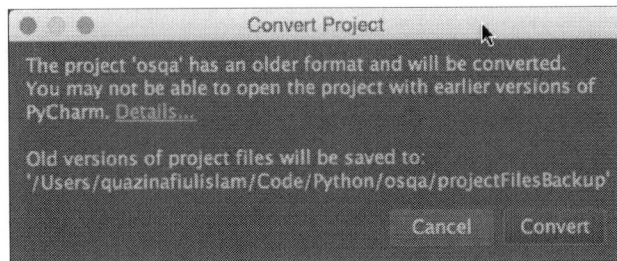

If we click on **Details...**, we will get a list of all the things that will be changed.

However, if PyCharm cannot recognize the project as a Django project, we need to point PyCharm to the correct locations inside **Languages & Frameworks | Django**.

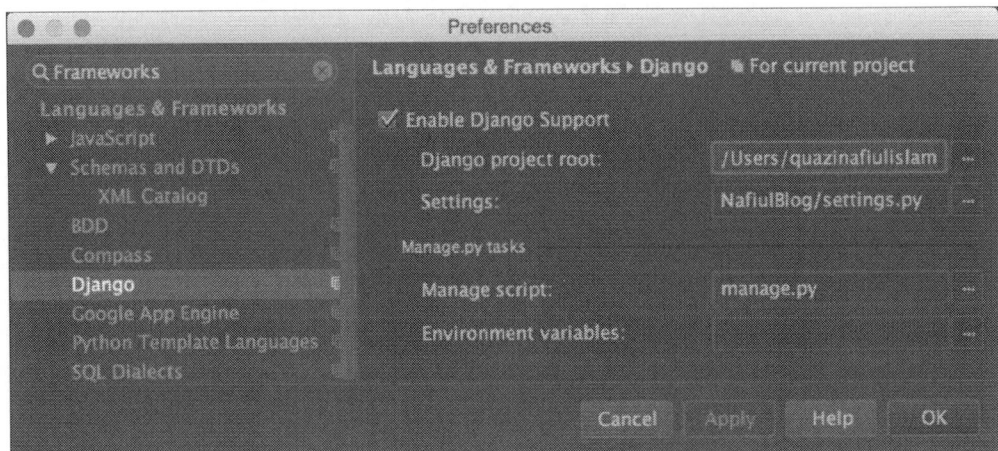

Model dependency diagrams

PyCharm allows us to take a look at how Django models are related. All we need to do is right-click on any Django model to see the models inside a certain package.

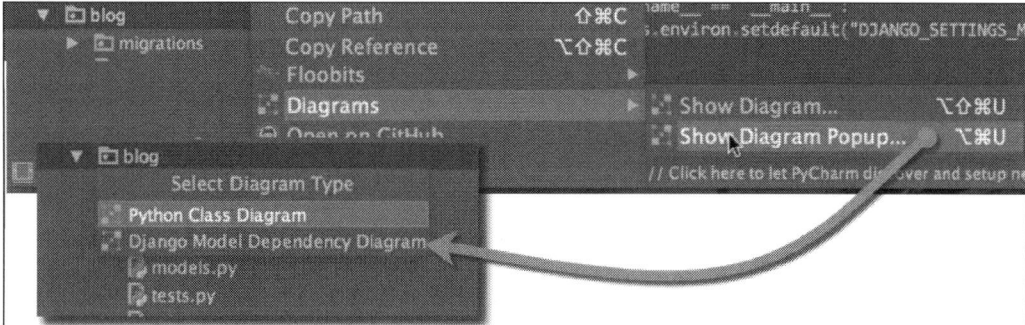

This will show the dependency diagram for all the Django models that will be created using Python `manage.py` migrate for that particular package. We can even generate diagrams for individual models (by right-clicking on the relevant class and then selecting the visualization option that we want).

This will generate a model dependency diagram, but only for the model `Post` in the preceding example.

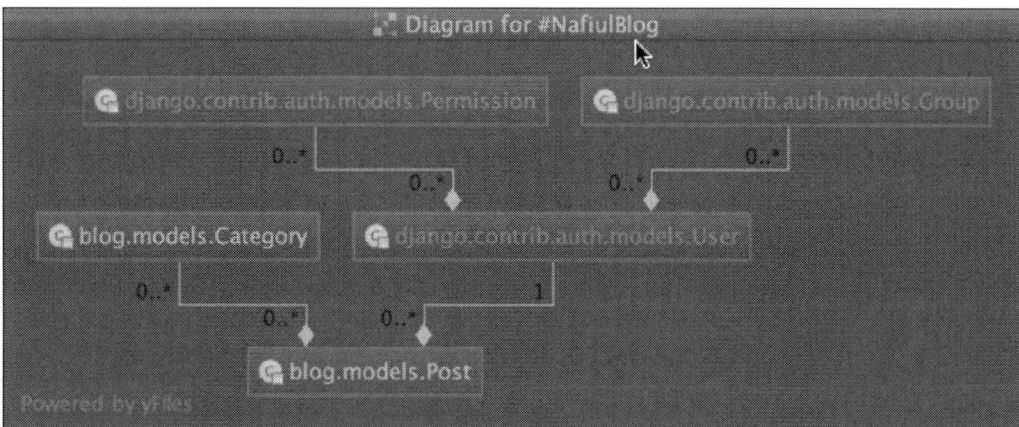

Manage.py tasks

PyCharm allows you to quickly execute manage.py tasks from a window (*Alt + R*).

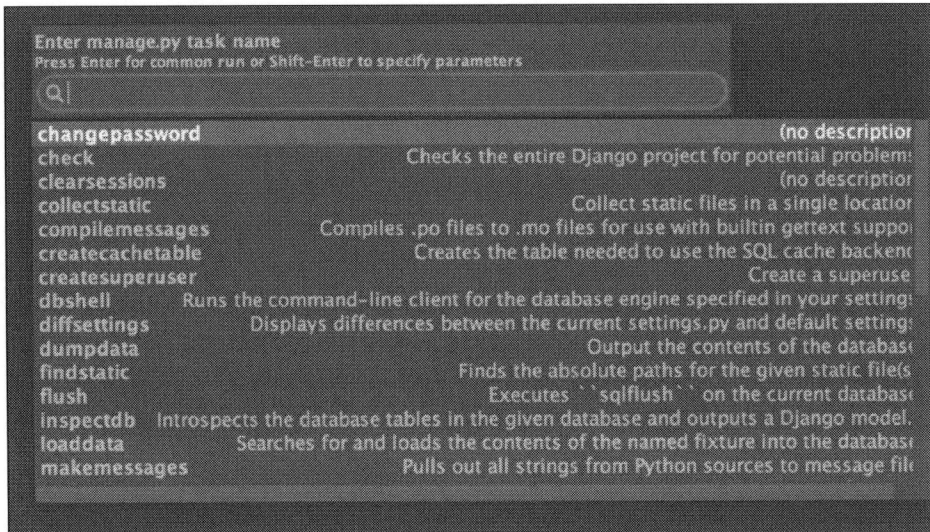

In my own development, I almost never use this. I instead opt to use the command line and run the manage.py script myself. However, this can be very useful for Windows systems since you don't have handy tools such as workon, which automatically links your virtualenv to your project.

Django Console

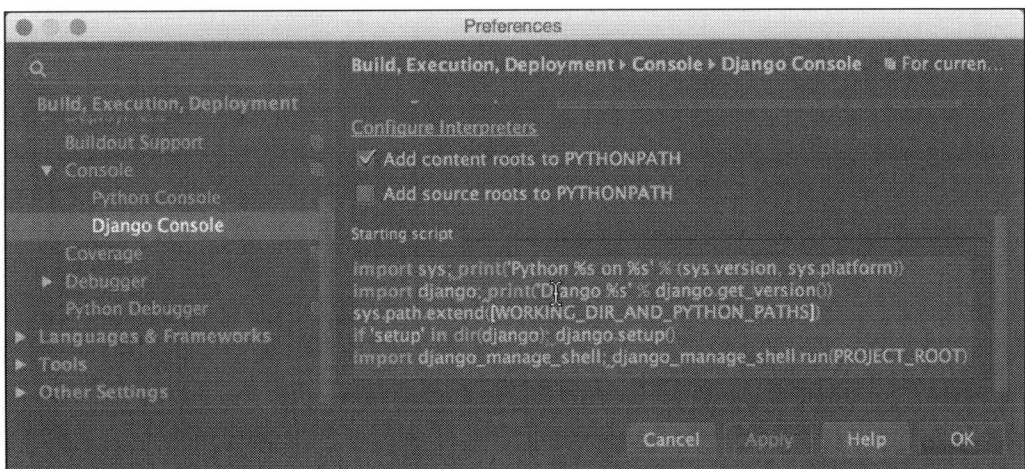

Whenever we open up the console for a Django project, we are going to get a specialized console for Django that is essentially a PyCharm version of the `manage.py` shell. What this basically means is that we get all the benefits of using manage.py's shell command as well as the code completion in the console session. We can even modify it inside the **Django Console** settings. In the previous versions of PyCharm, the **Django Console** was a separate console to the Python console, but in the newer versions, they have been merged.

Summary

In this chapter, we looked at PyCharm's powerful web-centric tools. Databases are well supported and there are many framework-agnostic tools that we can take advantage of. These tools are useful for frameworks that aren't officially supported by PyCharm. We also looked at the Django support that PyCharm provides.

What I love best about Django support is the automatic project creation, support in the console, and amazing code completion for Django ORM models (which are also present for SQLAlchemy).

PyCharm's support for web development and its approach to decoupled features allow developers to quickly get up to speed with most of the feature sets.

Index

About Packt Publishing

Packt, pronounced 'packed', published its first book, *Mastering phpMyAdmin for Effective MySQL Management*, in April 2004, and subsequently continued to specialize in publishing highly focused books on specific technologies and solutions.

Our books and publications share the experiences of your fellow IT professionals in adapting and customizing today's systems, applications, and frameworks. Our solution-based books give you the knowledge and power to customize the software and technologies you're using to get the job done. Packt books are more specific and less general than the IT books you have seen in the past. Our unique business model allows us to bring you more focused information, giving you more of what you need to know, and less of what you don't.

Packt is a modern yet unique publishing company that focuses on producing quality, cutting-edge books for communities of developers, administrators, and newbies alike. For more information, please visit our website at www.packtpub.com.

Writing for Packt

We welcome all inquiries from people who are interested in authoring. Book proposals should be sent to author@packtpub.com. If your book idea is still at an early stage and you would like to discuss it first before writing a formal book proposal, then please contact us; one of our commissioning editors will get in touch with you.

We're not just looking for published authors; if you have strong technical skills but no writing experience, our experienced editors can help you develop a writing career, or simply get some additional reward for your expertise.

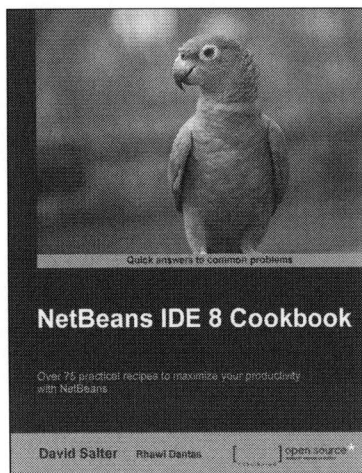

NetBeans IDE 8 Cookbook

ISBN: 978-1-78216-776-1   Paperback: 386 pages

Over 75 practical recipes to maximize your productivity with NetBeans

1. Increase developer productivity using features such as refactoring and code creation.

2. Test applications effectively using JUnit, TestNG, and Arquilian.

3. A recipe-based guide filled with practical examples to help you create robust applications using NetBeans.

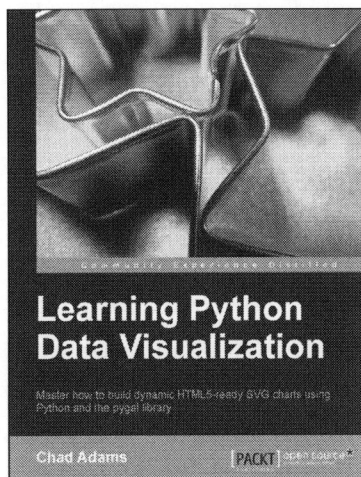

Learning Python Data Visualization

ISBN: 978-1-78355-333-4   Paperback: 212 pages

Master how to build dynamic HTML5-ready SVG charts using Python and the pygal library

1. A practical guide that helps you break into the world of data visualization with Python.

2. Understand the fundamentals of building charts in Python.

3. Packed with easy-to-understand tutorials for developers who are new to Python or charting in Python.

Please check **www.PacktPub.com** for information on our titles

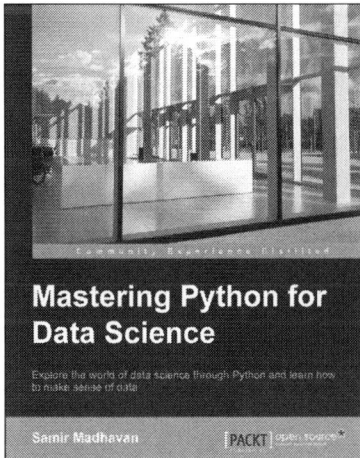

Mastering Python for Data Science

ISBN: 978-1-78439-015-0   Paperback: 294 pages

Explore the world of data science through Python and learn how to make sense of data

1. Master data science methods using Python and its libraries.

2. Create data visualizations and mine for patterns.

3. Advanced techniques for the four fundamentals of data science with Python—data mining, data analysis, data visualization, and machine learning.

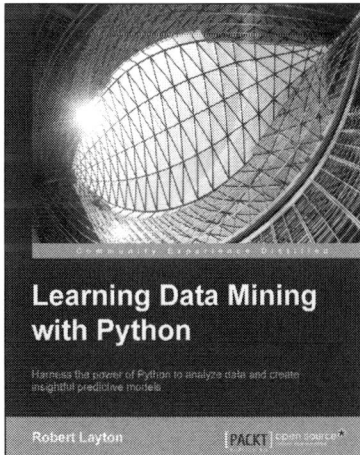

Learning Data Mining with Python

ISBN: 978-1-78439-605-3   Paperback: 344 pages

Harness the power of Python to analyze data and create insightful predictive models

1. Learn data mining in practical terms using a wide variety of libraries and techniques.

2. Learn how to find, manipulate, and analyze data using Python.

3. Step-by-step instructions on creating real-world applications of data mining techniques.

Printed in Great Britain
by Amazon